Grierson on Documentary

Also by Forsyth Hardy
—
JOHN GRIERSON: A Documentary Biography

GRIERSON
ON
DOCUMENTARY

Edited with an Introduction
by
FORSYTH HARDY

FABER AND FABER
London & Boston

First published by Collins in 1946
Revised edition published in 1966
by Faber and Faber Limited
3 Queen Square London WC1N 3AU
Abridged edition 1979
Printed in Great Britain by
Whitstable Litho Ltd Whitstable Kent
All rights reserved

British Library Cataloguing in Publication Data

Grierson, John
Grierson on documentary. – Abridged ed.
1. Moving-pictures, Documentary – Production
and direction – Collected works
I. Hardy, Forsyth
791.43'53   PN1995.9.D6

ISBN 0–571–11367–2

Acknowledgements

Much of the material comprising this volume appeared in journals in which Grierson had a close personal interest: *Cinema Quarterly*, *World Film News*, and *Documentary News Letter*. Details of the published sources are set out in the Appendix: grateful acknowledgements are due to the editors and publishers concerned.

Contents

Contents

Introduction

The word documentary, its generally accepted definition being 'the creative treatment of actuality', was first used in a film sense by John Grierson when writing in the New York *Sun* (8 February 1926) about Robert Flaherty's *Moana*. 'Being a visual account of the daily life of a Polynesian you'h', he wrote, the film 'has documentary value.' Documentary was to become a movement in Britain in the 1930s, while the use of the film for social comment, developed by the movement, was to spread to most countries throughout the world and eventually to move out of the cinema into television.

Throughout his life (1898–1972), John Grierson was the focal point of the movement, its main driving force. The influences which fostered it began with his upbringing by radically-minded Scottish parents, both teachers, his service in mine-sweepers during the First World War and his experiences as post-war student at Glasgow University when industrial depression and social deprivation produced the Red Clydeside movement. To these were added his observation of immigration problems in Chicago when he went in 1924 to the United States as a Rockefeller Research Fellow in social science and his studies of the popular press and eventually of the cinema which led him to write first of the movies as a hobby and later to examine the reactions of the film-going masses as measured by the box-office.

Two film-makers in particular affected his early thinking and, directly and indirectly, the movement he founded. In New York Grierson met Robert Flaherty who, in *Nanook of the North* and *Moana*, had shown how the camera could be used to bring the beauty of the natural world to the screen: his approach was in total contrast to Hollywood's studio reconstruction. Grierson helped to prepare Eisenstein's *Potemkin* for its release in the United States and observed at first hand how the principles of symphonic structure and dynamic editing were applied for persuasive purposes. Flaherty's approach and the technique of the Russian directors were to continue as significant influences.

When Grierson returned to Britain in 1927 his intentions had clarified. To him films were primarily a means of reaching and influencing public opinion: 'I look on cinema as a pulpit and use it as a propagandist.' His first opportunity to put his ideas into practice came in the unlikely form of the Empire Marketing Board, an agency

Introduction

of the British Government established in 1926 to promote the marketing of Empire products. His fire and enthusiasm for the use of the cinema convinced the Board's secretary, Sir Stephen Tallents, and his proposal for a film on the Scottish herring fisheries was accepted. The result was *Drifters* (1929) which he wrote, directed, partly photographed and edited.

In the British cinema, then an anaemic photograph of the London West End theatre, *Drifters* was revolutionary in its rough reality. It drew its drama from workaday Britain; and it used a technique derived from the Russian directors and unlike anything in contemporary native film-making. For the first time the working man in Britain saw and recognised himself on the screen; and for the first time young British film-makers, attracted by the potential of a still young art form and aware of its possible use for social purposes, had proof that both could be combined in a way which they found exciting.

Grierson could have made more films like *Drifters*. Instead he decided to devote himself to teaching and persuaded Tallents to engage other young men who, like himself, wanted to use film rather than make films: '. . . sociologists, a little worried about the way the world was going'. Among the earliest to join him were Basil Wright, John Taylor, Arthur Elton, Edgar Anstey and Paul Rotha (who later independently followed a complementary path in documentary). Stuart Legg, Harry Watt, Donald Taylor, Evelyn Spice, Stanley Hawes, Humphrey Jennings, and his sisters, Ruby and Marion Grierson, were among others who worked with him. Flaherty joined the unit and for a brief period lent the inspiring vision of 'the finest eyes in cinema'. And when, on the demise of the Empire Marketing Board in 1933, the film unit went with Sir Stephen Tallents to the General Post Office and acquired its own sound system, Alberto Cavalcanti came from France to contribute his knowledge and skill.

As the building and training continued, the films began to appear. Among the first group were the Flaherty-Grierson *Industrial Britain* (1933) and Basil Wright's lyrical *O'er Hill and Dale* (1932). For the G.P.O. Grierson produced *Night Mail* (1936), an account of the overnight journey of the mail train between London and Scotland, on which all the members of the unit worked and to which Benjamin Britten and W. H. Auden contributed memorably. Of all the hundreds of films which emerged from the documentary movement in the 1930s it has most securely stood the test of time. No less distinguished was Basil Wright's *Song of Ceylon* (1935). The range of the unit's work was extended when Len Lye, the New Zealand artist, was given the

12

opportunity to experiment in the use of abstract colour images and Norman McLaren was brought from Scotland to develop his ideas of film animation. Grierson imposed no rigid pattern. 'The documentary idea,' he wrote, 'demands no more than that the affairs of our time shall be brought to the screen in a fashion which strikes the imagination and makes observation a little richer than it was. At one level, the vision may be journalistic, at another, it may rise to poetry and drama. At another level again, its aesthetic quality may lie in the mere lucidity of its expression.'

Grierson's was the main voice raised in exposition of the documentary idea, although Sir Stephen Tallents in *The Projection of England* and the leading members of the unit were also active in writing and lecturing. Grierson set out the principles of documentary theory, published originally in *Cinema Quarterly*, and these early articles form the first section of this volume. They helped to make the documentary idea more widely known, in Britain and increasingly in overseas countries.

In Britain the movement had spread beyond the inevitably cramping limits of Government departmental sponsorship. The movement's sociological concern found expression in such films as *Housing Problems* (1935), *Enough to Eat?* (1936), *Children at School* (1937), *The Smoke Menace* (1937) and *The Londoners* (1939). When Grierson resigned from the G.P.O. Film Unit in June, 1937, there was already a larger volume of documentary production outside than inside Government sponsorship. To meet the need for a cental co-ordinating body Grierson set up Film Centre, in association with Arthur Elton, Stuart Legg and J. P. R. Golightly. It acted as a consultative and policy-forming centre for the growing number of national corporations and public bodies using the documentary film for their purposes. Among the services Grierson rendered was to act as production adviser to the first Films of Scotland Committee and the group of seven films which resulted in 1938 remain a remarkably comprehensive record of a country's achievement and outlook.

Over ten years Grierson had seen the documentary movement grow in Britain to a point where it seemed as natural to find public issues being examined on the screen as it is today in television. One consequence was that on the outbreak of war there was a generation of film-makers in Britain trained in the use of the film for informational and inspirational purposes.

Meanwhile, Grierson was looking beyond Britain. A commission from the Imperial Relations Trust to report on the film situation in

Introduction

Canada, Australia, New Zealand and South Africa coincided with an invitation from the Canadian Government to prepare a plan for the development of Canadian film production. His proposals for Canada were accepted and in May, 1939, the National Film Board of Canada was established. As he was on the point of leaving for Australia to continue his work for the Imperial Relations Trust Grierson accepted a pressing invitation to become the Board's first Film Commissioner. The appointment was for a period of six months but was later extended to cover the war period.

With energy and zeal which astonished everyone in Canada, from the Prime Minister to the civil servants accustomed to the undemanding tempo of life in Ottawa, Grierson accepted the challenge and seized the opportunity to re-develop the documentary movement in virgin territory. The organisation was 'pulled off the sky'. To the experienced Stuart Legg, Stanley Hawes, Raymond Spottiswoode and Norman McLaren Grierson added young Canadians of like mind and temperament. The first recruits were Ross McLean, Donald Buchanan, Donald Fraser and James Beveridge and they were soon joined by Tom Daly, Stanley Jackson, Sydney Newman, Guy Glover, Evelyn Spice (Cherry), Gudrun Bjering (Parker) and Margaret Ann Bjornson (Lady Elton). In a remarkably short time they had launched two series of films, *Canada Carries On*, on Canadian life and achievement and addressed to Canadians, and *World in Action*, on world affairs, discussed from a Canadian point of view. To these films for the theatres was added a steadily increasing flow of productions for the well organised rural circuits and other specialised audiences.

The National Film Board gave Grierson the advantages of centralised and co-ordinated control of a nation's film activities—something he had not had in Britain—and the use he made of his opportunity underlined the compelling nature of his social conscience and the breadth of his vision. 'The main thing,' he wrote, 'is to see this National Film Board plan as a service to the Canadian public, as an attempt to create a better understanding of Canada's present, and as an aid to the people in mobilising their imagination and energy in the creating of Canada's future. . . . A country is only as vital as its processes of self-education are vital.' Before the end of the war the National Film Board was outstripping in enterprise and achievement its equivalent organisations in Britain and the United States.

Grierson's intellectual energy during these peak years of his personal achievement is reflected in the papers he wrote and the addresses he gave, either as Film Commissioner or as General Manager of

Introduction

Canada's Wartime Information Board. In these papers, which form the main section of the book, he expressed his belief that education was the key to the mobilisation of men's minds to right ends or wrong ends and urged that the times called for a change in thinking and in values. The old individualist and nationalist viewpoints, he suggested, were incapable of mastering current problems. In one of the last of these papers, 'The Challenge of Peace', he wrote of a new phase of rehabilitation and reconstruction calling for the highest order of heart and mind and he suggested that the workers in every medium had a crucial contribution to make.

This was the measure of Grierson's thinking when he decided to resign as Canada's Film Commissioner at the end of the war and to establish in New York International Film Associates, a base for international documentary film production. 'What determined my decision to extend the range of documentary,' he wrote to me at the time, 'was the realisation that our work could not depend on a single national sponsorship, however strong, but only on the international reality created by the common interests of the common people everywhere.' But his ambitious plans foundered, partly because of his appearance at the Gouzenko spy trial in Ottawa and the consequent effect on opinion in the United States, already, in the pre-McCarthy period, sensitive about Communist involvement; and partly because of a diminished appetite in the post-war cinema for documentary and the discussion of public affairs, about to move into television.

In February, 1947, Grierson accepted an invitation from Julian Huxley, Director-General of UNESCO, to be the Organisation's first Director of Mass Communications and Public Information. After a frustrating year, attempting to cope with procedures involving forty member states, he returned to Britain to take overall charge of the planning, production and distribution of Government films—a move for which his former associates had been campaigning. The high hopes he had when he arrived and his increasing disillusionment with the situation he found are reflected in the surveys of documentary film production he wrote for the Edinburgh International Film Festival's annual publication and which are included in this volume.

Film as an international force was still at the forefront of Grierson's thinking and while at the Central Office of Information in London he lent his vision to every undertaking which would extend the use of film internationally. One of these was the film committee of the Brussels Treaty Organisation whose pioneering work in the co-production of cultural and educational films was taken over, first by

15

Introduction

Western European Union and later by the Council of Europe. He also found time to complete his investigation for the Imperial Relations Trust, interrupted by the war, by visiting South Africa. He was beginning to be a familiar figure at international film festivals and continued to be for the rest of his life, meeting there friends and associates in international documentary who respected him as founder and leader of the movement.

In 1951 the British Government set up, as one of the agencies of the National Film Finance Corporation, Group 3, designed as a training ground for young directors in making low-budget fiction films, and invited Grierson, with John Baxter, to control production. Grierson saw it as an opportunity to give young directors, many of whom had begun in documentary, the experience of working with a dialogue script and actors and perhaps to bring into fiction film-making something of his teaching. Philip Leacock, Cyril Frankel, John Eldridge, John Guillermin, Wolf Rilla and Pennington Richards were among the directors who grasped the opportunities which Group 3 offered. Grierson himself got most satisfaction out of making *The Brave Don't Cry* (1952), a reconstruction of an Ayrshire mine disaster and rescue, a subject to which, because of his upbringing in a mining area, he could bring a personal understanding.

It was inevitable that Grierson should be thinking more and more of television as it captured the mass audience from the cinema. He recognised that it was the logical alternative means of distribution, especially for documentary, although with foresight he urged (in 1953) that any form of television which diminished the vital development of the art of the cinema meant a loss to the creative life of the nation. He himself became directly involved in television when, in October 1957, he launched a weekly programme called *This Wonderful World* on Scottish Television. It was an immediate success and for the next ten years he introduced to a new documentary audience 'the wonderful things, the strange and beautiful things, the camera has seen'. A programme which began in Scotland was later networked and through it he reached a vast public, composed of hundreds of thousands of small family groups, to whom he talked in an intimate, persuasive way. It was a new pulpit and his congregation was larger than ever before. The chapter, 'Learning from Television', gives some of his conclusions at the mid-way stage of the programme's long run.

For the programme he travelled widely in Europe and further afield, seeing thousands of films, and consequently was uniquely well informed about world film-making in the 1960s. Through attendance at

Introduction

film festivals and international assemblies, his contacts with documentary film-makers remained fresh.

Some aspects of Grierson's work in the last years of his life are not represented in this collection of his papers. Among these is his service to his native country through his active membership of the Films of Scotland Committee, recognised when he was made a Commander of the Order of the British Empire in July, 1961. In 1968, after he had received the Golden Thistle Award for outstanding achievement in the cinema at the Edinburgh Film Festival, he accepted an invitation to lecture on mass communications at McGill University in Montreal. He attracted a class of some seven hundred students, the largest in the university's records, and continued to teach there until shortly before his death in Bath on 19 February 1972. He died as he had lived, giving of himself. His personal story will be found in *John Grierson: A Documentary Biography*.

Those to whom he had given so much quickly took steps to ensure that his teaching would not be forgotten. The Grierson Memorial Trust was formed in London and an annual Grierson Award initiated. A Grierson Archive was established at Stirling University with an associated and complementary Grierson Project at McGill University. Perhaps most significantly the head of features at Granada Television, speaking at the opening of the Grierson Archive in Stirling, said: 'The Grierson ideal of art and entertainment married to social purpose is alive, reasonably well and living in television'.

Grierson's lucid and compelling exposition of its aims contributed much to the development of documentary. His writings have been a source of stimulus and enrichment for those who were outside the range of his personal influence. Individually they enunciated principles which conditioned the whole trend of the movement and set a pace for it. Together they still constitute the most solid and penetrating analysis yet made of the film as an instrument affecting public opinion.

From this abridged collection of his papers, the film reviews he contributed to a number of journals in the early 1930s have been omitted, the intention being to publish a companion volume, *Grierson on the Movies*. Perhaps that volume will appropriately bear witness to the affection Grierson always had for 'the living quicksilver of the medium itself', to which he refers in the Preface he wrote for the first edition of *Grierson on Documentary*.

Forsyth Hardy.

Edinburgh.
15 July 1978.

17

1 'Drifters'

Drifters is about the sea and about fishermen, and there is not a Piccadilly actor in the piece. The men do their own acting, and the sea does its—and if the result does not bear out the 107th Psalm, it is my fault. Men at their labour are the salt of the earth; the sea is a bigger actor than Jannings or Nitikin or any of them; and if you can tell me a story more plainly dramatic than the gathering of the ships for the herring season, the going out, the shooting at evening, the long drift in the night, the hauling of nets by infinite agony of shoulder muscle in the teeth of a storm, the drive home against a head sea, and (for finale) the frenzy of a market in which said agonies are sold at ten shillings a thousand, and iced, salted and barrelled for an unwitting world—if you can tell me a story with a better crescendo in energies, images, atmospherics and all that make up the sum and substance of cinema, I promise you I shall make my next film of it forthwith.

But, of course, making a film is not just the simple matter of feeling the size of the material. If that were so every fool who fusses over a nondescript sunset, or bares his solar plexus to the salt sea waves on his summer holiday, would be an artist. I do not claim the brave word, though I would like to, but I think I know what it mostly means. It has very little to do with nondescript enthusiasm, and a great deal to do with a job of work.

In art, as in everything else, the gods are with the big battalions. You march on your subject with a whole regiment of energies: you surround it, you break in here, break in there, and let loose all the shell and shrapnel you can (by infinite pushing of your inadequate noddle) lay hands on. Out of the labour something comes. All you have to do then is to seize what you want. If you have really and truly got inside, you will have plenty—of whatever it is—to choose from.

So in this rather solid adventure of the herring fishery I did what I could to get inside the subject. I had spent a year or two of my life wandering about on the deep sea fishing-boats, and that was an initial advantage. I knew what they felt like. Among other things they had

A Movement is Founded

developed in me a certain superior horsemanship which was proof against all bronco-buckings, side-steppings and rollings whatsoever. I mention this because the limiting factor in all sea films is the stomach of the director and his cameramen. It is a super fact, beyond all art and non-art. Of my cameramen one also was an ex-seaman. The other, for all his bravery, was mostly unconscious.

In this matter I was altogether to blame. What I know of cinema I have learned partly from the Russians, partly from the American westerns, and partly from Flaherty, of *Nanook*. The westerns give you some notion of the energies. The Russians give you the energies and the intimacies both. And Flaherty is a poet.

The net effect of this cinematic upbringing was to make me want a storm: a real storm, an intimate storm, and if possible a rather noble storm. I waited in Lowestoft for weeks till the gale signal went up, and I got it. So did the cameramen. The wild Arabian breeze of the drifter's bilges did not help matters.

Taking the film as a whole I got the essentials of what I wanted. I got the most beautiful fishing-village in the world—I found it in the Shetlands—for a starting point. I staged my march to the sea, the preparations, the procession out. I ran in detail of furnace and engine-room for image of force, and seas over a headland for image of the open. I took the ships out and cast the nets in detail: as to the rope over the cradle, the boy below, the men on deck against the sea; as to the rhythm of the heaving, the run on the rollers, the knotted haul of each float and net; as to the day and approaching night; as to the monotony of long labour. Two miles of nets to a ship: I threw them in a flood of repetition against a darkening sky.

The life of Natural cinema is in this massing of detail, in this massing of all the rhythmic energies that contribute to the blazing fact of the matter. Men and the energies of men, things and the functions of things, horizons and the poetics of horizons: these are the essential materials. And one must never grow so drunk with the energies and the functions as to forget the poetics.

I had prepared against that as best I knew how. Image for this, image for that. For the settling of darkness, not darkness itself, but flocks of birds silhouetted against the sky flying hard into the camera: repeated and repeated. For the long drift in the night, not the ship, not the sea itself, but the dark mystery of the underwater. I made the night scene a sequence of rushing shoals and contorting congers. For the dawn, not a bleary fuss against the sky (which in cinema is nothing), but a winding slow-rolling movement into the light. Then a bell-buoy.

Then a Dutch lugger rolling heavily into the light. Three images in a row.

You can never have your images too great, and I think there are none of us poets enough to make cinema properly. It is in the end a question of suggesting things, and all the example of Shakespearian metaphor is there to tell you how short we stand of the profundities.

The most solid scene, I would say, was the spectacle of the hauling. Camera and cameraman were lashed on top of the wheelhouse, and the nets came up through the heavy sea in great drifts of silver. We got at it from every angle we could and shot it inside-out with the hand camera; and, put together, it made a brave enough show. But even then the fact of the matter, however detailed, however orchestrated, was not enough. The sea might lash over the men and the ship plunge, and the haul of the nets tauten and tear at the wrists of the men: it was still not enough. This business of horizons had to be faced over again. By fortune a whale came alongside to clean the nets, and I used it for more than a whale. I used it for a ponderous symbol of all that tumbled and laboured on that wild morning. It adds something, but it is possible that something else, had I but felt it properly, would have carried the scene still further to that horizon I speak of. Images, images—details and aspects of things that lift a world of fact to beauty and bravery—no doubt half a hundred passed under my nose, and I did not see them.

So through the procession into harbour, and the scenes in the market-place at Yarmouth—fact joined to fact and detail to detail. But here, of course, because of the size and variety of the scene, rather greater possibilities in the matter of orchestration. The gathering procession of buyers and sellers on the quayside, the procession of ships through the harbour mouth: the two processions interwoven. The selling itself, the unloading, the carrying: mouth work and shoulder work interwoven, made complementary to each other, opposed to each other as your fancy takes you. Rivers of fish, being slid into a ship's hold, cartfuls of baskets, girls gutting, barrels being rolled: all the complex detail of porterage and export dissolved into each other, run one on top of the other, to set them marching. It is the procession of results. Cranes and ships and railway trains—or their impressionistic equivalents—complete it.

The problem of images does not arise so plainly here, for cinematic processions, if you bring them off, are solid affairs that carry their own banners. Two, however, I did try. As the labour of the sea turned to the labour of the land, I carried forward a wave theme. It is played

21

heavily for accompaniment as the ships ride in; but as life on the quayside takes charge of the picture, it is diminished in strength till it vanishes altogether. Through breaking waves the buyers and sellers go to their business. Count that, if you will, for an image of opposition. It is a far cry from the simple and solid labour of the sea to the nepman haggling of the market-place.

The last was of a similar type. As the catch was being boxed and barrelled I thought I would like to say that what was really being boxed and barrelled was the labour of men. So as the herring were shovelled in, and the ice laid on, and the hammer raised to complete the job, I slid back for a flash or two to the storm and the hauling. The hammer is raised on mere fish: it comes down on dripping oilskins and a tumbling sea. This notion I kept repeating in flashes through the procession of barrels and the final procession of railway trucks. The barrels of the dead pass for a second into the living swirl of a herring shoal, in and out again; the smoke in a tunnel dissolves for a moment into the tautened wrist of a fisherman at the net-rope.

I cannot tell you what the result of it all is. Notions are notions and pictures are pictures, and no knowledge of cinematic anatomy can guarantee that extra something which is the breath of life to a picture. If I raise this matter of images it is rather to give you some idea of how the movie mind works. It has to feel its way through the appearances of things, choosing, discarding and choosing again, seeking always those more significant appearances which are like yeast to the plain dough of the context. Sometimes they are there for the taking; as often as not you have to make a journey into a far country to find them. That, however, is no more difficult for cinema than for poetry. The camera is by instinct, if not by training, a wanderer.

2   The Russian Example

In *One Family*, which sets out to bring our modern Empire alive, to seize and hold and shape the dramatic material of the Empire's commerce, the difficulty is to find a dramatic mould into which one can pour the ordinary business of orchard harvests, prairie harvests, plantation harvests and the like. It sounds easy as pie, I know, for these on the face of them are noble subjects, with the earth under, and the sky over, and a multitude of human lives in and around. The earth gives forth, the ships carry, the millions in the market place black each other's eyes for the profit and loss. Yes, but Canada and the Antipodes, Africa and the Indies—who will discover and map the common streams of dramatic life in a world so wide, and present them for the Congo rivers they are? That would be a large work indeed and in criticizing *One Family*, one should consider as much the size of the job involved as any tendency to shortcoming.

It may be—and what I understand of aesthetic bids me believe—that in making art in our new world we are called upon to build in new forms altogether. Fantasy will not do, nor the dribblings of personal sentiment or personal story. The building of our new forms has been going on, of course, for a long time in poetry and the novel and architecture, and even within such limitations of medium as one finds in painting and sculpture. We have all been abstracting our arts away from the personal, trying to articulate this wider world of duties and loyalties in which education and invention and democracy have made us citizens.

It would, I know, be easy to find a description of the problem as far back as Socrates. Was there not something to the effect that everything I have comes from the state, that in the state is my only self worth worrying about, and that my all must be for the state? I forget the lines, but where the state is so much vaster and more complex than the one-horse town of Athens, and the work of learning how to govern it decently is so important and so pressing, there is an urgency in the problem of articulating it to ourselves which is without parallel in the history of citizenship. What sentiments will we have in this new world

23

to warm and direct our will in it? How shall we crystallize them and teach them if we are to stave off chaos?

Do not believe it if people tell you we have only to go to the Russians for our guide. The Russians are naturally on the same job as ourselves, and more deliberately, and with less patience of the reactionary and sentimental Poets-in-Blazers who take the honours of art in our own country. But, looking at the core of the problem, what in fact have they given us? Pudovkin is only D. W. Griffith in Revolutionary garb, with the sensation of a Revolutionary victory by arms to balance the Ride of the Klansmen and the other fake climaxes of Griffith cinema. Who in the name of sense can believe in revolution as a true climax? As a first act climax perhaps, but not as a fifth. By these terms Pudovkin is, *qua* artist, no revolutionary at all. The pastures of his art are old pastures, eaten to the roots.

Eisenstein is something different, if on the whole not quite so successful. He plays the mass and thinks without a doubt in the mass, but again the fake climax of Revolution in *Potemkin*. And when he had a chance to make a climax of peace-in-the-mass instead of war-in-the-mass, he failed. *The General Line* is no less in its fundamentals a failure than Creighton's *One Family*. This is a hard saying with so many brilliant criticisms about on the subject, but I shall stand by it; and the Russians, I know, will take my point. Eisenstein does not get inside his Russian peasants nor, with true affection, inside the problem of co-operating them. He is looking at their peace drama from the outside, being clever about it, even brilliant about it, but from the outside. The struggle of their communal farms strikes no fire in him.

There is, I believe, only Turin and *Turksib* which for all its patches of really bad articulation is the single job that takes us into the future. *Turksib* is an affair of economics, which is the only sort of affair worth one's time or patience.

My only warning in that matter is that it makes the job of building its Railroad a great deal easier from the dramatic point of view, by its drought, its sandstorms, its icestorms, its rock-blastings, and its quite sensational railway ride. They are all handled supremely well, and no one before, of course, thought of making a high spot of either rock-blasting or an engine solo. But you will see one's difficulty in following out its method if I set you the problem of, say, London's commerce—today's London commerce—and not any special Christmas or Easter day of London commerce—and ask you to find the physical, that is to say the movie, equivalent for these droughts and sandstorms, etcetera. Turin had a desert, and we have a doorstep. Fundamentally it is no matter in art how far or near or easily romantic or difficultly romantic your subject is : the affair, if it is a real affair—an affair of State in the good sense of that phrase—can be dramatized somehow. But plainly, and I have been saying all this to say so, it is not easy.

I remember sitting with a couple of Russian directors discussing the set-backs which accompanied the production of *The General Line.* They knew, as I knew, how it had fallen short of expectations, but at the end of our talk the position of Eisenstein as a master of cinema had been unassailed. The size of the job, the difficulties of the job : these were the matters they talked of. I had a picture of a bunch of directors (the left-wing school of the Russian cinema) disagreeing in many things, achieving quite various successes and publicities, but working together as one on a problem they faced in common. We have no such grouping of directors in this country and no such grouping of dramatic loyalties where the cinema of public affairs is concerned. Any one of us who starts in on the job, starts in at scratch ; the difficulty of our art, the size and life-giving power of our art ignored by the classes who have Power of the Militia (financial and all else) in this ribald State of England. We work ignominiously, half artists and half, for our living, errand-boys to the dickering doddering half-witted old Status Quo.

It would take a giant in such circumstances to produce anything comparable with the Russian films (and they are fools who expect it), for there would be no public thought or public urging behind the job. That is what we lack, and if the critics can create it, so much the better for all of us.

* * *

Dovzhenko's *Earth* is, I think, quite certainly one of the great films. I shall not guarantee that others will react to it as I did, but it may be decent to record that I have seen few films that have been responsible for the same renewal of cinematic energy. When I find a film that acts like a Salvation Army band on the weak and the wicked, I am content to avoid criticism and call it art.

Earth is a Russian film. It is tied to the Bolshevik idea as usual, but in some strange manner it manages to escape from it. There is just a possibility that the Russians accused it of Menshevik tendency and called for a more vigorous push on the Ukranian film front. The film tells the story of the struggle between kulak and peasant in the Ukranian villages : it is, in the upshot, rather more concerned with the Ukranian villages than with the struggle between kulak and peasant. The kulak, poor devil, who goes mad at the loss of his boundaries, is treated almost sympathetically. The local priest is for a brief but bright moment—before the Bolshevik code takes hold and forces Dovzhenko to make a 'heavy' of him—just the good stupid old village priest he was bound to be. Feeling a little out of it when the pagan youths order no prayer from him, unhappy, a figure—it is amusing to note—of Tchekov tragedy.

All this is rather fresh and with all my respect for Bolshevik ideology and the political righteousness with which it is pursued, I am tempted to take a step to the right and chortle for Dovzhenko's demonstration of the continuity of history. It means that Russian art threatens to leave melodrama and become—probably much too soon from a political point of view—humanist again.

Dovzhenko is a fine poet. His struggle between kulak and peasant is not really dramatic at all. The village people bring along a tractor; the tractor ploughs over the kulak's lands; the kulak shoots the fair-haired youth of the village in a crazy moment of drunken anger; and the young people of the village bury his body with hymns and speeches to the future. But all this will give you no idea whatever of the quality of *Earth*; and just because Dovzhenko is not a dramatist but a poet. The theme is right enough and good for deepening. It is in the deepening, however, in the attendant circumstances and accompanying image, that Dovzhenko shows his quality.

That other side of the film runs somewhat as follows:

It is autumn, apples are falling from trees, an old peasant is dying. The people of the village are gathered round him, talking easily, as peasants do, in the presence of death. The old man has laboured in the field for sixty-odd years, and should he not get a medal for that? He thinks he would prefer a pear. The sequence is quiet, and plainly done. Corn in three or four shots, apples in three or four more, the faces of the old man with only the faintest and subtlest changes of expression to carry the titles. A study in stills.

The villagers going off to fetch their tractor, low in the frame with a 90 per cent sky, the peasant ploughing with his solitary horse, high and heavy on the round of the hill for contrast. Space.

The tractor, after some trouble with radiators and a replenishment of radiators which is strictly censorable in England, arrives. The people in gala dress run to meet it, white and flashing in the sun, children young in the sun, dressed and decorative but with emphasis on light.

The tractor at work. Ploughing and reaping and threshing mixed up anyhow, and why not. Set against the stolid labours of a man with a scythe who refuses to be impressed. A fast sequence but no more

26

brilliant in cutting than many another. The speed picked up by inclusion of a man running, cut progressively faster and faster with the delving plough. A trick initiated by Turin.

Women bind the stooks high against the sky, laughing; the thresher is fed high against the sky, not too panchromatic and dropsical. There is wind and action and light, and a detail or two of bare peasant legs and blowing skirts. This, on the other hand, is Dovzhenko and important. He likes legs and blowing skirts and replenished radiators, rather decently. These details save the sequence from a certain lack of open spectacle. The women tie their stooks, standing to the camera, high, with their hands accurately in focus. This is one way of doing it and not the best. The emphasis, however, remains with wind, skirts, legs and sunlight.

The day is over and the labour done, and Dovzhenko is more at home than ever. The peasant youths stand statuesque in the dusk, each with his woman. From one point of view it is slightly implausible that youths and their women should so insist on the statuesque, for I cannot think that Russian ploughmen are inferior to our native ones, but with Dovzhenko the effect is right. The dusk is the coagulated sort of dusk which belongs to the country. Through it and down the road from the village the boy comes. He is foot-loose, he breaks into a dance, the dust swirls white under his feet.

The shot that kills him does not mean a thing in comparison. It is an excuse for a pagan burial, with apple trees brushing across the face of the dead and sunflowers in the background, with a bunch of youngsters singing about the future, an embryo commissar hitting up a peroration, and the older men, by the power of it, believing implicitly. The kulak who buries his head madly in the earth he has lost, who falls symbolically in a heap among the graveyard crosses of an older régime, is relatively unimportant. Even the old priest whose business is so tragically taken out of his hands is unimportant. The emphasis is on the apple trees and the sunflowers, and, lest there be any mistake about it, it remains there to the end.

The finale is of apples, of rain pouring crescendo on apples, of rain stopping and the sun brightening on apples. For 150 feet. The sequence is possibly the simplest example of easy dramatization in the history of cinema.

Technically it was for any of us to do this last sequence and we have not done it. This, I imagine, is the measure of Dovzhenko. There is nothing complex or difficult about his material, his method, or his mind; there is only a directness of sympathy and precision of method

A Movement is Founded

which one rather envies. Other films like *Turksib* have been more exciting technically; and they will have progeny more numerous than *Earth*. But none of them has been quite so satisfying since Flaherty walked out of *White Shadows* and lost himself in Samoa. For there is this similarity between Dovzhenko and Flaherty that both are lyricists. Dovzhenko is stagier and more apparently camera-conscious; but he is, on the other hand, more sensitive to the flash of action.

It is perhaps a pity that *Earth* is not an English film, for there is very little in it (except the faith in the future) which could not be paralleled in our own villages. I have known people talk as familiarly in the presence of death and behave in graveyards not dissimilarly to the old man who bent down his head to catch the words of the departed patriarch. For the rest we have all the apples, and corn, and peasants with bellies to the earth and heads to the sky, that any lyrical mind could wish for. We have also a history, of invasions and wars and plagues of one sort and another that have gone over the land and left the local gods of birth and death undaunted. We only lack the common faith in the future to complete our material.

It is an important lack, and it seems to a semi-alien like myself that the English mind will have to do something about it. It has lost the capacity for taking a chance on enthusiasms; so much so that even this emphasis on *Earth* will be suspect. It should have qualifications. It should leave a loop-hole in case of this, that, or the other thing; always unspecified. So with dearth of belief, action perishes, and the replenishing of radiators is impossible. The tractor cannot work and the village fête is a frizzle. And the English wind, of course, will not blow the skirts of the women with any decency, and English men and women will not stand to the camera statuesque in the dusk. For the little, England loses the lot.

*　　*　　*

3 Flaherty

A happy fortune has at last brought Robert Flaherty to England. Flaherty was the director of *Nanook* and *Moana*, the originator of *White Shadows of the South Seas*, the co-director, with Murnau, of *Tabu*. He was the initiator of the naturalist tradition in cinema, and is still the high-priest of the spontaneities. The happy fortune lies in the fact that of all distinguished foreign directors he is the one whose sympathies are most nearly English. Technically, he is American, but the major part of his life has been spent exploring or filming within the British Empire.

This long association, together with his explorer's hatred of Hollywood artificialities, makes him the one director whose cinematic persuasion is most likely to benefit our present England. He comes to London for the first time with an eye for its authority in the world, which adds fantasy to the most familiar. He has seen Eskimos travel a thousand miles to buy an English blanket which would last them a lifetime, when the shoddy article of more recent commercial tradition was at their igloo doors. He has eaten out an Arctic winter on the superior construction of English bully-beef tins, which refused to rust with foreign competitors. He has blessed the name of England ten thousand miles away for the one glue in the world which the tropics could not melt.

I knew Flaherty in New York, and he was the only man I knew there whom Babel did not enthral. This seemed to me a most perverse feat of the mind at the time, but in these later days I would more sensibly describe it as a feat of most necessary simplicity. It is only now apparent how the Blazonry of American ballyhoo was selling a generation into slavery. Flaherty used to say: 'They are a tribe of sharks preying on the weakness of their neighbours. This is their way of being ferocious.' He contrasted the public decency of Polynesians. Economics, of which he professes nothing, have most strangely found him right. I know not how many millions the American people will have to pay their irresponsible exploiters when prosperity comes again; for goods consumed.

29

A Movement is Founded

Now in London I find Flaherty's eye for things as fascinating as before. He tells me that wholesomeness went out of American humour when Mark Twain died, and that behind all the flashing wit of American cross-talk is an essential unkindliness. He tells me that England is dirty and scrambled, that its humour is simple, but that this original human wholesomeness remains to it. He tells me that English faces retain an individuality which stands up to the buildings as American faces cannot. He contrasts the manicured landscape of the Continent with the informality and intimacy of the Chilterns. He praises, most unfashionably, craftsmanship.

These hints and emphases are very close to the problem we have to solve in our English cinema, for we are more than ever in search of the national certainties we are to proclaim. We have not yet evolved a *style*. We imitate Hollywood, and occasionally we imitate Neubabelsburg and Moscow. There is some original lack of affection for our own English worth, a lack of knowledge of it, a lack of bravery in it which prevents our bringing beauty, and convincing beauty, out of the films we make.

It is, I know only too well, difficult to be sure of one's attitudes in a decade like this. Can we heroicize our men when we know them to be exploited? Can we romanticize our industrial scene when we know that our men work brutally and starve ignobly in it? Can we praise it—and in art there must be praise—when the most blatant fact of our time is the bankruptcy of our national management? Our confidence is sapped, our beliefs are troubled, our eye for beauty is most plainly disturbed: and the more so in cinema than in any other art. For we have to build on the actual. Our capital comes from those whose only interest is in the actual. The medium itself insists on the actual. There we must build or be damned.

Flaherty's most considerable contribution to the problem is, as always, his insistence on the beauty of the natural. It is not everything, for it does not in the last resort isolate and define the purposes which must, consciously or unconsciously, inform our craftsmanship. But it does ensure that the raw material from which we work is the raw material most proper to the screen. The camera-eye is in effect a magical instrument. It can see a thousand things in a thousand places at different times, and the cunning cutter can string them together for a review of the world. Or he can piece them together—a more difficult task—for a review of a subject or situation more intricate and more intimate than any mortal eye can hope to match. But its magic is even more than this. It lies also in the manner of its observation, in the

30

strange innocence with which, in a mind-tangled world, it sees things for what they are. This is not simply to say that the camera, on its single observations, is free from the trammels of the subjective, for it is patent that it will not follow the director in his enthusiasms any more than it will follow him in the wide-angled vision of his eyes. The magical fact of the camera is that it picks out what the director does not see at all, that it gives emphasis where he did not think emphasis existed.

The camera is in a measure both the discoverer of an unknown world and the re-discoverer of a lost one. There are, as everyone knows, strange moments of beauty that leap out of most ordinary news reels. It may be some accidental pose of character or some spontaneous gesture which radiates simply because it is spontaneous. It may be some high angle of a ship, or a crane, or a chimney stack, or a statue, adding some element of the heroic by a new-found emphasis. It may be some mere fore-shortening of a bollard and a rope that ties a ship to a quay in spirit as well as in fact. It may be the flap of a hatch cover which translates a gale. It may be the bright revelation of rhythms that time has worn smooth: the hand movement of a potter, the wrist movement of a native priest, or the muscle play of a dancer or a boxer or a runner. All of them seem to achieve a special virtue in the oblong of the screen.

So much Flaherty has taught us all. If we add to it such instruction as we have taken from Griffith and the Russians, of how to mass movement and create suspense, of how to keep an eye open for attendant circumstance and subconscious effect, we have in sum a most formidable equipment as craftsmen. But the major problem remains, the problem I have mentioned, the problem the critics do not worry their heads over, though creators must: what final honours and final dishonours we shall reveal in this English life of ours: what heroism we shall set against what villainy. The field of cinema is not only a field for creators but also for prophets.

The method followed by Flaherty in his own film-making might give us a most valuable lead. He took a year to make his study of the Eskimos and this after ten years' exploration in the Eskimo country of Labrador and Baffin Land. He took two years to make his study of Samoan life, and only now, after three more years in the South Seas, feels he could do justice to it. He soaked himself in his material, lived with it to the point of intimacy and beyond that to the point of belief, before he gave it form. This is a long method, and may be an expensive one; and it is altogether alien in a cinema world which insists on forcing a pre-conceived shape (one of half a dozen rubber-stamped dramatic shapes) on all material together. Its chief claim to our regard, however, is that it is necessary, and particularly necessary in England. We know our England glibly as an industrial country, as a beautiful country of this epic quality and that; we know it by rote as a maker of Empire and as a manipulator of world-wide services. But we do not know it in our everyday observation as such. Our literature is divorced from the actual: it is written as often as not in the south of France. Our culture is divorced from the actual: it is practised almost exclusively in the rarefied atmosphere of country colleges and country retreats. Our gentlemen explore the native haunts and investigate the native customs of Tanganyika and Timbuctoo, but do not travel dangerously into the jungles of Middlesbrough and the Clyde. Their hunger for English reality is satisfied briefly and sentimentally over a country hedge.

We might make an English cinema, as we might make English art again, if we could only send our creators back to fact. Not only to the old fact of the countryside which our poets have already honoured, but to the new fact of industry and commerce and plenty and poverty which no poet has honoured at all. Every week I hear men ask for films of industry. They want it praised and proclaimed to the world, and I would like to see their money used and their purposes fulfilled. But what advice can I give them? We can produce them the usual slick rubbish, some slicker, some less slick; but who of us knows an industry well enough to bring it alive for what it is? And what statescraft is willing to send a creator into an industry, so to know it: for a year, for two years perhaps, for the length of a hundred thousand feet of film and possibly more. Our businessmen expect a work of art to schedule, as the housewife expects her daily groceries. They expect it of a new medium. They expect it from raw material which they in their own hearts despise.

Flaherty, as an individual artist, cannot answer the whole problem. He knows his primitives and will do a job for them out of the strength of his affection. He could do a job for English craftsmanship and for the tradition of quality in English work, and for the native solidity in English institutions, and English criticism and character; but he is of a persuasion that does not easily come to grips with the more modern factors of civilization. In his heart he prefers a sailing barge to a snub-nosed funnel-after, and a scythe to a mechanical reaper. He will say that there is well-being associated with the first and none with the second, and in a manner he is right: right in his emphasis on well-being.

Flaherty

But how otherwise than by coming to industry, even as it is, and forcing beauty from it, and bringing people to see beauty in it, can one, in turn, inspire man to create and find well-being? For this surely is the secret of our particular well-being, that men must accept the environment in which they live, with its smoke and its steel and its mechanical aids, even with its rain. It may not be so easily pleasant as the halcyon environment of Tahiti, but this is beside the point.

I think in this other matter one may turn to the Russians for guidance rather than to Flaherty. Their problem, of course, is different from ours. The industrial backwardness of the country, the illiteracy of their people, and the special factors of Russian psychology make for a rhetoric in their cinema which we cannot blindly imitate. Apart from this national difference, which is in effect their *style*, there is an ardour of experiment in their treatment of industrial and social material. They have built up rhythms from their machinery; they have made their work exciting and noble. They have made society on the move the subject-matter of art. Their sense of rhythm is not necessarily our sense of rhythm. Their sense of nobility and sense of social direction need not be identical with ours. The essential point, however, is that they have built up this rhythm and nobility and purpose of theirs by facing up to the new material. They have done it out of the necessity of their social situation. No one will say that our own necessity is less than theirs.

When I spoke with Flaherty on the Aran Islands he was full of the possibilities of the British documentary cinema. If on these islands—only so many hours from London—there was this story of romantic life ready to the camera, how many more must there be! He mentioned the Hebrides and the Highlands, and sketched out a film of Indian village life. He spoke of the tales of fine craftsmanship which must be tucked away in the Black Country. But first, he emphasized, there must be the process of discovery and freedom in discovery: to live with the people long enough to know them. He talked with a certain rising fury of the mental attitude of the studio-bred producer who hangs a slicked-out story of triangles against a background of countryside or industry. Rather must the approach be to take the story from out the location, finding it essentially there: with patience and intimacy of knowledge as the first virtues always in a director. He referred to a quotation I once wrote for him in New York, when his seemingly tardy method of production was first an issue in the studios. It was Plato's description of his metaphysics where he says that no fire can leap up or light kindle till there is 'long intercourse with the thing itself, and it has been

33

lived with'. No doubt the studios, with their slick ten- or fifteen-day productions of nothing-in-particular, still disagree with Flaherty and Plato profoundly. His idea of production is to reconnoitre for months without turning a foot, and then, in months more perhaps, slowly to shape the film on the screen: using his camera first to sketch his material and find his people, then using his screen, as Chaplin uses it, to tell him at every turn where the path of drama lies.

No director has the same respect as Flaherty for the camera; indeed very few of them even trouble to look through the camera while it is shooting their scenes. Flaherty, in contrast, is always his own 'first cameraman'. He spoke almost mystically of the camera's capacity for seeing beyond mortal eye to the inner qualities of things. With Fairbanks he agrees that children and animals are the finest of all movie actors, because they are spontaneous, but talks also of the movements in peasants and craftsmen and hunters and priests as having a special magic on the screen because time or tradition has worn them smooth. He might also add—though he would not—that his own capacity for moving the camera in appreciation of these movements is an essential part of the magic. No man of cameras, to my knowledge, can pan so curiously, or so bewilderingly anticipate a fine gesture or expression.

Flaherty's ideal in the new medium is a selective documentation of sound similar at all points to his selective documentation of movement and expression in the silent film. He would use the microphone, like the camera, as an intimate attendant on the action: recording the accompanying sounds and whispers and cries most expressive of it. He says the language does not matter at all, not even the words, if the spirit of the thing is plain. In this point as in others, Flaherty's cinema is as far removed from the theatrical tradition as it can possibly be. His screen is not a stage to which the action of a story is brought, but rather a magical opening in the theatre wall, through which one may look out to the wide world: overseeing and overhearing the intimate things of common life which only the camera and microphone of the film artist can reveal.

4   First Principles of Documentary

Documentary is a clumsy description, but let it stand. The French who first used the term only meant travelogue. It gave them a solid high-sounding excuse for the shimmying (and otherwise discursive) exoticisms of the Vieux Colombier. Meanwhile documentary has gone on its way. From shimmying exoticisms it has gone on to include dramatic films like *Moana*, *Earth*, and *Turksib*. And in time it will include other kinds as different in form and intention from *Moana*, as *Moana* was from *Voyage au Congo*.

So far we have regarded all films made from natural material as coming within the category. The use of natural material has been regarded as the vital distinction. Where the camera shot on the spot (whether it shot newsreel items or magazine items or discursive 'interests' or dramatised 'interests' or educational films or scientific films proper or *Changs* or *Rangos*) in that fact was documentary. This array of species is, of course, quite unmanageable in criticism, and we shall have to do something about it. They all represent different qualities of observation, different intentions in observation, and, of course, very different powers and ambitions at the stage of organizing material. I propose, therefore, after a brief word on the lower categories, to use the documentary description exclusively of the higher.

The peacetime newsreel is just a speedy snip-snap of some utterly unimportant ceremony. Its skill is in the speed with which the babblings of a politican (gazing sternly into the camera) are transferred to fifty million relatively unwilling ears in a couple of days or so. The magazine items (one a week) have adopted the original 'Tit-Bits' manner of observation. The skill they represent is a purely journalistic skill. They describe novelties novelly. With their money-making eye (their almost only eye) glued like the newsreels to vast and speedy audiences, they avoid on the one hand the consideration of solid material, and escape, on the other, the solid consideration of any material. Within these limits they are often brilliantly done. But ten in a row would bore the average human to death. Their reaching out for the flippant or popular touch is so completely far-reaching that it dislocates something.

A Movement is Founded

Possibly taste; possibly common sense. You may take your choice at those little theatres where you are invited to gad around the world in fifty minutes. It takes only that long—in these days of great invention —to see almost everything.

'Interests' proper improve mightily with every week, though heaven knows why. The market (particularly the British market) is stacked against them. With two-feature programmes the rule, there is neither space for the short *and* the Disney *and* the magazine, nor money left to pay for the short. But by good grace, some of the renters throw in the short with the feature. This considerable branch of cinematic illumination tends, therefore, to be the gift that goes with the pound of tea; and like all gestures of the grocery mind it is not very liable to cost much. Whence my wonder at improving qualities. Consider, however, the very frequent beauty and very great skill of exposition in such Ufa shorts as *Turbulent Timber*, in the sports shorts from Metro-Goldwyn-Mayer, in the *Secrets of Nature* shorts from Bruce Woolfe, and the Fitzpatrick travel talks. Together they have brought the popular lecture to a pitch undreamed of, and even impossible in the days of magic lanterns. In this little we progress.

These films, of course, would not like to be called lecture films, but this, for all their disguises, is what they are. They do not dramatize, they do not even dramatize an episode: they describe, and even expose, but in any aesthetic sense, only rarely reveal. Herein is their formal limit, and it is unlikely that they will make any considerable contribution to the fuller art of documentary. How indeed can they? Their silent form is cut to the commentary, and shots are arranged arbitrarily to point the gags or conclusions. This is not a matter of complaint, for the lecture film must have increasing value in entertainment, education and propaganda. But it is as well to establish the formal limits of the species.

This indeed is a particularly important limit to record, for beyond the newsmen and the magazine men and the lecturers (comic or interesting or exciting or only rhetorical) one begins to wander into the world of documentary proper, into the only world in which documentary can hope to achieve the ordinary virtues of an art. Here we pass from the plain (or fancy) descriptions of natural material, to arrangements, rearrangements, and creative shapings of it.

First principles. (1) We believe that the cinema's capacity for getting around, for observing and selecting from life itself, can be exploited in a new and vital art form. The studio films largely ignore this possibility of opening up the screen on the real world. They photograph acted stories against artificial backgrounds. Documentary would photograph the living scene and the living story. (2) We believe that the original (or native) actor, and the original (or native) scene, are better guides to a screen interpretation of the modern world. They give cinema a greater fund of material. They give it power over a million and one images. They give it power of interpretation over more complex and astonishing happenings in the real world than the studio mind can conjure up or the studio mechanician recreate. (3) We believe that the materials and the stories thus taken from the raw can be finer (more real in the philosophic sense) than the acted article. Spontaneous gesture has a special value on the screen. Cinema has a sensational capacity for enhancing the movement which tradition has formed or time worn smooth. Its arbitrary rectangle specially reveals movement; it gives it maximum pattern in space and time. Add to this that documentary can achieve an intimacy of knowledge and effect impossible to the shim-sham mechanics of the studio, and the lily-fingered interpretations of the metropolitan actor.

I do not mean in this minor manifesto of beliefs to suggest that the studios cannot in their own manner produce works of art to astonish the world. There is nothing (except the Woolworth intentions of the people who run them) to prevent the studios going really high in the manner of theatre or the manner of fairy tale. My separate claim for documentary is simply that in its use of the living article, there is *also* an opportunity to perform creative work. I mean, too, that the choice of the documentary medium is as gravely distinct a choice as the choice of poetry instead of fiction. Dealing with different material, it is, or should be, dealing with it to different aesthetic issues from those of the studio. I make this distinction to the point of asserting that the young director cannot, in nature, go documentary and go studio both.

In an earlier reference to Flaherty, I have indicated how one great exponent walked away from the studio: how he came to grips with the essential story of the Eskimos, then with the Samoans, then latterly with the people of the Aran Islands: and at what point the documentary director in him diverged from the studio intention of Hollywood. The main point of the story was this. Hollywood wanted to impose a ready-made dramatic shape on the raw material. It wanted Flaherty, in complete injustice to the living drama on the spot, to build his Samoans into a rubber-stamp drama of sharks and bathing belles. It failed in the case of *Moana*; it succeeded (through Van Dyke) in the case of *White Shadows of the South Seas*, and (through Murnau)

37

in the case of *Tabu*. In the last examples it was at the expense of Flaherty, who severed his association with both.

With Flaherty it became an absolute principle that the story must be taken from the location, and that it should be (what he considers) the essential story of the location. His drama, therefore, is a drama of days and nights, of the round of the year's seasons, of the fundamental fights which give his people sustenance, or make their community life possible, or build up the dignity of the tribe.

Such an interpretation of subject-matter reflects, of course, Flaherty's particular philosophy of things. A succeeding documentary exponent is in no way obliged to chase off to the ends of the earth in search of old-time simplicity, and the ancient dignities of man against the sky. Indeed, if I may for the moment represent the opposition, I hope the Neo-Rousseauism implicit in Flaherty's work dies with his own exceptional self. Theory of naturals apart, it represents an escapism, a wan and distant eye, which tends in lesser hands to sentimentalism. However it be shot through with vigour of Lawrentian poetry, it must always fail to develop a form adequate to the more immediate material of the modern world. For it is not only the fool that has his eyes on the ends of the earth. It is sometimes the poet: sometimes even the great poet, as Cabell in his *Beyond Life* will brightly inform you. This, however, is the very poet who on every classic theory of society from Plato to Trotsky should be removed bodily from the Republic. Loving every Time but his own, and every Life but his own, he avoids coming to grips with the creative job in so far as it concerns society. In the business of ordering most present chaos, he does not use his powers.

Question of theory and practice apart, Flaherty illustrates better than anyone the first principles of documentary. (1) It must master its material on the spot, and come in intimacy to ordering it. Flaherty digs himself in for a year, or two maybe. He lives with his people till the story is told 'out of himself'. (2) It must follow him in his distinction between description and drama. I think we shall find that there are other forms of drama or, more accurately, other forms of film, than the one he chooses; but it is important to make the primary distinction between a method which describes only the surface values of a subject, and the method which more explosively reveals the reality of it. You photograph the natural life, but you also, by your juxtaposition of detail, create an interpretation of it.

This final creative intention established, several methods are possible. You may, like Flaherty, go for a story form, passing in the ancient manner from the individual to the environment, to the environment transcended or not transcended, to the consequent honours of heroism. Or you may not be so interested in the individual. You may think that the individual life is no longer capable of cross-sectioning reality. You may believe that its particular belly-aches are of no consequence in a world which complex and impersonal forces command, and conclude that the individual as a self-sufficient dramatic figure is outmoded. When Flaherty tells you that it is a devilish noble thing to fight for food in a wilderness, you may, with some justice, observe that you are more concerned with the problem of people fighting for food in the midst of plenty. When he draws your attention to the fact that Nanook's spear is grave in its upheld angle, and finely rigid in its down-pointing bravery, you may, with some justice, observe that no spear, held however bravely by the individual, will master the crazy walrus of international finance. Indeed you may feel that in individualism is a yahoo tradition largely responsible for our present anarchy, and deny at once both the hero of decent heroics (Flaherty) and the hero of indecent ones (studio). In this case, you will feel that you want your drama in terms of some cross-section of reality which will reveal the essentially co-operative or mass nature of society: leaving the individual to find his honours in the swoop of creative social forces. In other words, you are liable to abandon the story form, and seek, like the modern exponent of poetry and painting and prose, a matter and method more satisfactory to the mind and spirit of the time.

Berlin or the Symphony of a City initiated the more modern fashion of finding documentary material on one's doorstep: in events which have no novelty of the unknown, or romance of noble savage on exotic landscape, to recommend them. It represented, slimly, the return from romance to reality.

Berlin was variously reported as made by Ruttmann, or begun by Ruttmann and finished by Freund: certainly it was begun by Ruttmann. In smooth and finely tempo'd visuals, a train swung through suburban mornings into Berlin. Wheels, rails, details of engines, telegraph wires, landscapes and other simple images flowed along in procession, with similar abstracts passing occasionally in and out of the general movement. There followed a sequence of such movements which, in their total effect, created very imposingly the story of a Berlin day. The day began with a processional of workers, the factories got under way, the streets filled: the city's forenoon became a hurly-burly of tangled pedestrians and street cars. There was respite for food: a various respite with contrast of rich and poor. The city started work again, and a shower of rain in the afternoon became a considerable event. The city stopped work and, in further more hectic processional of pubs and cabarets and dancing legs and illuminated sky-signs, finished its day.

In so far as the film was principally concerned with movements and the building of separate images into movements, Ruttmann was justified in calling it a symphony. It meant a break away from the story borrowed from literature, and from the play borrowed from the stage. In *Berlin* cinema swung along according to its own more natural powers: creating dramatic effect from the tempo'd accumulation of its single observations. Cavalcanti's *Rien que les Heures* and Léger's *Ballet Mécanique* came before *Berlin*, each with a similar attempt to combine images in an emotionally satisfactory sequence of movements. They were too scrappy and had not mastered the art of cutting sufficiently well to create the sense of 'march' necessary to the genre. The symphony of Berlin City was both larger in its movements and larger in its vision.

There was one criticism of *Berlin* which, out of appreciation for a fine film and a new and arresting form, the critics failed to make; and time has not justified the omission. For all its ado of workmen and factories and swirl and swing of a great city, Berlin created nothing. Or rather if it created something, it was that shower of rain in the afternoon. The people of the city got up splendidly, they tumbled through their five million hoops impressively, they turned in; and no other issue of God or man emerged than that sudden besmattering spilling of wet on people and pavements.

I urge the criticism because *Berlin* still excites the mind of the young, and the symphony form is still their most popular persuasion. In fifty scenarios presented by the tyros, forty-five are symphonies of Edinburgh or of Ecclefechan or of Paris or of Prague. Day breaks—the people come to work—the factories start—the street cars rattle—lunch hour and the streets again—sport if it is Saturday afternoon—certainly evening and the local dance hall. And so, nothing having happened and nothing positively said about anything, to bed; though Edinburgh is the capital of a country and Ecclefechan, by some power inside itself, was the birthplace of Carlyle, in some ways one of the greatest exponents of this documentary idea.

The little daily doings, however finely symphonized, are not enough. One must pile up beyond doing or process to creation itself, before one hits the higher reaches of art. In this distinction, creation indicates not the making of things but the making of virtues.

And there's the rub for tyros. Critical appreciation of movement they can build easily from their power to observe, and power to observe they can build from their own good taste, but the real job only begins as they apply ends to their observation and their movements. The artist need not posit the ends—for that is the work of the critic—but the ends must be there, informing his description and giving finality (beyond space and time) to the slice of life he has chosen. For that larger effect there must be power of poetry or of prophecy. Failing either or both in the highest degree, there must be at least the sociological sense implicit in poetry and prophecy.

The best of the tyros know this. They believe that beauty will come in good time to inhabit the statement which is honest and lucid and deeply felt and which fulfils the best ends of citizenship. They are sensible enough to conceive of art as the by-product of a job of work done. The opposite effort to capture the by-product first (the self-conscious pursuit of beauty, the pursuit of art for art's sake to the exclusion of jobs of work and other pedestrian beginnings), was always a reflection of selfish wealth, selfish leisure and aesthetic decadence.

This sense of social responsibility makes our realist documentary a troubled and difficult art, and particularly in a time like ours. The job of romantic documentary is easy in comparison: easy in the sense that the noble savage is already a figure of romance and the seasons of the year have already been articulated in poetry. Their essential virtues have been declared and can more easily be declared again, and no one will deny them. But realist documentary, with its streets and cities and slums and markets and exchanges and factories, has given itself the job of making poetry where no poet has gone before it, and where no ends, sufficient for the purposes of art, are easily observed. It requires not only taste but also inspiration, which is to say a very laborious, deep-seeing, deep-sympathizing creative effort indeed.

The symphonists have found a way of building such matters of common reality into very pleasant sequences. By uses of tempo and rhythm, and by the large-scale integration of single effects, they capture the eye and impress the mind in the same way as a tattoo or a military parade might do. But by their concentration on mass and movement, they tend to avoid the larger creative job. What more attractive (for a man of visual taste) than to swing wheels and pistons about in ding-dong description of a machine, when he has little to say about the man who tends it, and still less to say about the tin-pan product it spills? And what more comfortable if, in one's heart, there

41

is avoidance of the issue of underpaid labour and meaningless production? For this reason I hold the symphony tradition of cinema for a danger and *Berlin* for the most dangerous of all film models to follow.

Unfortunately, the fashion is with such avoidance as *Berlin* represents. The highbrows bless the symphony for its good looks and, being sheltered rich little souls for the most part, absolve it gladly from further intention. Other factors combine to obscure one's judgment regarding it. The post-1918 generation, in which all cinema intelligence resides, is apt to veil a particularly violent sense of disillusionment, and a very natural first reaction of impotence, in any smart manner of avoidance which comes to hand. The pursuit of fine form which this genre certainly represents is the safest of asylums.

The objection remains, however. The rebellion from the who-gets-who tradition of commercial cinema to the tradition of pure form in cinema is no great shakes as a rebellion. Dadaism, expressionism, symphonics, are all in the same category. They present new beauties and new shapes; they fail to present new persuasions.

The imagist or more definitely poetic approach might have taken our consideration of documentary a step further, but no great imagist film has arrived to give character to the advance. By imagism I mean the telling of story or illumination of theme by images, as poetry is story or theme told by images: I mean the addition of poetic reference to the 'mass' and 'march' of the symphonic form.

Drifters was one simple contribution in that direction, but only a simple one. Its subject belonged in part to Flaherty's world, for it had something of the noble savage and certainly a great deal of the elements of nature to play with. It did, however, use steam and smoke and did, in a sense, marshal the effects of a modern industry. Looking back on the film now, I would not stress the tempo effects which it built (for both *Berlin* and *Potemkin* came before it), nor even the rhythmic effects (though I believe they outdid the technical example of *Potemkin* in that direction). What seemed possible of development in the film was the integration of imagery with the movement. The ship at sea, the men casting, the men hauling, were not only seen as functionaries doing something. They were seen as functionaries in half a hundred different ways, and each tended to add something to the illumination as well as the description of them. In other words the shots were massed together, not only for description and tempo but for commentary on it. One felt impressed by the tough continuing upstanding labour involved, and the feeling shaped the images, determined the background and supplied the extra details which gave colour to the whole. I do not urge the example of *Drifters*, but in theory at least the example is there. If the high bravery of upstanding labour came through the film, as I hope it did, it was made not by the story itself, but by the imagery attendant on it. I put the point, not in praise of the method but in simple analysis of the method.

*   *   *

The symphonic form is concerned with the orchestration of movement. It sees the screen in terms of flow and does not permit the flow to be broken. Episodes and events, if they are included in the action, are integrated in the flow. The symphonic form also tends to organize the flow in terms of different movements, e.g. movement for dawn, movement for men coming to work, movement for factories in full swing, etc., etc. This is a first distinction.

See the symphonic form as something equivalent to the poetic form of, say, Carl Sandburg in *Skyscraper*, *Chicago*, *The Windy City* and *Slabs of the Sunburnt West*. The object is presented as an integration of many activities. It lives by the many human associations and by the moods of the various action sequences which surround it. Sandburg says so with variations of tempo in his description, variations of the mood in which each descriptive facet is presented. We do not ask personal stories of such poetry, for the picture is complete and satisfactory. We need not ask it of documentary. This is a second distinction regarding symphonic form.

These distinctions granted, it is possible for the symphonic form to vary considerably. Basil Wright, for example, is almost exclusively interested in movement, and will build up movement in a fury of design and nuances of design; and for those whose eye is sufficiently trained and sufficiently fine will convey emotion in a thousand variations on a theme so simple as the portage of bananas (*Cargo from Jamaica*). Some have attempted to relate this movement to the pyrotechnics of pure form, but there never was any such animal. (1) The quality of Wright's sense of movement and of his patterns is distinctively his own and recognizably delicate. As with good painters, there is character in his line and attitude in his composition. (2) There is an over-tone in his work which—sometimes after seeming monotony —makes his description uniquely memorable. (3) His patterns invariably weave—not seeming to do so—a positive attitude to the material, which may conceivably relate to (2). The patterns of *Cargo*

A Movement is Founded

from Jamaica were more scathing comment on labour at twopence a hundred bunches (or whatever it is) than mere sociological stricture. His movements—(*a*) easily down; (*b*) horizontal; (*c*) arduously 45° up; (*d*) down again—conceal, or perhaps construct, a comment. Flaherty once maintained that the east-west contour of Canada was itself a drama. It was precisely a sequence of down, horizontal, 45° up, and down again.

I use Basil Wright as an example of 'movement in itself'—though movement is never in itself—principally to distinguish those others who add either tension elements or poetic elements or atmospheric elements. I have held myself in the past an exponent of the tension category with certain pretension to the others. Here is a simple example of tension from *Granton Trawler*. The trawler is working its gear in a storm. The tension elements are built up with emphasis on the drag of the water, the heavy lurching of the ship, the fevered flashing of the birds, the fevered flashing of faces between waves, lurches and spray. The trawl is hauled aboard with strain of men and tackle and water. It is opened in a release which comprises equally the release of men, birds and fish. There is no pause in the flow of movement, but something of an effort as between two opposing forces, has been recorded. In a more ambitious and deeper description the tension might have included elements more intimately and more heavily descriptive of the clanging weight of the tackle, the strain on the ship, the operation of the gear under water and along the ground, the scuttering myriads of birds laying off in the gale. The fine fury of ship and heavy weather could have been brought through to touch the vitals of the men and the ship. In the hauling, the simple fact of a wave breaking over the men, subsiding and leaving them hanging on as though nothing had happened, would have brought the sequence to an appropriate peak. The release could have attached to itself images of, say, birds wheeling high, taking off from the ship, and of contemplative, i.e. more intimate, reaction on the faces of the men. The drama would have gone deeper by the greater insight into the energies and reactions involved.

Carry this analysis into a consideration of the first part of *Deserter*, which piles up from a sequence of deadly quiet to the strain and fury—and aftermath—of the strike, or of the strike sequence itself, which piles up from deadly quiet to the strain and fury—and aftermath —of the police attack, and you have indication of how the symphonic shape, still faithful to its own peculiar methods, comes to grip with dramatic issue.

The poetic approach is best represented by *Romance Sentimentale* and the last sequence of *Ekstase*. Here there is description without tension, but the moving description is lit up by attendant images. In *Ekstase* the notion of life renewed is conveyed by a rhythmic sequence of labour, but there are also essential images of a woman and child, a young man standing high over the scene, skyscapes and water. The description of the various moods of *Romance Sentimentale* is conveyed entirely by images: in one sequence of domestic interior, in another sequence of misty morning, placid water and dim sunlight. The creation of mood, an essential to the symphonic form, may be done in terms of tempo alone, but it is better done if poetic images colour it. In a description of night at sea, there are elements enough aboard a ship to build up a quiet and effective rhythm, but a deeper effect might come by reference to what is happening under water or by reference to the strange spectacle of the birds which, sometimes in ghostly flocks, move silently in and out of the ship's lights.

A sequence in a film by Rotha indicates the distinction between the three different treatments. He describes the loading of a steel furnace and builds a superb rhythm into the shovelling movements of the men. By creating behind them a sense of fire, by playing on the momentary shrinking from fire which comes into these shovelling movements, he would have brought in the elements of tension. He might have proceeded from this to an almost terrifying picture of what steel work involves. On the other hand, by overlaying the rhythm with, say, such posturing or contemplative symbolic figures, as Eisenstein brought into his *Thunder Over Mexico* material, he would have added the elements of poetic image. The distinction is between (*a*) a musical or non-literary method; (*b*) a dramatic method with clashing forces; and (*c*) a poetic, contemplative, and altogether literary method. These three methods may all appear in one film, but their proportion depends naturally on the character of the director—and his private hopes of salvation.

I do not suggest that one form is higher than the other. There are pleasures peculiar to the exercise of movement which in a sense are tougher—more classical—than the pleasures of poetic description, however attractive and however blessed by tradition these may be. The introduction of tension gives accent to a film, but only too easily gives popular appeal because of its primitive engagement with physical issues and struggles and fights. People like a fight, even when it is only a symphonic one, but it is not clear that a war with the elements is a braver subject than the opening of a flower or, for that matter, the opening of a cable. It refers us back to hunting instincts and fighting instincts, but these do not necessarily represent the more civilized fields of appreciation.

It is commonly believed that moral grandeur in art can only be achieved, Greek or Shakespearian fashion, after a general laying out of the protagonists, and that no head is unbowed which is not bloody. This notion is a philosophic vulgarity. Of recent years it has been given the further blessing of Kant in his distinction between the aesthetic of pattern and the aesthetic of achievement, and beauty has been considered somewhat inferior to the sublime. The Kantian confusion comes from the fact that he personally had an active moral sense, but no active aesthetic one. He would not otherwise have drawn the distinction. So far as common taste is concerned, one has to see that we do not mix up the fulfilment of primitive desires and the vain dignities which attach to that fulfilment, with the dignities which attach to man as an imaginative being. The dramatic application of the symphonic form is not, *ipso facto*, the deepest or most important. Consideration of forms neither dramatic nor symphonic, but dialectic, will reveal this more plainly.

5 The E.M.B. Film Unit

In official records you would find the E.M.B. Film Unit tucked away in a long and imposing list of E.M.B. Departments and Sub-Departments, forty-five all told. The Film Unit was number forty-five. 'Research and Development' interests accounted for the first twenty-four. There the major part of E.M.B. work was done. In one respect or another it helped to integrate or promote all the major researches across the world which affected the production or preservation or transport of the Empire's food supplies. Consideration of cinema was, properly, junior to the consideration of such matters as entomological, mycological, and low temperature investigation.

So, through considerations of Tea, Rice, Sugar, Tobacco, Tung Oil, and Forest Products, to 'Marketing Economic Investigation and Intelligence': Marketings of home agricultural produce, regional sales drives, marketing inquiries in general, and market intelligence services for fish, fruit, dairy produce, dried and canned fruits in particular, world surveys of production and trade, retail surveys, accounts of wastage in imported fruit, experimental consignments, and I know not what all. Then 'Publicity', banner-heading the departments of newspaper advertisement, posters, recipes, leaflets, lectures, broadcasts, exhibitions, shopping weeks, and trade meetings.

After the trade meetings, cinema. I give you its place not in humility, but for proportion. It was a department among other departments, and part of a very much larger scheme of educational and propaganda services. Whatever its pretentions in purely cinematic terms, it was dedicated and devoted to the usual cold-blooded ends of Government.

Of the fifteen hundred tyros who applied for jobs in the E.M.B. Film Unit, fifteen hundred exactly expressed their enthusiasm for cinema, for art, for self-expression, and the other beautiful what-nots of a youthful or simply vague existence. Not one considered this more practical relationship of commissions to be served, nor the fact that Treasury money, and opportunity to make any films at all, were entirely conditioned by these commissions to be served. The point is important. In Britain, as in any other country, there is little or no

47

money for free production. There is money for films which will make box-office profits, and there is money for films which will create propaganda results. These only. They are the strict limits within which cinema has had to develop and will continue to develop.

The principal point of interest about the E.M.B. Film Unit is that, within such necessary propaganda limits, it was permitted a unique measure of freedom. The dogs of the commercial world are harried and driven to quick box-office results. The dogs of the propaganda world are more wisely driven to good results, for half the virtue of propaganda is in the prestige it commands. Another point: the commercials are interested only in the first results of their films: that is to say, in the amount of money a film takes in a twelvemonth. The long-range propagandists are not. Quick takings are a guarantee of immediate public interest and are therefore important, but the persistence of a film's effect over a period of years is more important still. To command, and cumulatively command, the mind of a generation is more important than by novelty or sensation to knock a Saturday night audience cold; and the 'hang-over' effect of a film is everything. In this sense the propaganda road to cinema has certain advantages. It allows its directors time to develop; it waits with a certain patience on their experiments; it permits them time to perfect their work. So by all logic it should do, and so it did at the E.M.B. If the E.M.B. was an exception in the degree of its patience and the extent of the freedom which it permitted, it was because the E.M.B. at the time was the only organization outside Russia that understood and had imagination enough to practise the principles of long-range propaganda. It was not unconscious of the example of Russia.

These more imaginative interpretations of the methods of propaganda were entirely due to Sir Stephen Tallents, whose book on the Projection of England indicated only slimly the creative work he did for the mobilization of the arts in the national service. The points of contact of E.M.B. publicity, education, and propaganda were so many and various that I doubt if even the war of 1914–18 produced so widely ranged or so penetrating a system. The fact that it worked in a lower key and without drawing attention to itself in easy species of ballyhoo was the measure of its strength as a peacetime activity. The ballyhoo method does for a pinch, but only so.

Its principal effect in six years (1928–33) was to change the connotation of the word 'Empire'. Our original command of peoples was becoming slowly a co-operative effort in the tilling of soil, the reaping of harvests, and the organization of a world economy. For the old flags of exploitation it substituted the new flags of common labour; for the old frontiers of conquest it substituted the new frontiers of research and world-wide organization. Whatever one's politics, and however cynical one might be about the factors destructive of a world economy, this change of emphasis had an ultimate historical importance. History is determined by just such building of new sentiments. It was clear that we had to learn to make our building deliberate.

I give you this conception of the E.M.B. as a world force, without apology. I cannot speak for the various official intentions nor, for that matter, guarantee that they understood the implication of the E.M.B.'s growing proportions, but so it existed in some of our minds, and with consequent direction in most of the things we did.

In cinema we got the very brief commission 'to bring the Empire alive'. We were instructed, in effect, to use cinema, or alternatively to learn to use it, to bring alive the industries, the harvests, the researches, the productions, the forward-looking activities of all kinds; in short, to bring the day-to-day activities of the British Commonwealth and Empire at work into the common imagination. The only conditions laid down were that we should have the good sense to explore a few preliminary avenues, work for a period experimentally, and remember the sensitive nerves of Treasury officials: Mr. Hildred being the unhappy financial Atlas appointed to carry this new and incomprehensible infant on his shoulders. I cannot say we succeeded at first with this neurological aspect of our work. We were confused in Mr. Hildred's mind (and possibly very rightly) with the people who take snapshots at the seaside; and he was not sure that our results should cost any more than the customary five for a shilling. Whitehall, we discovered, was longer by a bittock than the road to Damascus, and sky splitting an even more valuable art than cinema. But we did, and for two long years, explore the avenues.

Before the E.M.B. Unit was formed for continuous production, Walter Creighton and I wandered about looking at things. I think we must have seen every propaganda film in existence between Moscow and Washington. We certainly prepared the first surveys of the propaganda and educational services of the principal Governments. We ran, too, a school of cinema where all the films we thought had a bearing on our problem were brought together and demonstrated in whole or part, for the instruction of Whitehall. *Berlin, The Covered Wagon, The Iron Horse*, the Russians; we had all the documentaries and epics worth a damn; though, in calculation of our audience, we had perforce to change a few endings and consider some of the close-ups among the less forceful arguments. In effect, we sold our idea of cinema sufficiently well to get cash in hand for our first experimental productions. Creighton plumped for fantasy and I for documentary: Creighton making *One Family*, a seven-reel theatrical, with B.I.F., and I *Drifters* with New Era.

The choice of documentary was made partly on personal grounds, and partly on grounds of common financial sense. A Government department cannot, like the commercial gamblers, take a rap: or at least its powers of resistance are keyed only to the very smallest raps. Alternatively, if the Civil Service or any other public service must have its illegitimate infants, it is best to see that they are small ones. Documentary is cheap: it is, on all considerations of public accountancy, safe. If it fails for the theatres it may, by manipulation, be accommodated non-theatrically in one of half a dozen ways. Moreover, by reason of its cheapness, it permits a maximum amount of production and a maximum amount of directorial training against the future, on a limited sum. It even permits the building of an entire production and distribution machine for the price of a single theatrical. These considerations are of some importance where new experiments in cinema are concerned. With one theatrical film you hit or miss; with a machine, if it is reasonably run, the preliminary results may not be immediately notable or important, but they tend to pile up. Piling up they create a freedom impossible on any other policy.

The fact that documentary was the genre most likely to bring method and imagination into such day-to-day subjects as we dealt with was, of course, a final argument.

On these high conceptions, the unit continued to operate. The problem was not so much to repeat the relative success of *Drifters* but to guarantee that, with time, we should turn out good documentaries as a matter of certainty. It was a case of learning the job, not on the basis of one director, one location, and one film at a time, but on the basis of half a dozen directors with complementary talents, and a hundred and one subjects along the line. And because the job was new and because it was too humble to appeal to studio directors, it was also a question of taking young people and giving them their heads.

That was in 1930. In the three years that followed we gathered together, and in a sense created, Basil Wright, Arthur Elton, Stuart Legg, and half a dozen others. Wright was the best lyrical documentary director in the country, Elton the best industrial, and Legg the best all-rounder. One or two others, it seemed, would presently be heard from.

The E.M.B. Film Unit

Their record at that date was not, of course, a huge one, and in the circumstances could not be. It comprised *Industrial Britain* (with Flaherty), *Big Timber, O'er Hill and Dale, Country Comes to Town, Shadow on the Mountain, Upstream, Voice of the World,* and *The New Generation.* Wright was working on three films from the West Indies (*Cargo from Jamaica, Windmill in Barbados, Liner Cruising South*), Elton a five-reel account of aeroplane engines (*Aero-Engine*), and Legg two films on the Post Office. Edgar Anstey made *Uncharted Waters,* a film of Labrador exploration. J. N. G. Davidson made *Hen Woman,* the unit's only story documentary. D. F. Taylor had a film on the stocks (for the Travel Association) dealing with the changing landscape of Lancashire (*Lancashire at Work and Play*). Evelyn Spice was working on a new series of films for schools, covering the English seasons and the economic areas of England. To these add two or three odd films for the Ministry of Agriculture, sundry experiments in abstract films by Rotha and Taylor, and non-theatrical makings or re-editings at the rate of about fifty a year. That was the production account, and it was fair enough for the period involved. Two years' apprenticeship, or even three, was a short time for the exploration of a new craft, and the maturing of new talent, and I doubt if we expected anything considerable or exciting in less than five.

What was important was that this was the only group of its kind outside Russia: that is to say, the only group devoted deliberately, continuously, and with hope, to the highest forms of documentary. And its policy was in this respect unique, that so long as the film's general aim was served, no consideration of a mere popular appeal was allowed to enter. The director, in other words, was free in his manner and method as no director outside the public service can hope to be. His only limits were the limits of his finance, the limits of his aesthetic conscience in dealing so exclusively with an art of persuasion, and the limits of his own ability. In the practical issue they might sometimes embarrass, but did not seem to prevent a reasonably good result.

6 Summary and Survey: 1935

An artist in this art of cinema may whistle for the means of production. A camera costs a thousand pounds, a sound-recording outfit three times as much, and the brute cost of every second of picture shot is sixpence. Add the cost of actors, of technicians, of the thousand-and-one technical processes which come between the conception and the finished film, and the price of production is already a matter of high finance. A poet may prosper on pennies. A film director, even a bad director, must deal in thousands. Six thousand or so will make a quickie to meet the English quota laws. With sixty thousand one is reaching to the *Chu Chin Chows*. The more garish efforts of the Napoleonic de Mille cost two hundred and more. *Ben Hur* at more than a million and *Hell's Angels* at nearly a million are exceptions, but they happened. The cost of a film ranges between the price of a hospital and the estimated cost of clearing the slums of Southwark.

The most interesting point about these huge production costs is that they can be recovered. *Ben Hur* made money. This fact must be realized, and, with it, the one consideration which controls the cinema and dictates its relation to the artist: that a film is capable of infinite reproduction and infinite exhibition. It can cross boundaries and hold an audience of millions. The world's cinema audience is 250 millions a week, each and all of these myriads paying his yen or rupee or shilling or quarter for the privilege. Chaplin's *City Lights* was seen by fifteen millions in Britain alone. Where the prize of popularity is so gigantic, considerations of art and public service must, of course, be secondary. The film people are businessmen and, by all law of commerce, their spiritual researches are confined to those common factors of human appeal which ensure the rattle of ten or twenty or fifty million sixpences across the world. In this respect they pursue the same principles as Woolworth and Ford. They have rationalized the hopes-and-dreams business: a more plainly dangerous development, if entered lightly into, than all other rationalization whatsoever.

There are, among the common factors of human appeal, higher factors like humour and religion. There are the lower common factors of sentimentality and sensationalism. In the practical issue, nothing is quite so diffident as a million dollars. There is a certainty about the lower factors which the higher cannot pretend. Who—particularly a financier—can recognize the genuine prophet from the fake? Cinema has, on the whole, lost so much on its mistakes of prophecy that its simpler instinct is to avoid all prophecy together.

Humour it has held to, and faithfully. Epic—in twenty years or so—it has learned to distinguish from melodrama. These, in their blessed combination of simplicity and depth, have a sure record in commercial cinema: comedy in particular. They represent the two points at which wide human appeal may also have the quality of depth. And, so far from breaking through the economic law, it has been proved by Chaplins and Covered Wagons that they even more generously fulfil it. Simple inspiration, as priests and medicine men once discovered, was always a better box-office bet than simple entertainment.

But there, in comedy and epic, is the limit. Great cameramen contribute their superb craftsmanship, great story-tellers their invention, great art directors their splendour of décor, and the patience and skill which build even the average film are miracles to wonder over; but, at centre, in the heart and theme of the commercial film the financial consideration rules. It is a consideration of largest possible audiences and widest possible appeal. Sometimes, in comedy and epic, the result is in its simple way splendid. Nearly always the technical splendours of cinema loom gigantically over trivial and contemptible issues.

Only, therefore, in comedy, in epic, in occasional idyll does the commercial cinema touch the world of art, and is cinema possible for the artist. And epic and idyll being near to the problems of prophecy (note for example the difficulties of Robert Flaherty), comedy is of these the surest ground. Chaplin, Disney, Laurel and Hardy and the Marx Brothers are the only relatively footloose artists in cinema today. They are, in fact, free up to the point of satire. There, comedy merges with those deeper considerations of which finance must necessarily be sensitive. Footloose they are, these comedians, till in a moment of more considered fancy the Marx Brothers decide to play ducks and drakes with the banking system, Walt Disney with the American constitution, and Laurel and Hardy with the N.A.M.

Epic, too, can have its way if it is as rough-shod as *The Covered Wagon*, as sentimental for the *status quo* as *Cavalcade*, as heroic in the face of hunger as *Nanook*. Heaven defend it if, as once happened in

A Movement is Founded

Griffith's *Isn't Life Wonderful?*, the hunger is not of Eskimos but of ourselves. Perhaps it is that people do not want to see the world in its more sordid aspects, and that the law of widest appeal does not permit consideration of either our follies or our sorrows. Certain it is that the magnates of cinema will deplore the deviation. Theirs the dream of shop-girl and counter-clerk, and exclusively they pursue it. The films of our modern society are set among braveries too detached for questioning. The surroundings vary, and they sometimes reach to the mills and factories and hospitals and telephone exchanges of common life. They even reach back to include the more solid pageantries of history. But seldom is it that a grave or present issue is struck. Industry and history might assuredly bring to dramatic point those matters which more nearly concern us. In film they do not, because the financiers dare not. These backgrounds are façades only for an article which—though in comedy and epic it may not be trifling—is invariably safe.

This is not to convict the film producers of a great wrong. Like other businessmen, they serve their creed and ensure their profit and, on the whole, they do it very well. In one sense even, the financier might regard himself as a public benefactor. In an age when the faiths, the loyalties and the purposes have been more than usually undermined, mental fatigue—or is it spiritual fatigue—represents a large factor in everyday experience. Our cinema magnate does no more than exploit the occasion. He also, more or less frankly, is a dope pedlar.

This, then, is the atmosphere in which the maker of films is held, however noble his purpose or deep his inspiration. He is in a closed circle from which he can only by a rare failure of the system escape. It is a threefold circle. The financier-producer will prevent him going deep lest he becomes either difficult or dangerous. But beyond the producer lies the renter who, skilled only in selling dope, is unfitted for stimulants. If the film deviates in any way he will either curse it as a changeling or, in an effort to translate it into his own salesman terms, deceive and disappoint exhibitor and public alike. In this way *Moana* was mis-sold as 'the Love Life of a South Sea Syren'. The exhibitor is the third circle. He is by nature and circumstance more nervous than either producer or renter. He could, of course, combine the capacities of teacher and showman. He could, by articulating unusual virtues in a film, introduce them to the public. He could thereby create a more discriminating and critical public. But the exhibitor follows, like his brothers, the line of least resistance. The more imaginative points of showmanship are not for him when the brazen methods of ballyhoo are so patently effective. He is, he will say in self-defence, 'in the entertainment business' or, sometimes, 'in the entertainment catering business'. Entertainment may be as rich as inspiration, but, being a complacent fellow in his world of sensational superlatives, it is difficult to convince him.

The wise director will accept these conditions from the beginning. Production money, renting facilities, theatre screens, with the qualifications I have noted, are held against any divergence from the common law. His stuff must be popular stuff and as popular as possible. It must also be immediately popular, for the film business does not allow of those long-term policies and belated recognitions so common to art. A film is out and away and in again in twelve months, and the publicity which is so necessary to wide and sensational success promotes a sally rather than a circulation. The system does not allow of that slow penetration which is the safeguard of the painter and poet.

In spite of all this, the system does sometimes fail and unexpected things come through. The fit of scepticism which overtook Germany after 1918 had the effect of encouraging a seriousness of outlook which was altogether novel in the commercial world. Theatres and studios combined in the contemplation of Fate, and the cinema had its only period of tragedy. *Caligari*, *Destiny*, *The Joyless Street*, *The Grey House*, were the great films of this period. They were humourless and sombre but they were imaginatively done. They added power to cinema and celebrity to directors. Hollywood almost immediately acquired the celebrity. Murnau, Pommer, Jannings, Pola Negri, Lubitsch went over but, subjected to the brighter air of Hollywood and the wider insistence of its international market, their skill was quickly chained to the normal round. The system, as it continuously does with able aliens, absorbed them or broke them. After a struggle Pommer returned to Europe, but could not rebuild the tradition he had deserted. Murnau also struggled and in a last attempt at escape produced, with Flaherty, *Tabu*: too late, perhaps, for the expensive and shallow outlook of the studios had caught him. Lubitsch discovered a genius for comedy and was whole-heartedly absorbed. The rule obtains whether it is the artist or only his story that passes to the commercial atmosphere. Like the Celtic warriors, 'when they go into the West they seldom come back'.

The other exceptions are individual ones. Occasionally a director has money enough to back his own venture. Distribution may be lacking: but he can in the meantime have his fling. Occasionally a director is able to convince or deceive a producer into doing something more solid than usual. Occasionally, the publicity value attaching to a great reputation may overcome commercial scruples. In these categories come certain deviations of Fairbanks, King Vidor, D. W. Griffith, von Sternberg and Jean Renoir and responsible versions of H. G. Wells and Eugene O'Neill and Bernard Shaw. Sometimes, again, the personal toughery or insistence of a director has managed a deeper result than was contemplated or wanted. In this category are some of the films of von Stroheim, the best films of von Sternberg, Flaherty's *Moana*, Dreyer's *Joan of Arc* and some of the best of King Vidor and D. W. Griffith. But even the toughs do not last long. These men have done much for cinema and Griffith is the greatest master cinema has produced, but only Sternberg seems to have any assurance of continuity. He is the golden producer of the golden Dietrich. As a parting shot from his retirement Griffith has announced that one line of Shakespeare's poetry is worth all that the cinema ever produced.

To be absorbed or eliminated is the only choice in the commercial cinema, for it has the virtue of singleness of purpose. It has no ambition to specialize for specialized audiences. It has no reason to exploit the artist for the individual or creative quality of his inspiration. It is a big racket, they say, and you must play it big: which is to say that you must play it good and wide and common to the exclusion of all height and handsomeness. Within its lights and limits the commercial cinema is right. The artist is an economic fool who confuses financial dealings with patronage and exploitation with understanding.

Commercial cinema, being the monstrous undisciplined force it is, has done a great deal of harm. It has also done a great deal of simple good. Even in the world of sentimentality and sensationalism its narrative is racy, its wit is keen, and its types have more honest human gusto than their brothers and sisters of the stage and popular novel. The vast array of thwarted talent so expresses itself. If cinema has not debunked the greater evils of society it has very successfully debunked some of the lesser ones. It has given many salutary lessons in critical citizenship, for it has taught people to question authority, realize the trickeries that may parade in the name of Justice, and recognize that graft may sit in the highest places. It has taught the common people to take account of themselves in their common manners, if not in their common rights. It has taught the world to dress better, look better, and, to some extent, behave better. It may not have added to the wisdom of the world but it has at least de-yokelized it. These are only some of the gifts of the commercial cinema. There is also the gift of beautiful women, of the fresh air of the Westerns, of much fine setting and brilliant décor. The skill and polish of its presentation, though only the professional may judge them properly, are a continuing delight. They may even exercise a continuing discipline.

The stars are not so easily included in the benefits of cinema. They are our version of the mythological figures who have at all times expressed the desires of primitive peoples. Here, as always, the figures of the imagination maintain the will. But to say so is to discover that other side of the picture which is not so beautiful. For loss and lack of other mythology, the millions are very deeply bound to their stars: not only in the matter of their dress and bearing but also in the ends they seek. On this criterion the stars are a queer lot. The inquiries of the Payne Trust in America discovered some interesting analyses in this connection, and I take the following excerpts more or less solidly from H. J. Forman's summing up of their findings. Thirty-three per cent of the heroines, 34 per cent of the villains, 63 per cent of the villainesses in one hundred and fifteen pictures—all these eminent protagonists—are either wealthy or ultra-wealthy. The 'poor' run only to 5 per cent. The largest classification for all characters combined is *no occupation. Commercial* comes next with ninety characters. *Occupation unknown* comes next with eighty. The gangsters, bootleggers, smugglers, thieves, bandits, blackmailers and prostitutes follow, also with eighty. *Theatrical, servants, high society*, the luxury trades in fact, follow, as one might imagine, the gangsters, the thieves and the bandits. These together account for six hundred and forty of a total character list of eight hundred and eighty-three. The remaining quarter of this crazily assorted population is scattered among many callings, notable in that common labour is not included in them at all. A few agricultural labourers exist, but only to decorate the Westerns. Mr. Forman adds: 'Were the population of the United States the population of the world itself, so arranged and distributed, there would be no farming, no manufacturing, almost no industry, no vital statistics (except murders), no economic problems and no economics.'

Dr. Dale contributes an even more entertaining analysis of *goals*. In his hundred and fifteen pictures, the heroes are responsible for thirteen good sound murders, the villains and villainesses for thirty. Heroines have only one to their credit. Altogether fifty-four murders are committed, to say nothing of fifty-nine cases of mere assault and battery. Thirty-six hold-ups are staged and twenty-one kidnappings, numerous other crimes scattering. The total score is remarkable. Forty-three crimes are attempted; four hundred and six are actually committed. And taking an analysis of forty pictures in which fifty-seven criminals are responsible for sixty-two crimes, it appears that of the fifty-seven only three were arrested and held, four were arrested and released, four others were arrested but escaped, seven were arrested and the punishment implied, twenty-four were punished by extra-legal methods. Fifteen criminals went wholly unpunished.

'The goals in the lives of these baseless ruthless people', says Mr. Forman, 'are often as tawdry as themselves. Of the social goals, the higher goals of mankind, the numbers are very small.' They are indeed, when one realizes that 75 to 80 per cent of the films deal more or less exclusively with sex and crime. Of the sixteen 'goals' figuring most frequently, *performance of duty* comes a miserable eighth in the order of merit. All the others are strictly personal. *Love* in its various forms is first, second, fourth, fifth, sixth, with *illicit love* quietly solid at tenth. 'Shoddy goals', says Mr. Forman, 'pursued frequently by highly objectionable human beings.' It is difficult not to agree, though economic estimate is, on the whole, more fruitful than moral indignation.

Out of this welter of influences for good and evil it is possible occasionally to isolate a dramatic film which is just a good honest film in itself—with spirit enough to dodge sociological criticism. The gangster films *Quick Millions* and *Beast of a City* were well done. So were the newspaper stories *Hi! Nellie*, *Five Star Final* and *The Front Page*. So were the convict films *I am a Fugitive* and *Twenty Thousand Years in Sing Sing*. So was the back-stage story *Forty-Second Street*. They have invention and gusto in the high degree we generally associate with Edgar Wallace. And this is as much as a wise critic will expect of the dramatic film. One film of the line did break through to subtler qualities. This was *Three-Cornered Moon*. It appeared humbly as a second feature and its deviation was plainly mistrusted, but it made a fine affair of family affection and said something quietly of the American depression. Among the sentimental romances there was *Ekstase*, not a film of the line but a freak of quality from Czechoslovakia. The commercial cinemas refused it. Sentimental romance does, however, vary a little. By dint of great directorial ambition (or is 'artistic' the word?) the sad, sad saccharine of *Seventh Heaven* becomes the sad, sad saccharine of *The Constant Nymph*. Here the object of the affection is no longer the rich young man next door: he is the poor young artist in the garret over the way. So the mind of the movies moves laboriously to higher things.

The creative reputations built on such foundations are, to say the least, slimly based. In great generosity the critics have made names for Milestone, Roland Brown, Mamoulian and others. They are great and skilled craftsmen certainly, but nothing of them remains at the midriff after a twelvemonth. Here perhaps the critics, finding no depth of theme for their consideration, have made a grave and continuing mistake. They have equated a mere skill of presentation with the creative will itself. So doing they have perverted criticism and misled at least one generation of willing youths into false appreciation. The only critic in Britain who has taken the proper measure of the movies is St. John Ervine. By blasting it for its shallowness he, by implication, defends a cinema which may yet—who knows—be measured to the adult mind. But it is the cinema-conscious and the cinema-critical who rise howling at his word. Our body of criticism is largely to blame. It is consciously or subconsciously influenced by the paid advertisement and the flattering hospitality of the trade. It is, consciously or subconsciously, affected by the continuing dearth of critical subject matter. The observation of technical skill is the only decent gambit available to a disheartening, sychophantic, and largely contemptible pursuit.

Outside the world of drama there are, of course, better things. There are the idylls, the epics and the comedies. Each has its own particular problems and troubles: financial in the case of idylls, as one might expect in a genre so near to poetry, technical in the cases of comedy and epic, because of the complications of sound. The great idyll of the period has been *Man of Aran*, and I precise its story for its bearings on the economic arguments I have laid. Flaherty came to Britain at the invitation of the old E.M.B. Film Unit, not of the cinema trade at all. He had done nothing in cinema since his co-operation with Murnau on *Tabu*: a film which was financed and made outside the commercial circle. Through the persistent efforts of Cedric Belfrage and Angus McPhail he passed to Gaumont-British, to be given *carte blanche* on the Aran Islands. This was altogether a freak happening in commercial cinema and entirely due to the supporting courage of Michael Balcon and McPhail at G.-B.

After two years the film came along. It was not altogether the film some of us expected. It made sensation of the sea, it restored shark-hunting to the Arans to give the film a high-spot, and Flaherty's genius for the observation of simple people in their simple manners was not, we felt, exercised to the full. But as a simple account of human dignity and bravery through the years, the film was a fine affair. There remained only the selling of it in a world inclined to be alien. Flaherty himself had to take up the necessary barn-storming tactics. He went through the country making personal appearances.

59

A Movement is Founded

Aran Islanders in home-spun and tam-o'-shanters attended with him and spoke at luncheons given to local Mayors. Flaherty's life story appeared in a Sunday newspaper and copies of it were handed out by cinema attendants dressed in fisherman's jerseys marked 'Man of Aran'. The champagne flowed and the critics raved. In the Edgware Road a now excited crowd tried to cut locks of hair from Tiger King the hero, and Maggie Durrane the heroine—a lovely creature—went on tour of Selfridge's under the *Daily Express*, to discuss silk stockings and the modern woman. So far as Britain was concerned the method worked. Salesman and exhibitor alike were driven into acquiescence and the British commercial cinema's only work of art was ballyhooed into appreciation. Without Flaherty behind it storming, raging, praying and publicizing, heaven knows what would have happened. The fate of the film in Paris is a fair guide. There the pessimism or inertia or stupidity of the commercial agent made all the difference. In a country more instructed than England in documentary, where *Nanook* and *Moana*, the other great films of Flaherty, had been running for twelve and eight years respectively, the commercial people cut down the film and billed it below the line as a subsidiary feature.

The cinema magnates, as I have noted, have been good to comedy, and so has the medium. It was, from the beginning, kind to the masks of clowns; its space and its movement gave the stage tumblers a more generous outlet; editing and trick work, from precising the throwing of pies, came to encourage a new ingenuity of comic event. The coming of sound was something of a disaster for the silent comedians like Chaplin, Keaton, Langdon, Griffith and Lloyd. The realism of the spoken word destroyed the more distant atmosphere in which the silent art created them, and none of them has had the ingenuity to develop a use of sound which would preserve the ancient quality of their mask and ballet. Cavalcanti's film *Pett and Pott* shows how this could effectively be done by formalizing the sound and making it contribute to the mute (*a*) in comedy of music, (*b*) in comedy of sound image, and (*c*) in comedy of asynchronism; but the studios have failed to experiment. Intoxicated by the novelty and ease of the spoken word they have not perhaps thought the old comedy of mask worth saving, and the mummers have not known how to save themselves. Their art is, for the moment, declining. The palm is passing to a new band of wisecrack comedians who, like the Marx Brothers, W. C. Fields, Schnozzle Durante, Burns and Allen, make as great a preciosity of talking as their predecessors did of silence. Laurel and Hardy do not depend quite so much on talk and the peculiar style of their comedy has allowed them to make a more effective use of sound. They are clumsy, they are destructive, they are in essence noisy people; the world of sound is theirs to crash and tumble over. By making sound an integral factor in their mumming, they have tumbled on a first creative use of sound.

Out of the possibilities of sound synchronization a world of sound must be created, as refined in abstraction as the old silent art, if great figures like Chaplin are to come again. It is no accident that of all the comedy workers of the new régime the most attractive, by far, is the cartoonist Disney. The nature of his material forced upon him something like the right solution. Making his sound strip first and working his animated figures in distortion and counterpoint to the beat of the sound, he has begun to discover those ingenious combinations which will carry on the true tradition of film comedy.

Epic, too, has had its setback since the coming of sound. There has been *Cimarron* to succeed *The Iron Horse* and *The Covered Wagon*, but nothing like the same continuity of great outdoor themes, in which continents were crossed, jungles penetrated and cities and nations built. There has been the technical difficulty that outdoor sound with its manifold of background noise has been difficult to register, but apart from this there has not been the same will to create in outdoor worlds as in silent days. The commercial cinema has come more than ever indoors to imitate in dialogue and confinement the charade of the theatre. The personal human story is more easily told in sound than it was in silence. Silence drove it inevitably to wider horizons, to issues of storm and flood, to large physical happenings. Silence could hardly avoid epic and sound can. Just as silence created its own tempo'd form and its own sense of distance, the new medium might present a deeply counterpointed consideration of great event. The voices of crowds and nations could be cross-sectioned; complex happenings could be dramatized by the montage of sound and voice, and by the many possibilities there are of combining, by sound, present fact with distant bearings. Experimenting in *Song of Ceylon*, Basil Wright crossed a chorus of market cries and a rigmarole of international commerce with a scene of Buddhist ceremonial. Lost in the ease of dialogue, the studios will have none of this.

Man of Aran, if we accept it as near to epic, is a silent, not a sound film: a silent film to which a background ribbon of sound has added nothing but atmosphere. Its story is a visual story. Its effects are achieved by the tempo'd technique built up by the Russian silent films. The sound script does not jump into the narrative to play the

A Movement is Founded

part it might easily do in building up the issue. In *Man of Aran* perhaps it was not necessary. In films of wider range it is plainly foolish to avoid the powers which lie ready to hand. Where a film combines in significance the highlights of a nation's history there is much which an imaginative use of sound cutting and sound orchestration might do. Of *Cimarron* one can remember only the rumble of wagons, the chatter of crowds, the beat of horses' hoofs, and some dialogue of personal story: unimportant, uncreative noises all of them, which did nothing to build the body of cinema epic. Whatever horizons were crossed cinema itself stayed halting at home. This neglect of the creative element of the new cinema proves, if proof were necessary, that if the deeper purpose were not there it is not likely that the medium will be deeply discovered.

Outside these fields of popular cinema—of which this all too qualified result can be expected—there has grown up another more independent cinema. I do not mean here the *avant garde* cinema which for a while flourished in France and has raised its head wherever family fortune and youthful enthusiasm have allowed it. The French *avant garde* with René Clair (the early René Clair of *The Italian Straw Hat*), Cavalcanti, Epstein and Jean Renoir, made its dash for liberty by exploiting its friends. Working on a shoestring it created its own little distribution and theatre system. It built its own faithful audience at the Ursulines and the Vieux Colombier. All the requisites of an independent cinema were there except principle, and the loyalty which goes with principle. In fact, the moment the businessmen of the group made money they invested it in popular films and abandoned art and audience alike. The *avant garde* movement blew up because its directors were economic innocents and, until they go to Hollywood, film directors only too often are. It blew up because the tie which bound the director and his agents was not the creative one they imagined. In a dilettante sense it may have been, but it had no social basis which could withstand commercial temptation.

Something more solidly founded than the *avant garde* cinema there has been, and that is the propagandist cinema. With the failure of the French movement, it became evident in at least one quarter that, if an independent cinema were to become possible, some other economic basis than the entertainment world and other than private philanthropy had to be discovered. Education was first considered but, being the poor, neglected, unimaginative world it is, was quickly discarded. The choice of propaganda was inevitable. It has been responsible for odd periodic excursions into cinema in a hundred

62

centres. The Canadian Government has a film bureau which produces films for its departments. Government departments in the United States, France, Germany and Italy have their annual issue of films on agriculture, health and industrial process. The vaults of great industrial houses are packed with the more or less pathetic efforts of commercial film companies (shooting at so much a foot) to make their processes and products exciting. But only in Britain—I except Russia—was propaganda deliberately exploited for the greater opportunity it presented to cinematic art, and made the basis for a school of cinema. This was at the Empire Marketing Board, under Sir Stephen Tallents, who is possibly the most imaginative and far-seeing of the masters of propaganda in Britain: certainly the only one who has considered how, and how deeply, propaganda may serve the State. He has maintained with John Stuart Mill that 'it is the artist alone in whose hands truth becomes impressive and a living principle of action'.

If you are to bring alive—this was the E.M.B. phrase—the material of commerce and industry, the new bewildering world of invention and science and the modern complex of human relationship; if you are to make citizenship in our vast new world imaginative and, therefore, possible, cinema is, on the face of it, a powerful weapon. But when the material of event has not yet been brought to imaginative form, research into new cinematic method is necessary. The example of the studios was not good enough, for it demonstrated little respect for common fact and less for common achievement. Its cameras and its technique had not prowled into this world of worker, organizer and discoverer. What was wanted was a cinema capable of building its art from subject matter essentially alien to the studio mind. On the bare evidence of Ruttmann's *Berlin*, Cavalcanti's *Rien que les Heures*, and with a side-glance at the Russians, the E.M.B. dived into what it called 'Documentary': giving a freedom to its directors never recorded before in cinema. Indeed it is a curious comment on our art that the only freedom given to directors since has also been by propagandist groups: by Shell, the B.B.C., the Ministry of Labour, the Ceylon Government, the Gas Light and Coke Co., and by certain shipping, creosoting and radio firms in Europe. It is, of course, a relative freedom only, for state propaganda has its own ideological limits. This, however, can be said for it: the freshness and even the difficulty of its material drive the director to new forms and rich perspectives.

Out of this world has come the work of Walter Ruttmann, Joris Ivens, Jean Lods, Basil Wright, Paul Rotha, Arthur Elton, Stuart Legg and Evelyn Spice. Save Ruttmann, they are all young people. They are all masters of camera and, more importantly, masters of *montage*. They have all learned how to make ordinary things stand up with a new interest, and make fine sequence of what, on the face of it, was plain event. They have begun to bring their observation of the world under their nose to an issue. Their documentary is not the idyllic documentary of Flaherty with its emphasis of man against the sky, but a documentary of industrial and social function, where man is more likely to be in the bowels of the earth.

Whatever the difference of their still developing styles—symphonic in Ruttmann, Ivens, Wright and Rotha, analytic in Elton and Legg and dialectical as yet in none of them—they have one achievement in common. They have taken the discursive cinema of the news reels, the scenics and the 'interests', and given it shape; and they have done it with material which the commercial cinema has avoided. They have not yet learned how to combine the lucid—and even academic— estimate of event in the body of imaginative work, but they are coming slowly nearer to the growing points of their social material.

The relationship between the artist and the themes of the community, so far from binding the artist, has opened new horizons for it. The documentary of work and workers has found endless possibilities stretching out before it: reaching not perhaps as its forebears did to halcyon horizons but by the nearest hole in the road to engineering master-works, and by the nearest vegetable store to the epics of scientific agriculture. And where there is so much occasion for observing the qualities of mankind, the human factor must be increasingly commanded. As though to demonstrate how in this seemingly sober world the mainspring of creation lies, it is remarkable how much quicker in the uptake this relatively small group has been in the exploitation of the new sound medium. The G.P.O. Film Unit, which succeeded the E.M.B. Film Unit, is the only experimental centre in Europe. Where the artist is not pursuing entertainment but purpose, not art but theme, the technique is energized inevitably by the size and scope of the occasion. How much further it reaches and will reach than the studio leap-frog of impotent and self-conscious art!

The near relationship to purpose and theme is even more plainly evidenced by the great Russian directors. They too were begun in propaganda and were made by it: in the size of their story and the power of their style. One cannot do less when recording a world revolution than develop a tempo to take it. But the most interesting story of the Russian film does not begin until after *Potemkin* and *The End of St. Petersburg*. These early films with their tales of war and sudden death provided relatively easy material, and did not diverge greatly in melodrama from the example of D. W. Griffith. There was the brighter cinematic style; there was the important creation of crowd character; but the whole effect was hectic and, in the last resort, romantic. In the first period of revolution the artists had not yet got down, like their neighbours, to themes of honest work; and it is remarkable how, after the first flush of exciting cinema, the Russian talent faded. Relating cinema to the less melodramatic problems of reconstruction was plainly a different matter.

Eisenstein set himself to tell the story of the Russian peasants, and had to discover wicked poisoning kulaks to make a case for co-operatives. He took three years to make a mull of *The General Line*. The truth was that he came to his subject from the outside and did not sufficiently appreciate either the peasants or their problems. Victor Turin, more luckily, had the shooting of the Turkestan-Siberian railway: where the specious and romantic appeal of drought and desert storm could give colour to his story. *Turksib* gave every impression of building a railway but the approach was again too detached to appreciate just how precisely or humanly it was built. H. G. Wells very properly remarked that its epileptic way of doing things was too much for him. Dovjenko missed his footing in the same way as Eisenstein. He only incidentally and crudely treated the question of peasant organization in *Earth*, by melodramatically associating it with the personal villainies of an individual kulak. And, as Flaherty might have done, he ran the film into a song of the seasons: so beautifully that only the dialecticians noticed his avoidance. Vertov, coming nearer to the problem, used every camera exhibitionism to tell in *Enthusiasm* how wonderful the worker's life was. But the heroic angle of his vision of workmen always failed to observe what the men were doing. Altogether, the Russian directors have been slow in coming to earth. Great artists they are, but alien for the most part to the material they are set. Only in Ermler's first crude *Fragment of an Empire*: in his more mature *Counterplan*: and in *Men and Jobs*—where the central issue in Russia of giving industrial skill to a peasant community is the dramatic issue of the film—does the future seem assured. Eisenstein, after Parisian adventuring in *Romance Sentimentale* (a description of the moods of a female pianist) and further wanderings in the exotic atmospheres of Hollywood and Mexico, is still planning a successor to *October*. Pudovkin's *Deserter* has not yet, like *Men and Jobs*, found those common issues in which alone the work of that great artist can develop.

A Movement is Founded

Pudovkin reveals more than any of the Russian directors the trouble which has faced them. Lacking a strong political head, he has blundered into the most curious and revealing mess which Russia has ever sent us—a film called *A Simple Case*. It was clearly Pudovkin's intention to demonstrate how the reactionary mind had faltered as it came to grips with the life of reconstruction. But this theme is based on a trivial personal story in which a Soviet soldier runs off with a vamp. The story, in other words, is not nearly large enough for the issue and, with heavy weather over nothing, the film fails. Not all Pudovkin's beautiful symbolic images of death and resurrection can save it. *Deserter* followed *A Simple Case*. It is also a personal story: of a German worker who deserted the class war in Hamburg for the ease of workers' emancipation in Russia. He finds in Russia, as one might expect, that the real thing is back on his own home front. The film is greatly spread; there are marchings and counter marchings, riots and revolutions in the grand manner; there is a scene in a Russian factory where the deadline for the completion of a giant generator is frantically kept. Indeed, one may only observe of Pudovkin at this stage that it is the foulest folly in industrial practice to keep any such deadline frantically. And his own recourse to Hamburg and the pyrotechnics of sudden death, when accurate industrial observation was open to him on his own doorstep, is the very desertion he is describing.

It is a commonplace of modern teaching that even with revolution, revolution has only begun. The Russian film directors do not seem to have appreciated the significance of this, for it would lead them to subject matter which, for the moment, they appear to avoid: to the common problems of everyday life and to the common—even instructional—solutions of them. But Russian directors are too bound up—too aesthetically vain—in what they call their 'play films' to contribute to Russia's instructional cinema. They have, indeed, suffered greatly from the freedom given to artists in a first uncritical moment of revolutionary enthusiasm, for they have tended to isolate themselves more and more in private impression and private performance. As much as any bourgeois counterpart, they have given themselves the airs and ribbons of art. This has been possible because the first five-year plan and the second have been too busy with essential services to get round to cinema. For the future, one may leave them safely to the consideration of the Central Committee. One's impression is that when some of the art and all of the bohemian self-indulgence have been knocked out of them, the Russian cinema will fulfil its high promise of the late twenties. It is bound to, for only its present romantic perspective prevents it coming to grips with the swift and deeply detailed issues around it. The revolutionary will must certainly 'liquidate', as they put it, this romantic perspective.

Of our own future there are two things to say, and the first has to do with sound. The habit is to consider sound-film as in some sense a progress on the silent form. What has happened of course is that the cheaper and easier uses of the silent film have been succeeded by the cheaper and easier uses of the sound-film. There has been as yet no succession to the mature use of silent cinema which slowly developed in Griffith, Sennett, Eisenstein, Pudovkin, in the great German school, in the French *avant garde*, and in the documentaries of Flaherty and Ruttmann. We have added sound and, in the process, have lost a great deal of our sense of visual form. We use sound to mouth a story from one more or less insignificant situation to another. We use music for atmosphere and sometimes to give tempo to our event. Our crowds roar and our carriages rumble. The shadows of our screen make noises now, and it is true that, at their best, they might be Shakespearean noises; but that is not to say we are thinking sound-film and properly using it. For sound-film is not simply an opportunity of doing what straight plays and magic lantern lectures have already done: it is, in its own right, an opportunity for something individual and different, and imaginatively so. A brief consideration of its physical nature will indicate this. The sound, like the mute, is visually registered on a strip of film. Like the images of the mute, the different stretches of sound can be cut up with scissors and joined by paste in any order one pleases. Any sound stretch can be laid over another and added to it. So natural sound, music, recital, dialogue can be orchestrated to the will of the artist; and his orchestrations may be in any relation he selects to the images which run alongside. A statue of the Buddha may be associated with religious music or with the sound of wireless signals relating to tea and international markets, or with some word spoken from a Buddhist gospel. An orator's speech can be variously associated with (*a*) its own noise, (*b*) a jazz band playing 'I Can't Give You Anything But Love, Baby', (*c*) the dictation of the secretary who determined its rhetoric, (*d*) a heavenly choir of female voices, (*e*) the applause or execration of a fifty-thousand crowd rolling up in carefully shaped waves, (*f*) any sound the artist cares to draw on the side of the film. A succession of Gs or Ks, for example, might make a remarkable and revealing accompaniment. The point is that one may add almost anything one chooses to an image or to a sequence of images; for there is, in sound-film, a power of selection which is denied the stage.

A Movement is Founded

With these immense powers available, it is fairly clear that the synchronized dialogue with which we are universally afflicted represents a crude use of the new medium, hardly better than the B.B.C.'s reproductive use of the microphone. What must come is a conception of the sound-film as a new and distinct art with a genius of its own; to be slowly discovered as the silent art of cinema had begun to be discovered. The fine abstraction of that art we have lost among the chattering voices. In the weird perspectives of sound-film we shall find it again.

And regarding the future, there is this second point to make: that the cinema will divide and specialize and the more ambitious parts of it will break—as much as may be—from the stranglehold of commercial interests. Cinema is neither an art nor an entertainment: it is a form of publication, and may publish in a hundred different ways for a hundred different audiences. There is education to serve; there is the new civic education which is emerging from the world of publicity and propaganda; there is the new critical audience of the film circles, the film societies and the specialized theatres. All these fields are outside the commercial cinema.

Of these, the most important field by far is propaganda. The circles devoted to the art of cinema mean well and they will help to articulate the development of technique, but the conscious pursuit of art carries with it, in periods of public difficulty, a certain shallowness of outlook. The surface values are not appreciated in relation to the material they serve, for there is avoidance of the central issues involved in the material. We need not look to the film societies for fundamentals. They will continue to be bright about trivialities of tempo and other technique, and their pleasant Sunday afternoons will continue to be innocuous. The 'grim and desperate education' of propaganda is another matter. It comes more and more to grips with the questions of public life and public importance, and cinema, serving it, reflects a certain solidity of approach. The facts are simple enough. In a world too complex for the educational methods of public speech and public writing, there is a growing need for more imaginative and widespread media of public address. Cinema has begun to serve propaganda and will increasingly do so. It will be in demand. It will be asked to create appreciation of public services and public purposes. It will be asked from a hundred quarters to create a more imaginative and considered citizenship. It will be asked, too, inevitably, to serve the narrower viewpoints of political or other party propaganda. But where there are wide fields, the participation of the artist can be various.

Summary and Survey: 1935

As I see it, the future of the cinema may not be in the cinema at all. It may even come humbly in the guise of propaganda and shamelessly in the guise of uplift and education. It may creep in quietly by way of the Y.M.C.A.s, the church halls and other citadels of suburban improvement. This is the future for the art of cinema, for in the commercial cinema there is no future worth serving. It represents the only economic basis on which the artist may expect to perform. Two possibilities there are which qualify this conclusion. The theatres, now so abandoned in their commercial anarchy, would, under any measure of national or international direction, be forced to larger considerations than they at present entertain. And the coming of television will bring a consideration of cinema as liberal at least as the B.B.C.'s present consideration of music. In these respects, the future is bright enough. But even under a controlled cinema and a televised cinema, it will be wise for the artist to organize his independence: going direct to public service for his material and his economy. There lies his best opportunity—and therefore his freedom.

1   The Course of Realism

Here is an art based on photographs, in which one factor is always, or nearly always, a thing observed. Yet a realist tradition in cinema has emerged only slowly. When Lumière turned his first historic strip of film, he did so with the fine careless rapture which attends the amateur effort today. The new moving camera was still, for him, a camera and an instrument to focus on the life about him. He shot his own workmen filing out of the factory and this first film was a 'documentary'. He went on as naturally to shoot the Lumière family, child complete. The cinema, it seemed for a moment, was about to fulfil its natural destiny of discovering mankind. It had everything for the task. It could get about, it could view reality with a new intimacy; and what more natural than that the recording of the real world should become its principal inspiration?

I remember how easily we accepted this in the tender years of the century when our local lady brought to our Scottish village the sensation of the first movies; and I imagine now it was long before the big towns like Edinburgh and Glasgow knew anything about them. These, too, were documentaries, and the first film I saw was none other than Opus 2 in the history of cinema—the Lumière boy eating his apple. Infant wonder may exaggerate the recollection, but I will swear there was in it the close-up which was to be invented so many years later by D. W. Griffith. The significant thing to me now is that our elders accepted this cinema as essentially different from the theatre. Sin still, somehow, attached to play-acting, but, in this fresh new art of observation and reality, they saw no evil. I was confirmed in cinema at six because it had nothing to do with the theatre, and I have remained so confirmed. But the cinema has not. It was not quite so innocent as our Calvinist elders supposed. Hardly were the workmen out of the factory and the apple digested than it was taking a trip to the moon and, only a year or two later, a trip in full colour to the devil. The scarlet women were in, and the high falsehood of trickwork and artifice was in, and reality and the first fine careless rapture were out.

70

The Course of Realism

Thinking back over the years of development, fresh air and real people do appear for periods at a time. Obviously the economics of production in the early days were more cheaply served by the natural exterior. Till we learned to create our own sunlight, the heavenly variety was cheaper; until we mastered the art of miniature and dunning and back projection, it was cheaper to take the story to a natural location than the other way round. And the effect was to give not only naturalism to the setting but naturalism to the theme. One remembers the early Danish school which exported so many films before 1914; later the Swedish school with its noble exploitation in photography and drama of the Swedish light; the early English school of *Coming Thro' the Rye*, and the early American school of *The Great Train Robbery*, slapstick, and the Westerns. There was fresh air in all of them, but, more importantly, there was some reflection of ordinary life in the drama. In *The Great Train Robbery* the engineers and telegraph men were contacts with the real thing, and unimportant as they now seem, it was a long time before they cropped up again. Once inside the studio the tendency of the cinema was to make the most of its powers of artifice, graduating from the painted backcloths and wobbly colonnades to the synthetic and more or less permanent near-realism of three-ply, plaster, and painted glass. The supers like *Dante's Inferno*, and the highly expansive struggles for expression in a new medium which characterized the silent epics—those sweeping movements, those cosmic gestures—struck the keynote of the new art.

Cinema, I am inclined to think, has been from the first not the guttersnipe we all suppose, but something of a prig. It was not Zukor, clever little man as he may be, who first thought of attaching famous players to famous plays. The grand people of the French and British theatres had been gesturing to the studio roof for years before, and always in the grandest of causes: dealing with the destinies of Julius Caesar twice, King Lear thrice, and Hamlet six times before poor Zukor had begun to think about the cinema at all. Those early days produced forty versions of Shakespeare—Dante, Napoleon, and Marie Antoinette scattering—with a gusto for celebrity to which even silence proved no obstacle. So far from the latter-day Copperfields and Romeos representing a special advance of the cinema into cultural grounds, they merely show us back at the old and original stand. We may have whored in our time, but we have always been snobs at heart. Here, the higher economics. Big names and celebrated subjects brought attention, and attention brought money. They were easier to sell, for salesmen had not yet learned the art of giving cosmic importance to nonsense and nonentities. But, driven by economics into artifice, the cinema has stayed there for other equally effective reasons. It has never been quite sure of itself, never quite believed in its separate and original destiny. This, no doubt, is the price we have paid for being a new art, but the fact that we have been so largely in the hands of international traders and salesmen may have operated too. Great qualities they have brought out: fervour and excitement to the salesmanship of cinema and a certain extravagance to our spectacle. But social confidence and an easy acceptance of the right to social observation could hardly be claimed for many of those otherwise brilliant men who have built up the cinema. *Esprit* they have had, but hardly spirit.

Looking down the history of the actuality films, of what has seemed on the surface most natural and most real, there was, until the late thirties, a lack of fibre. From the beginning we have had newsreels, but dim records they seem now of only the evanescent and the essentially unreal, reflecting hardly anything worth preserving of the times they recorded. In curiosity one might wish to see again the Queen's Jubilees and the Delhi Durbars—with coloured coats that floated in air a full yard behind the line of march—the Kaiser at manœuvres and the Czar at play. Once Lenin spoke, here and there early aeroplanes made historic landings and war cameras recorded, till war cameras record again, the vast futility of the dead. Exceptional occasions, yes, and the greatest shot I ever saw came out of it with the *Blücher* heeling over and the thousand men running, sliding, jumping over the lurching side to their death—like flies. A fearful and quiet shot. But among the foundation stones, the pompous parades, the politicians on pavements, and even among the smoking ruins of mine disasters and the broken backs of distressed ships, it is difficult to think that any real picture of our troubled day has been recorded. The newsreel has gone dithering on, mistaking the phenomenon for the thing in itself, and ignoring everything that gave it the trouble of conscience and penetration and thought.

But something more intelligent arrived. It crashed through from the America that succeeded the slump and learned with Roosevelt the simple braveries of the public forum. It was called the *March of Time* and so strong is the need it fulfils that it will soon be called by a dozen names—Window on the World, World Eye, Brave New World, and what not. *March of Time* does what the other news records have failed to do. It gets behind the news, observes the factors of influence, and gives a perspective to events. Not the parade of armies so much as the race in armaments; not the ceremonial opening of a dam but the full story of Roosevelt's experiment in the Tennessee Valley; not the launching of the *Queen Mary* but the post-1918 record of British shipping. All penetrating and, because penetrating, dramatic.

Only three years old (in 1937), it has swept through the country, answering the thin glitter of the newsreels with nothing on the face of it more dramatic than the story of cancer research, the organization of peace, the state of Britain's health, the tithe war in the English shires, the rural economy of Ireland, with here and there a bright and ironic excursion into Texas centennials and the lunatic fringe of politics. In no deep sense conscious of the higher cinematic qualities, it has yet carried over from journalism into cinema, after thirty-eight years, something of that bright and easy tradition of free-born comment which the newspaper has won and the cinema has been too abject even to ask for. There are proper limits, it is true, to freedom of speech which the cinema must regard. Its power is too great for irresponsible comment, when circulations like the *March of Time*'s may run to nine thousand theatres across an explosive world. But it seems sensible for the moment that the *March of Time* has won the field for the elementary principles of public discussion. The world, our world, appears suddenly and brightly as an oyster for the opening: for film people—how strangely—worth living in, fighting in and making drama about. And more important still is the thought of a revitalized citizenship and of a democracy at long last in contact with itself.

In easier fields the actuality film has found a larger career, and the easier the more brilliant. Whenever observation has been so detached from the social theme as to raise no inhibition, its place on the screen has been assured. Films disclosing scenery and the more innocuous habits of mankind have come by the thousand, beautiful in photography, idyllic in atmosphere, though never till latterly exciting in substance, each with its Farewell to So-and-So raising a pleasant ripple on the art's nostalgia. Finer still, more skilled in observation, because further from wretched mankind, there has been the long and brilliant line of nature films. Studies of bird life, life under the sea, microscopic, slow-motioned, and speeded-up adventures in plant life: how beautiful they have been, with Bruce Woolfe, Mary Field, and Percy Smith staking a claim for England better than any: more continuous in their work, less dramatic at all costs than either the Americans or the Germans, more patient, analytic, and in the best sense observant. Here, if anywhere, beauty has come to inhabit the edifice of truth. Nor could there be any obstacle to the highly efficient analysis in slow-motion of what happens to bullets, golfers' swings, and labourers at work. In these matters of utilitarian observation cinema has built up a wide field of service, helping the research man, as it brilliantly did in the film observations on cancer research by Dr. Canti at Bart's, helping equally the industrialist and the salesman.

But the devil of reality has even then not been content. Ruttmann for Germany, Flaherty for America, Eisenstein and Pudovkin for Russia, Cavalcanti for France, and myself, shall I say, for Britain, we have taken our cameras to the more difficult territory. We have set up our tripods among the Yahoos themselves, and schools have gathered round us. Our realist showing, if secondary to the main growth of cinema, has assumed a certain bravery.

Flaherty adopted one gambit with *Nanook of the North*. By profession an explorer with a long and deep knowledge of the Eskimos, he had the idea of making a story about people he knew—not foisting, studio fashion, a preconceived story on a background for the decorative quality it added, but taking his story from within. *Nanook of the North* took the theme of hunger and the fight for food and built its drama from the actual event, and, as it turned out, from actual hunger. The blizzards were real and the gestures of human exhaustion came from the life. Many years before, Ponting had made his famous picture of the Scott expedition to the South Pole, with just such material; but here the sketch came to life and the journalistic survey turned to drama. Flaherty's theory that the camera has an affection for the spontaneous and the traditional, and all that time has worn smooth, stands the test of more than twenty years, and *Nanook*, of all the films that I have seen—I wish I could say the same for my own—is least dated today. The bubble is in it and it is, plain to see, a true bubble. This film, which had to find its finance from a fur company and was turned down by every renter on Broadway, has outlived them all.

Moana, which Flaherty made afterwards, added the same thought to Samoa. *White Shadows of the South Seas*, *Tabu*, *Man of Aran*, and *Elephant Boy* succeeded. But it was no wonder that Hollywood doubted his outlook. In *White Shadows* and *Tabu* they saw to it that a director of the other and approved species accompanied him. *White Shadows* and *Tabu* were, therefore, not quite Flaherty and were none the deeper for it. Poor Hollywood. No stars to draw the crowd, no love story, not much to whet an appetite ballyhoo'd into a vicious selectivity—only the fight against hunger, only the bravery of the tattoo, only—in Aran—the timeless story of man against the sky. They have been all too novel for a showmanship built on garish spectacle and a red-hot presentation of the latest curves. Flaherty might well call for a new and maturer language of salesmanship which can articulate the wider and deeper ambitions of the cinema, for the old salesmanship has served him and all of us pretty badly. He might well, with such high authorities as Ned Depinet and Sam Goldwyn, demand a segregation of the audience, for this insane cluttering of all species of audiences, taste and mood together, has completed the evil. The sales machine is mentally geared to take us everywhere, or not at all.

The position of the Flaherty species of realism is best evidenced in *Elephant Boy*, a film made from Kipling's *Toomai of the Elephants* and done in conjunction with the studio-minded Zoltan Korda of London Films. *Elephant Boy* begins magnificently. Toomai is set on the back of the highest elephant of all Mysore: in his youth and innocence giving a dignity to the Indian people one has never seen before on the screen. One is prepared for anything. The great herd of wild elephants is signalled. There are expectations of a jungle more exciting than the jungle of *Chang*, and of a relationship between man and nature as deep again as *Nanook*. But the synthetic spectacle of studio camp scenes and West End voices brings the film at every turn to an artificial, different plane. It comes between the boy and the jungle, and the full perspective of reality is not realized. They say an elephant will go mad on the death of his master and that he will go more mysteriously mad *just before* the death of his master. Nothing of this. Synthesis steps in, and an actor, in a fake beard, lashes the elephant to give a more Occidental motive for madness. The jungle might have been with its thousand eyes the image of all young and ardent Odysseys. Nothing of this either. The film drives on under the lash of the synthesists to the mere circus excitements of an elephant hunt.

The studio people insist on a species of drama more familiar and more dear to them than the fate of a native in the jungle and the limitation of their scale of values is going to be difficult to overcome, unless a producer comes along who can wed studio and natural observation in a new and vital formula. The salesmen have learned brilliantly to sell what is already important or may easily be associated with the excitements of sex and sudden death. They show no great signs of equipping themselves for the special task which the quality of Flaherty's themes demands.

We have been luckier in the field of realism which Cavalcanti initiated with *Rien que les Heures*, Ruttmann continued with *Berlin*, and some of us have developed on more deliberate sociological lines in the British documentary. The basis of this other realism is different from Flaherty's. We neither attempted so large a scale in our film-making, nor did we go so far for our themes. Limiting our costs, we did not have to struggle so wearily with sales organizations; and, from the first, we created a large part of our circulation outside the theatres altogether.

Rien que les Heures came later than *Nanook* by five years and was the first film to see a city through the turn of the clock. Paris was cross-sectioned in its contrasts—ugliness and beauty, wealth and poverty, hopes and fears. For the first time the word 'symphony' was used, rather than story. Cavalcanti went on to the more ambitious *En Rade*, like Flaherty taking his 'story from within' on the dockside at Marseilles, but the symphony approach had a lasting influence. Ruttmann carried on the idea in a still more whirling round of day and night in *Berlin*. No film has been more influential, more imitated. Symphonies of cities have been sprouting ever since, each with its crescendo of dawn and coming-awake and workers' processions, its morning traffic and machinery, its lunchtime contrasts of rich and poor, its afternoon lull, its evening denouement in sky-sign and night club. The model makes good, if similar, movie. It had at least the effect of turning the tide of abstraction in the German cinema and bringing it back to earth. It initiated the tradition of realism which produced such admirable films as *Mutter Krausen* and *Kameradschaft*, and it set a mark for amateurs the world over.

The British effort, while it owes everything to Flaherty and Cavalcanti initiative—latterly joining forces with Flaherty and Cavalcanti themselves—has been less aesthetic and more social in its approach. The shape of *Drifters*, the first of the British documentaries, was, for all its difference of subject, closer to Eisenstein than to Cavalcanti or Ruttmann. Though each chapter was a deliberate study in movement, the film took care to lead up to and stage an event. More important still, as I have come to consider, it had a theme in social observation— the ardour and bravery of common labour—and simple themes of the same sociological bearing have served us ever since, giving each new slice of raw material a perspective and a life, leading us in each new adventure of observation to a wider and more powerful command of medium and material alike. *Drifters* seems simple and easy now, though I remember the effort it took to convince showmen of the time that an industrialized fishing fleet might be as brave to the sight as the brown sails of sentiment and that the rigours of work were worth the emphasis of detail. This, after all, was before machinery had become 'beautiful' and the workaday life was 'fit' material for the screen. Behind us were hundreds of industrial films which industrialists had sponsored in pride and film companies had made in contempt, more often than not without script or direction, on the dismal basis of so much a foot. Work and workers were so dull by repute that, I remember bitterly, two hundred feet in the pictorials was the dead limit which showmen would offer for anything of the kind. Any director worth his salt was so busy trying to make the limelight of studio publicities that there was none so poor as to do reverence to the working theme.

This may explain why *Drifters*, simple film as it was, was so much of a *succès d'estime*, and why it so quickly became more of a myth than a film. It had the rarity value of opening, for Britain, a new vista of film reference. It may explain, too, why the workers' portraits of *Industrial Britain* were cheered in the West End of London. The strange fact was that the West End had never seen workmen's portraits before—certainly not on the screen. *Industrial Britain*, significantly, was hailed as a patriotic picture and has been widely circulated to this day for British prestige abroad. In the films that followed, from the idyllic pictures of Scottish shepherds to the complex and more difficult cross-sections of shipyards, airlines, radio services, weather forecasts, night mails, international economics, etc., etc., we relied similarly, beyond renter and exhibitor alike, on the people, and their superior taste in realism. In the seven or eight years following *Drifters* we put together some two hundred films of the documentary type and at the end of that time it was no longer so difficult to get into the theatres. The working theme and the civic reference contained in all of them were widely recognized for the aesthetic as well as for the national character they brought to the British cinema.

But the welcome, as might have been expected, was not unanimous. When the posters of the Buy British Campaign carried for the first time the figure of a working man as a national symbol, we were astonished at the Empire Marketing Board to hear from half a hundred Blimps that we were 'going Bolshevik'. The thought of making work an honoured theme, and a workman, of whatever kind, an honourable figure, is still liable to the charge of subversion. The documentary group has learned freely from Russian film technique; the nature of the material has forced it to what, from an inexpert point of view, may seem violent technical developments. These factors have encouraged this reactionary criticism; but, fundamentally, the sin has been to make the cinema face life. This must inevitably be unwelcome to the complacent elements in society.

Documentary, like all branches of realism, has suffered from the inhibitions of the trade, and the inhibitions have in due course been exploited by the more irresponsible and reactionary representatives of the political world. All the documentary directors have at one time or another felt the pressure of this criticism from outside. We have not only had to fight our material—new and therefore difficult as it was—but time and again there has been an attempt to apply that narrow and false yardstick of party-political value referred to by Paul Valery[1] which is the death of art and the death of all true national education.

It is worth recalling that the British documentary group began not so much in affection for film *per se* as in affection for national education. If I am to be counted as the founder and leader of the movement, its origins certainly lay in sociological rather than aesthetic aims. Many of us after 1918 (and particularly in the United States) were impressed by the pessimism that had settled on Liberal theory. We noted the conclusion of such men as Walter Lippmann, that because the citizen, under modern conditions, could not know everything about everything all the time, democratic citizenship was therefore impossible. We set to thinking how a dramatic apprehension of the modern scene might solve the problem, and we turned to the new wide-reaching instruments of radio and cinema as necessary instruments in both the practice of government and the enjoyment of citizenship. It was no wonder, looking back on it, that we found our first sponsorship outside the trade and in a Government department, for the Empire Marketing Board had, from a governmental point of view, come to realize the same issue. Set to bring the Empire alive in contemporary terms, as a commonwealth of nations and as an international combine of industrial, commercial, and scientific forces, it, too, was finding a need for dramatic methods. For the imaginative mind of Sir Stephen Tallents, head of that department, it was a quick step to the documentary cinema.

Sir Stephen Tallents referred to Henry the Navigator and the School of Navigation by which he opened up the New World, and pointed to film, radio, poster, and exhibition as the sextant and compass which would manœuvre citizenship over the new distances. He inspired a freedom of treatment which has rarely been the lot of documentary film-makers. We brought in Flaherty from America and Cavalcanti from France to strengthen our hands; the Russian films were run at the E.M.B. before they even reached the Film Society, and Cabinet

---

[1] 'Political conflicts distort and disturb the people's sense of distinction between matters of importance and matters of urgency. What is vital is disguised by what is merely a matter of well being; the ulterior is disguised by the imminent; the badly needed by what is readily felt.'

ministers argued our theories. We were encouraged in every experiment which would help us to develop the new art. But the E.M.B. passed, and only the film section carried on its belief in the new instruments of civic enlightenment. The parochial voices of immediate departmental needs could at last be heard, and were. Later the inspiration was strong at the Post Office, but much less strong where nationally it could have been more useful: in Agriculture, Health, Transport, and Labour. The flame lit at the Empire Marketing Board dimmed, and the documentary film looked more and more outside the Government departments—to the vast operations of oil, gas, electricity, steel, and chemicals, to the municipal and social organizations, and to the journalistic treatment of public problems on *March of Time* lines.

It seemed at the time a pity that others should reap the full benefits of a medium which the Government service discovered but which it was not quite inspired enough to mature. Names like Basil Wright Paul Rotha, Arthur Elton, Stuart Legg, Harry Watt, Evelyn Spice, John Taylor and Alexander Shaw came out of it, and they represented together an outlook which, uniquely in the world of cinema, was as deeply based in public as aesthetic effort. Personally I regretted the Government retreat, for, as I know after many years, no service is so great or inspiring, and particularly for film-makers, as a service which detaches itself from personal profit. It frees one's feet for those maturing experiments which are vital to the new art. It makes a daily bravery of what, under British commercial film conditions, is a dull little muddle of private interests and all too personal vanities.

If I emphasize this British documentary overmuch it is because I know it best; and it serves as well as any school to indicate a social approach to the cinema which, in the late thirties, was springing up universally. The young men were taking command and, conscious of the problems of the day, were coming closer to the world without and to realism, resolved to give to cinema that commanding position in public description so well within its grasp.

The Russians, after a brilliant period in which the Revolution was starkly relived and all its triumphs registered, found it more difficult to come to grips with Peace. The realistic powers of *Potemkin*, *The End of St. Petersburg*, *Ten Days that Shook the World*, and *Storm Over Asia* were barely matched in *The General Line* and *A Simple Case*. Conscious of the weakness, the Russians showed for a time a tendency to slip back to the old victories, and *Thunder Over Mexico*, *The Deserter*, *Chapayev*, and *We from Kronstadt* were all, in this sense, epics of nostalgia. Conviction was lacking in the themes of peace. *Earth* was beautiful, but only managed to melodramatize the issue between peasant and kulak. *The Road to Life*, with its story of reformed strays, was in a Y.M.C.A. tradition of patronage. It seemed, in the middle thirties, that the technique of mass energies and significant symbols, suitable for the stress of revolution, only embarrassed the quieter issues of a peacetime life, which was of necessity more domesticated and personal.

Nevertheless the technique has been changing in younger hands. Films like *Men and Jobs* seem ordinary against the old fireworks and are deplored widely as representing an abject surrender to Hollywood. But Russia, like every other country, has been coming closer to the common life and, unspectacular as its new films may seem in comparison with the old days, they are nearer the mark. With the United States, the Soviet Union remains during this period the most exciting of film countries. For America has been changing front with a vengeance. It may not understand the realism of Flaherty, but it is building up another realism, of a power and quality affecting film production everywhere. The tradition of the epics, of *The Covered Wagon*, *The Iron Horse*, *Pony Express*, *North of '36*, in one line, and of *The Birth of a Nation* and *Isn't Life Wonderful?*, in another, has flowered again in the national renaissance which succeeded the slump.

It is difficult to know why this epic tradition failed for a time. One may blame equally the complacency of the golden years which preceded 1929 and the alien invasion which succeeded the success of *Vaudeville*. There was certainly a sudden end to the epics and to those small town comedies of Cruze and Langdon which kept Hollywood so close to America, and only the desolate sophistication of Lubitsch and his American imitators succeeded them. But now, in 1937, there are new and remarkable developments. Most significant of these is the rise of the small-part player to a degree of vitality and importance which he does not enjoy in any other country, save Russia. Call-boys and typists, garage hands and lorrymen are mobilized behind the star and there is a new contact with the ordinary. With every year from 1930 the films have become braver and more real, as though the old men were out and the young men in. In films like *42nd Street* the element of realism appears as only a more detailed and observant treatment of the old romantic set-up, but there has also been an eager absorption of contemporary problems and materials in the American scene. However diffidently the more difficult problems may be handled, they are not altogether avoided. Prison life, the plague of gangsterdom, the new police, unemployment, lynching and the secret societies, the

The Course of Realism

New Deal, finance, and Hollywood itself are inspiring writer and director alike. Stories of medicine and research, aviation and labour, are added in good measure. This is the period which has produced *The Good Earth*, with its long vista'd story of Chinese peasantry, its trial by wind and drought and plague of the commonest and most persisting loyalty of mankind, its deep-laid sympathy for what is ordinary yet so spectacular because it is linked with the elements.

In comparison with such work from America, the outlook of the British film is blank enough. We stretch back into things that were and forward into things to come; we have musicals and farces galore; but there is all too little of the real thing. There is Flaherty, as of old, freed from the shackles of the studio and bringing back his jungle realities, but just as surely shackled again on his return with studio sahibs and Oxford-accented head-men. There is Gracie Fields doing her Saturday night turn in a Lancashire parlour, and George Formby following, and the East End of Max Miller debunking propriety in a check suit and grey bowler. The English music hall, at least, is in the line of direct observation—and not least when it breaks through and takes charge of the higher history of Henry the Eighth. There is the documentary, that too in the real line, but tight, tidy and removed in its own separate finances, and too wisely mistrustful of the commercial scramble to join hands with it. There is John Baxter with films sentimental to the point of embarrassment; but at least about real people's sentimentalities.

These are all we have to set at this time against the American wave of realism. Such flags of vitality as are flown over the British cinemas, in spite of quotas, city millions, and alien adventurers, are still, even increasingly, American flags. One reason lies with the foreigners. There are too many of them, cosmopolites of the world's cities, to whom Lancashire is only Gracie Fields's hundred-thousand a year and the men of the Clyde not even a whisper in consciousness. How could it be otherwise? If they had been artists, they might have sensed the *condition humaine* across the distance of nationality, but they are only promoters. Yet I do not blame the foreigners altogether. They are only abetted in their unrealities by their English allies. The West End stage, for all the presence of Bridie and O'Casey, has lost the accent of the people. As for the literary men, half a dozen have power together to blow the unreality to smithereens, but they are not so much in love with reality as to think the explosion worth their effort. Fantastic fees and flattering attentions are no irritant.

Even these factors are consequents rather than causes. At the back of the scene is a weakness in contemporary English life which those who, like myself, came to it from the outside, have never ceased to feel. The social and aesthetic leadership, as perhaps befits an old and, in itself, brilliant tradition, has long lost that proud contact with simple labour which characterizes the younger countries, and particularly America. The Labour movement, from which great aesthetic influence might have been expected, has only contrived to join forces with the old leadership. Artists who, by destiny, are the solvents of such detachment, remain, on the whole, a peculiar people in England. Following social rather than aesthetic distinctions, they reflect only a distance from the reality they should serve. The significant dramatists of this period, when they are not Americans, are, not strangely, Irishmen, Scotsmen, and far Northern provincials, deriving from traditions in which contact with the ordinary life has always been closer and less ashamed.

But I do not despair. All over Britain critics and leaders of opinion are conscious of the lack I have indicated and are hammering away at the forces governing our films. The championship by members of the Moyne Committee of a cinema closer to the national life is particularly significant. With such support, and in spite of all the artifices, inhibitions, inferiorities, snobberies, censorships, alien controls, and misguided party-political interventions, the British cinema may yet come, in realism, alive.

2   Battle for Authenticity

With its insistence on authenticity and the drama that resides in the living fact, the documentary film has always been in the wars. As the forces of propaganda closed round it at the end of 1938, the battle for authenticity became more arduous than ever.

Not so long ago, the materials of steel and smoke were not considered 'romantic' enough for pictures, and the documentary film was supposed to be engaged on a sleeveless errand. Today, people find industry and the skills that reside within it, magical and exciting. But it was relatively easy to find the beauty in the lives of fishermen and steel workers. Their dramatic atmosphere was ready-made. Documentary moved on to more difficult work when it proceeded to dramatize the daily activities of great organizations (*B.B.C.—The Voice of Britain, 6.30 Collection, Weather Forecast, A Job in a Million, Night Mail*, etc.). It was a unique achievement when, in *Big Money*, it made a fine, exciting story of the Accountant-General's Department of the Post Office—surely, on the face of it, one of the dullest subjects no earth.

Behind the three or four hundred documentaries made in Britain up to the end of 1938, there was this constant drive to attack new materials and bring them into visual focus on the screen. Clerks and other suburban figures were more difficult to present than fishermen and steel workers, till the documentary men got the hang of the work they did and began to understand how to attach the importance of the great public organizations they operated to the seeming dullness of their daily darg. All this meant time, research, and getting accustomed to human materials which had never been creatively treated before.

Yet, I think the greatest advance of all came with two little films which, except among the far-seeing, went almost unnoticed. One was called *Housing Problems* and the other *Workers and Jobs*. I think I am right in saying that the credit of the first goes to John Taylor whose first film it was. The second was Arthur Elton's. They took the documentary film into the field of social problems, and keyed it to the task of describing not only industrial and commercial spectacle but social truth as well.

Documentary Achievement

These simple films went deeper than earlier films like *Drifters* and later films like *Night Mail* and *North Sea*. They showed the common man, not in the romance of his calling, but in the more complex and intimate drama of his citizenship. See *Industrial Britain*, *Night Mail*, *Shipyard* and *North Sea* alongside *Housing Problems*. There is a precious difference. *Housing Problems* is not so well made nor so brilliant in technical excitements, but something speaks within it that touches the conscience. These other films 'uplift'. *Housing Problems* 'transforms' and will not let you forget.

I have watched the various documentary men come to this point of distinction. They know that a thousand easy excitements lie right to their hand. A dozen I could name could possibly out-Bolshevik the Bolsheviks and out-Nazi the Nazis in highfalutin parades against the skyline. But they do not do it. Shunning the meretricious attractions of the easy excitements, they have kept to the line which *Housing Problems* first defined.

The powerful sequence of films which appeared during the late thirties about nutrition and housing and health and education were the measure of their achievement. Significantly enough, the big films of 1938 hardly deviated into the 'epic' of industry at all. They were *The Londoners*, a film describing London's fifty years of local government; the G.P.O. film on national health; *New Worlds for Old*, Rotha's discussion of the public utility of the fuel resources; and the films of economic reconstruction, education, and agriculture, made in Scotland.

These films of social reconstruction and the growing points thereof became a powerful force for the public good. They found their place in the cinemas; they had a vast audience outside the cinemas; they were attracting more and more attention and prestige abroad. Other countries made documentaries, but no documentary movement anywhere was so deliberately constructive in public affairs, or had so many powerful national allies as ours. Above all, its continuous and unremitting description of Britain's democratic ideals and work within those ideals, had a special pertinence at the time.

This policy was not popular in all quarters. Though the Minister of Health expressed publicly his gratitude for the Nutrition film, it is wise to remember that, when that film was first made, it was branded by political busybodies as 'subversive'. Silly enough it sounds, but obstacle after obstacle was put in the way of the documentary film whenever it set itself to the adult task of performing a public service. Sometimes it came in the cry of the Censor that the screen was to be kept free of what was called 'controversy'. More often it was in the whispered obstruction emanating from Conservative Party politicians.

For the documentary men, whose vision has sought to go beyond party politics to a deeper sort of national story altogether, the path has not been comfortable. It has taken a good deal of persistence to maintain that a full and true story of British life is more likely to describe our virtues as a democracy, and that the richest picture to present in Britain and other countries lies in the actual bone and substance of British life.

In many of the documentary films, the country is shown tearing down slums and building anew, or facing up to unemployment and reorganizing economically: in general, passing from the negative to the positive. It is in this, precisely, that most of us have felt that the strength of democratic Britain is made manifest.

In the time of which I write I feared one thing. The unofficial censorships had sought to embarrass this honest picture of Britain which we had then partially achieved, and had been anxious to substitute for the heartfelt interpretation of responsible artists the synthetic lie of partisan interests. There was always, however, the graver danger that they would seek, in presenting Britain abroad, to show only the superficial and bombastic elements in the British scene. No country is greater in tradition and ceremonial than Britain, and we may well be proud of it. Fine pictures might be made of it, and there is no documentary man who would not wish to join in making them. It was another matter, however, to have the ceremonial of Britain made the be-all and end-all of Britain's picture abroad. It could only be an unsubstantial and silly meal for intelligent foreigners. The monotony of Soviet propaganda at one period, and the monotony of Nazi and Fascist propaganda in the immediate pre-war years, were ample of evidence of that.

If we are to describe the panoply of power and forget the living, working, everyday Britisher in the process of projection, our picture will be both false and, from the point of view of international relations, foolish. People of goodwill, and the wiser heads of the State, will, I am sure, keep that truth before them, and resist distortion. As for the documentary men, they have been fighting synthetic nonsense all their lives. By their very principles, they cannot be a party to false witness.

* but how 'real' was this view — see Orwell

1 The Film at War

The day war with Germany broke out, I was in Hollywood. I suppose everyone will remember that day in minute personal detail. It was the same on 4th August 1914. We all sensed, like a cloud on the mind, that here was the end of one epoch, the beginning of another, and all our personal worlds might never be the same again.

On 4th August 1914 I was on the coast of the Scottish Hebrides and the war was very near. I spent the whole day watching the trawlers and the drifters breasting the tide, puffing their way back in hundreds to become minesweepers and anti-submarine patrols. But on 3rd September 1939 I was in Hollywood, 6,000 miles away from the Scottish coast, and the seat of war. No minesweepers or anti-submarine patrols. Only white yachts, gliding along on a smooth blue Pacific. California was sunning itself on the beaches and Hollywood was behind me, the city of unreality, stardust, and people's dreams.

Yet instead of feeling a world away from the war, I felt no distance at all. I knew very well that there beside me in Hollywood was one of the greatest potential munition factories on earth. There, in the vast machinery of film production, of theatres spread across the earth with an audience of a hundred million a week, was one of the great new instruments of war propaganda. It could make people love each other or hate each other. It could keep people to the sticking point of purpose.

And that is how it is in our modern world. Like the radio and the newspaper, the film is one of the keys to men's will, and information is as necessary a line of defence as the army, the navy, and the air force. The leaders responsible for the conduct of war have to ask new kinds of questions. Which nation puts its case insistently and well and makes converts and allies? Who arouses the national loyalty? Who makes purpose commanding? Who mobilizes the patrol ships of the human mind? These are vital considerations among statesmen today. In the thirties European politics seemed to turn on the effect of propaganda and every nation was fighting for command of the international ether. Even the issue of the war may turn on the skill and imagination with which we formulate our aims and maintain our spirit.

In the early months of the war the film was mobilized like the newspaper and the radio alongside the fighting forces of the nations. Even Hollywood, far from the battlefront, was immediately affected. I never saw so great a scurry in my life as in that first week of war in the chambers of Hollywood's magnates. A third of their world market had vanished overnight or become completely uncertain. Who knew when the bombs would be raining from the sky and making theatres in the European cities untenable? The black-outs had driven people from the screen romance to sit waiting by their radios for the latest war news.

Hollywood was so nervous that it had a new idea every day. The first reaction was to draw in its economic horns, make cheaper pictures, intensify its American market. There was some talk of forgetting its international role and going all American. The result of that policy was seen in more pictures of North American history, more pictures of South America. Hollywood even began, in a sudden burst of light, to remember that Canada was a North American country.

There was another school of thought in Hollywood which remembered the war of 1914–18 and how the frothier kinds of entertainment had prospered. A great deal was heard in these first days about stopping serious pictures and giving people nothing but light-hearted ones —to permit them to forget their worries. 'Give them more fluff' was the way Hollywood described it. But not for long. The more modern school of production, the younger men, argued vehemently in every studio. They said, I think wisely, that people would be asking more questions in this war, and that this policy of froth and fluff would be an insult to the intelligence of the people. I confess I was greatly interested to hear how seriously these younger producers talked—the men like Walter Wanger. There was no question of avoiding world responsibility, no desire whatever to forget the war and make a false paradise of neutrality. In Wanger's office we installed a ticker service from the United Press and daily we sat around it, reading the war news, considering how best the film might serve mankind in this new situation. Everyone in this particular group was for going into propaganda of some kind, but everyone I noticed was for avoiding hatred. No *Beast of Berlin* and other childish exaggerations this time, they said. And through all their thoughts I noticed there ran the theme: 'Let us do something to keep the decent human values alive. Let us so maintain men's sanity that when it comes to peace, we shall know how to make it stable.'

The warring nations had to be much more direct. They reached out, at once, to make the film their recruiting sergeant. In the newsreels they made the film an instrument of international information by which they could tell the world about their efficiency, their power, their confidence, and their will to win.

That new mood was apparent in two of the first films to come from Britain. There was not much peace in *The Warning*. It was a picture of England preparing for death and disaster; and you saw the old England made grotesque by war as in a distorting mirror. There was no peace in *The Lion Has Wings*. That work of film documentation was Britain actually at war, zooming and roaring above the clouds. It was also the film at war. There would be more and more as the days went on. And they would be far more real, far more documentary, these films of war, than any seen before from British studios.

I have been for a long time interested in propaganda and it is as a propagandist I have been from the first interested in films. I remember coming away from the last war with the very simple notion in my head that somehow we had to make peace exciting, if we were to prevent wars. Simple notion as it is, that has been my propaganda ever since— to make peace exciting. In one form or another I have produced or initiated hundreds of films; yet I think behind every one of them has been that one idea, that the ordinary affairs of people's lives are more dramatic and more vital than all the false excitements you can muster. That has seemed to me something worth spending one's life over.

I should have been an unhappy person if I had thought all this vanished with the war. Strangely enough the war seemed only to accentuate people's hunger for reality. It was proper that the film should take its place in the line of defence, as in duty bound. It was proper that it should use its powers to mobilize the full effort of the nation. But—so it seemed in these early months—one way, too, in which we could maintain our defences and keep our spirit for the struggle ahead was to remember that the aims of our society lie beyond war and in the love of peace. It would be a poor information service, it seemed, which kept harping on war to the exclusion of everything, making our minds narrow and anæmic. It would be a poor propaganda which taught hatred, till it violated the sense of decency which ten thousand years of civilization have established. It would be an in-efficient national information which did not keep the home fires of national activity burning, while the men were off to the war. In war as in peace, strength lies in hope, and it is the wisest propaganda which keeps men rich in hope.

The war would have achieved its final feat of destructiveness, and we should have been brought to the very brink of spiritual suicide, if we had lost the sense of what we were defending.

On this serious question of the relation of peace thoughts and war thoughts, I am going to quote from the great French writer, Giraudoux. Addressing the children of France, as Director of the French Ministry of Information, at the opening of their school year, he said:

'Thirty-eight thousand of your teachers have had to take machine-gun, bomb, and grenade and all the abhorred tools of destruction to form a rampart behind which you will be sheltered this winter—to learn from the masters left to you—and from your school books—your country's inviolable love of peace. . . . Young sentinels, learn a true history, a true geography, a moral without hatred, lessons in things which have nothing to do with gunpowder and bayonets.'

So there you have it. There are two sides to propaganda, and two sides to the film at war. The film can be mobilized to give the news and the story of a great historical event. In that sense our aim was to use it for all its worth to secure the present. But my hope has been that the film would also be used more and more to secure the future and serve the still wider needs of the people of Canada. War films, yes, but more films, too, about the everyday things of life, the values, the ideals which make life worth living. I hoped that we could use the film to give visual significance to the words of the Canadian Prime Minister when he said that the spirit of mutual tolerance and the respect for fundamental rights are the foundation of the national unity of Canada.

In that way I have thought to rescue from these barren days of trouble something we could hand on to the future.

2 Searchlight on Democracy

I write this in Canada and Canada is a good country in which to study the terms of democracy. Here you have a people strung out along three thousand miles of railroad. In the middle, between Winnipeg and Ottawa, there is a sort of no-man's-land. It is not like the States. It has no Middle West, no meeting place between peoples of the west and east.

The physical distances are so great that they place a heavy burden on the processes of democracy. People cannot come very easily together to discuss things. National committees can meet only rarely. If a committee decision is to be carried out, the gap between the decision and the action is accentuated by the sheer difficulty of mileage.

I cite this case of Canada, because it demonstrates how much the democratic way of discussing things and doing things depends on a quick and living system of communications. In Canada the difficult problem of yesterday is being liquidated to some extent under one's eyes. The new factor which has come into the situation is the airplane and airplanes are meaning more to Canada than to any country I can think of. This country of many days' journeys is being concertina'd dramatically. People are getting together more quickly. National discussion is becoming easier to arrange. Understanding between isolated localities and centres of opinion is becoming a simpler matter than it was yesterday. The tempo of consequent action which is the bugbear of the democratic method must inevitably become faster.

In one way or another this problem of communications is vital to every democratic society. Getting together is important. Getting our ideas together is important. Once good feelings and good ideas move like wildfire across the democratic sky, we are half-way towards building a community worth living in.

In this respect we depend more deeply on our system of communications than do the authoritarian states. It is true that the dictator needs his radio. The word from on high must be heard by all. The rhetorical moment must be enjoyed *en masse*. The band must beat out its rhythm across the entire domain. But the subtler and richer forms of communication are less necessary. It is not so vital to spread ideas or to spread initiative. It is not so vital to put upon the individual citizen the responsibility of taste and good feeling and judgment. In a democracy it *is* vital, and this responsibility for spreading good feelings and taste and judgment is the whole responsibility of a democratic education.

Your dictator with a wave of the hand can clear a slum or rebuild a town—and this is always an attractive prospect to people who want slums cleared and towns rebuilt. But the communication of dictatorship is of orders given and of organization set in motion. Our democratic interest in communications is very different. It is integral to the democratic idea that constructive action shall bubble up all over the place. Initiative must be not only central but local. By the mere acceptance of democracy we have taken upon ourselves the privilege and the duty of individual creative citizenship and we must organize all communications which will serve to maintain it.

I know the waving hand of the dictator can more spectacularly clear the slums, if—and who can ensure it?—it is disposed to clear the slums. I know that efficiency is attractive and the beat of feet marching in unison is a remarkable source of persuasion. I know, too, that when, in the democratic way, we leave so much initiative to the individual and the locality, the result is sometimes only too local. Local taste may be terrible to the metropolitan æsthete. The perfectly sound scientist will be challenged by rustic pigheadedness. But what we lose perhaps in efficiency and taste—and it is just possible that the dictator may be a man of taste—what we lose with our shabby local methods, we gain in spirit. It may be poor but it is our own.

The moment we accept this decision a great obligation is laid upon education in a democracy. It must perfect its system of communication so that individuals and localities may draw from the deepest source of inspiration. It must create a flow of initiative and ideas which, while maintaining the vitality of democracy, will help it to challenge authoritarian standards in quality and efficiency. This is a tall order but I can see no way out of it. In the first place it means reorientation of our education policy and a conception of education as an active constructive system in the maintenance of democracy. The detached view will no longer serve. Either education is for democracy and against authoritarianism, or it is for authoritarianism. The day of standing aside is over because the issue has become too vital. It is from now on an instrument of state with a part to play in fulfilling the democratic idea. It has the job of relating the individual to the responsibilities of that idea.

Development in Canada

I think all of us realize that we have in the past laid too much emphasis on a narrow view of individualism. We have geared our educational processes to the person in private rather than to the person in public. Haunting our minds and our policies has been the concept of a leisure-time education and not of a working-citizen education. Our ideal has been the cultured individual, the gentlemen in a library. We have made much of accurate information and the somewhat questionable efficacy of deductive logic. We have held before us the ideal of rational citizenship, where the individual, like a lone ranger on a detached horizon—which he never is—makes a cold judgment on the facts. We have pictured our educated man as someone with a knowledge of the classics and capable of polite conversation on literature and the arts. Inspired by these thoughts, we have proudly introduced our working man to Plato and the philosophies. I have seen some of that myself. I have gone through the farce of teaching *A Midsummer Night's Dream* to evening-school brush workers, and Plato to tired labourers. It was a pretty conceit: but we have, I think, all come to appreciate how detached from reality such an outlook on education is. This education is like a rose without a smell. It misses the essence of common thinking and common doing. It lacks integral contact with the living processes of citizenship. It approaches the labourer—and I can only think of it as a highly insulting approach—with the intention of improving him and of shaping him in an image which could never be his reality. He may be a fine labourer and a fine man: he will at best be but a poor gent in a library—and who wants to be that anyway? It is an anæmic conception. It lacks what seems to me respect for the labourer as such and for the man that is in him, and for the part he can play in his own community. It does not create an image in his mind of what he, himself, on his own doorstep, and out of his own rich human character, could do and enjoy within the community. It is education with its roots in the air.

On the other hand, if education is to be an active instrument of the democratic idea, it must first be socialized. By that I mean that it must at every turn take hold of its role as a social instrument. It is one of the remarkable revolutions of our time how all branches of human thought and activity are coming to appreciate their active relation to social forces. The scientist has come out of his cell. Each branch of science is losing the atmosphere of mere scholastic inquiry and academic discipline. It has become just one other aspect of the pursuit of human well-being. You see, particularly, how science is lending its aid to housing and health and establishing new measurements of well-being by which the individual must live. You see the same revolution in medicine, in the overnight change from curative to preventative health service.

You see it in the new conception of living architecture, in which architecture is no longer a matter of mere building but a creative process of community planning in which the scientist, the doctor, the builder, the transport expert, the psychologist, the teacher, the public administrator and the citizenry are partners in a joint enterprise.

Education has been as conscious as any other field of the need for a new social outlook. But it has tended to be borne down by its own traditional emphasis on knowledge and books. Out in Kent, where I practised some part of my citizenship, we spent a vast sum (I think it was £50,000) running books out from Maidstone to our hamlets. But certainly, in my own village, it was not books we talked about and not books we wanted. We were all farmers and that was our principal world of discourse. We were interested in the things of the land and in every species of new magic which affected the land. What we most wanted to know was what they were doing at East Malling and Wye and other research stations. We wanted a more living discourse than books. We wanted, for example, a picture service through the winter nights which would show us what others were doing and what the scientists had to tell us, and so give us an opportunity for discussion and argument. But somehow or other that would not quite be education, and there was no £50,000 for the information we needed. Even in Kent where we were educationally progressive, the burden of the books was still upon us.

How then are we to twist the outlook of education so that it will become a more real power in the maintenance of democracy? I was discussing this with my friend, George Ferguson, the editor of the *Winnipeg Free Press* and one of Canada's most stalwart champions of the democratic idea. He said that the only thing you have to set against the spectacular appeal of the totalitarian state is the spectacle of liberty. I think the idea is worth examining. Looking back on our own documentary films, I know I have tried to do something of this sort in every film with which I have been concerned. I have asked the directors to call down a cinematic blessing on the fact that people in our world are so natively out of step. I have asked them to express the beauty that goes with the tatterdemalion good humour of a London bank holiday. We have in our own fashion and in a hundred ways described those manifestations of the human spirit which are not mobilized, not regimented, not dictated from without. We like, in our

Development in Canada

group, to quote the story of the fine housing estate which the beautiful
æsthete of an architect designed, for it shows much of what we in our
documentary films have tried to say. This architect had his design so
sweetly planned that it was already decided in the blueprint which
tenants were to have brown curtains, and which blue. One thing came
unstuck and that was the tenants. They said, Hell, they would submit
to having baths and one thing and another but curtains were private
and they would do what they pleased with them. The architect said
all right, but no lace. And the tenants said Hell again, if we like lace
we will have lace. And that's the way it turned out. When the curtains
went up they were every colour of the rainbow and a good few were
lace. And the pleasure of the event was that the moment they did go
up, the beautiful design of the architect got what it most needed. It
came alive.

One would expect the democratic educational system to preach just
such liberty and keep the æsthetes and other superior people in their
places. I hope that as we blueprint for the community life, we will
realize, the specialists among us, that we are specialists for and on
behalf of people and not specialists from without. I hope that we, at
all costs, see to it that people have the full freedom of their initiative
and judgment and have the power to invest whatever is done with
their own rich notion of life. In that sense, education has a great deal
to do with the expression and maintenance of liberty.

It is the same thing when your educational system gives voice to the
notion of fraternity or equality. In the democratic definition of these
things, nothing very definite or spectacular can be said about either.
Our conceptions of fraternity and equality are essentially undemonstrative. When you think of it, the dictator states did a magnificent
job in presenting their own brand of fraternity. They had their
comrade-in-arms gambit. They had the spectacle of men joining together in the religious brotherhood of the blood. Their fraternity was
expressed in exciting forms like parades, flags and mutual salutes. One
does not wonder for a moment if it seems to fill a gap and meet a need
for recognizable comradeship which our own system lacks. It seems
to me, however, that the democratic idea must shrink a little from the
outstretched hand, the hearty backslap, or any such form of mania.
I like to think that in our presentation of the democratic idea we will
know how to present fraternity and a common feeling for one's neigh-
bour with a degree of diffidence. But it puts a heavy burden on
democratic statement when the very essence of it is that it should not
be melodramatic and should not be spectacular.

94

Searchlight on Democracy

We are faced indeed with a very difficult problem. It means that people must be taught to appreciate that being together, talking together, living together and working together in common undemonstrative harmony is the whole fraternity. It means that we must praise and encourage every little grouping of common spirits who ride their bicycles out into the country, or hike across the downs, or meet in the local to organize a cricket team or hoist a pint. It means that we are concerned with a multitude of ordinary things and that the very secret of them is their ordinariness. We are led inevitably to the conclusion that if such simple human elements are to be made the basis of loyalty, then we must learn to make a drama and a poetry from the simple.

As in the case of liberty and fraternity, so with equality. One drives on inevitably to the conception that we cannot present a rich interpretation of dramatic virtues except we produce a poetry and a drama of ordinary things. The spectacular appeal, the organized uplifting emotion which the totalitarian system provided in its education could, I believe, be matched and could be matched tomorrow if the writers and the poets and the picture men among us would seize upon the more intimate and human terms of our society.

Our searchlight on democracy will in the end turn out to be a quiet soft light under which little things are rounded in velvet and look big.

As I review the special problems of education, I find myself involuntarily altering many of the literary measurements which I was taught. I find myself laying less emphasis on the Renaissance and on the great expression of the human spirit which it fired. I find myself drawing a distinction which is not in the copy-books, between the court traditions of English literature and the common or garden expression which is at all times bound up with villages and music halls. I find myself less interested at the moment in Milton and Shakespeare than in Crabbe and Burns. To use Gogarty's word, the *graffiti* of the people were never more important than now. It seems to me that the emotional and spiritual maintenance of democracy depends on an absolute acceptance of the idea that a man is a man for a' that, and that the most important poetry or beauty in the end is that which bubbles traditionally—and not always academically—out of ordinary people. It will mean a widening of our educational view in half a dozen classes of curriculum. It will mean that the pictures of Jimmy Cagney will jostle for attention in the presence of Shakespeare himself, and that when Cézanne is being discussed, the beauties of public house art will not be forgotten. If any complain of the vulgarity of the project I can only answer that the vulgarization of education is in the logic

95

of our time and that it will bring with it—this outlook on the actual—a deep inspiration that we need.

I began by saying that democratic education needed its own vital system of communications—its own system of wildfire across the sky. I have tried to suggest that the wildfire we need will not, by the very nature of democracy, be that spectacular answer to the authoritarian challenge which people today are asking for. Our searchlight on democracy, I have suggested, will be a quiet and intimate light as befits the idea we serve, though it will make up in its width of sympathy and in the far-reaching subtlety of its detail what it lacks in emphasis.

But how is our system of education to bring this art of democracy into being? It calls obviously for a change of outlook and of heart, involving the newspaper story, the poster, the radio, and the terms of instruction as well as the more permanent arts of poetry, drama and picture. How can we establish this change of outlook and of heart which will give a true and moving picture of our democracy?

You cannot go out in cold blood to create such a new appreciation of the ordinary. Art does not happen like that. It is not taken by assault. It is a better rule to say that art comes as a by-product of the more pedestrian task. I think that the way and the means become apparent when you look closely into the more specific problems of democratic education. In solving each problem as it comes up, I think that you will find that you are involved willy nilly in the creation of an art and that the solution of each problem will be a contribution to the spectacle you are asking.

Let me distinguish the principal problems of education in a democracy. Firstly, you must inspire interest in the community life. Secondly, by creating such warm sentiments in regard to one or other aspect of the community life, you will inspire that initiative which is the heart and soul of the democratic idea. Thirdly, you must help in creating common standards of community thinking and community doing, if democracy is to be not only spirited but fine. Firstly: *Interest*. Secondly: *The participation which emanates from interest*. Thirdly: *Standards of judgment*.

Look at what they involve. If you are to create interest in the community life, you are face to face with the Herculean task of articulating this monstrous new metropolitan world which we have built for ourselves. You must bring it alive, so that people will live intimately in it and will make an art of life from it. And you cannot do it by information alone or analysis alone, for the life escapes. You can only do it in those dramatic terms which present the life of the thing and the purpose of the thing and make intimacy possible. The radio, the picture, the poster, and the story are the more obvious instruments in your hands and art has become inevitably half of your teaching.

Let me be specific. You will not succeed in bringing things alive in a general spate of new enthusiasm. Things do not happen that way either: vague enthusiasms are not the best of guides. As educationalists, you are concerned at every point with specific areas of interest. The child has to be prepared for citizenship in field or town. The world which has to be brought alive to him will, if you are wise, have a good deal to do with that field or that town, and only later with those wider perspectives of citizenship which reach out from it. The citizen, similarly, has his factory, his union, his family, his neighbours, his traditions, his news, his hobbies, his specialized world of discourse, his movies, his pub, his relationship with taxes and votes, and other aspects of local or national government. Perhaps he even has his church. These are the terms of his life and in each and every aspect of it his understanding is not so great that it cannot be greater or his harmony so assured that it cannot be brighter. At a hundred points education can touch the quick of his life and light the way for him. It may excite him a bit more about his neighbourhood. It may encourage him in his skill—as I kept asking the Kent County Council to encourage me in my strawberry-growing. It may, in general, make his world a more exciting place than it seems.

But again and again you will find yourself concerned with a dramatic or living process rather than a pedagogic or merely informational one. And I am thinking not only of the power of the movie and the newspaper. I am thinking of arts as separate as private discussion and child welfare: gardening and sport and music hall. These and a thousand more represent openings for your imagination as educationists, for they are the opportunity and the substance of the work you must finally do. All are media of communication and a way to the art and spectacle of democracy.

In my own field of documentary film-making, this is the inspiration on which we operate and I am not sure we may not have done just enough (since 1929) to prove its truth. We have been concerned with those very problems of bringing specific fields of modern activity alive to the citizen. We have worked in a dozen very different areas, and made a first tentative shot at picturing the worlds of communication and science, public administration and social welfare. We have followed along the perspective of modern life and sought to find themes which gave a new significance to the terms of ordinary living. Sometimes we have approached the task on a journalistic level or poetic level or analytical level or more dramatic level, but always we have been concerned to find a degree of beauty in the process and make our own contribution to the spectacle of democracy at work. It can be done and it can be done more widely. And all the thousand arts of human discussion and intercourse have their own special contribution to make.

I shall dismiss the creation of initiative by simply repeating that if you crystallize sentiments, you establish will power: if you create interest, you inevitably inspire initiative.

It is in the third field, the communication of *standards*, that education can find its other great opportunities for presenting a living expression of democracy.

When we were considering the creation of interest, we were involved at every point in bridging gaps between the citizen and his community. This is a general process. All of us need in general to know and feel intimately how the world we live in gets along.

But it is also a specialized process, for all of us have specialized interests. We need to equip ourselves better in terms of our agriculture, our care of children, our educational activity and so forth. There are, in fact, a thousand other gaps to bridge between, shall we say, the farmer and the research station, between the citizen and better practice. Our system of communications must provide for a rich flow of living records from which each of us, in our own separate interest, learns what the other fellow is doing and is thereby enabled to pull up our own standards. Leeds, they tell me, is away ahead in certain aspects of housing, with special arrangements for old people and for people disposed to tuberculosis. Leeds, in that case, is an important growing point of housing initiative. And it would be good for every municipality to have the sight of it in their eyes. Kensal House in London represents a vital experiment and achievement in community living. Here again, a living record of it will brace the spirit of similar experimenters elsewhere.

We arrive inevitably at the thought that propaganda or education in a democracy must operate on a large number of specialized levels and should be deliberately organized on a large number of levels. There must, of course, be a general spate of information and uplift, affecting the minds of general audiences: and you have the film and radio organized for that purpose. But I like to think that those of us who are interested in special aspects of the community life will develop our own systems of communications and that film and radio and other media of vital communication will do much for us.

When you see this from the international viewpoint, you will realize how much these specialized services could mean to international understanding and to the expression of the democratic idea. Wandering about the world, one finds that while countries differ in their expression and in their local idioms, they are in one respect identical. We are all divided into groups of specialized interests and we are all, at bottom, interested in the same things. There are the same essential groups everywhere. Here is a group interested in town planning, or in agriculture, or in safety in mines or in stamp collecting. Whatever the different language they speak, they speak the common language of town planning, agriculture, safety in mines, and stamp collecting. In that sense, one never thinks of Geneva as representing the real internationalism. The real internationalism is in the manias we share with each other.

How great is the opportunity this provides for the creation of the democratic picture! Several years ago Basil Wright and I suggested a scheme to the International Labour Office. We said, in effect: 'Why do you not create a great international interflow of living documents by which specialized groups will speak to their brethren in the fifty countries that operate within your system? You are anxious to raise the common standard of industrial welfare. Why do you not use the film to do it? If France has the best system of safety in mines, let other countries have the benefit of this example. If New Zealand is a great pioneer of ante-natal care, let other countries see the record of its achievement.'

I hope the I.L.O. will do something about that, but I would not simply leave it to the I.L.O. Britain is now engaged in far-reaching efforts of education and propaganda. There has been a lot of talk about the projection of Britain. I say frankly that I do not think anyone in high quarters has seriously thought about how it should be performed in a truly democratic way, or has seen the enormous advantage in international communication which the democratic idea gives us. In Whitehall there is no philosophy of propaganda and certainly none that is recognizably democratic as distinct from authoritarian. There is the same exhausting effort to look spectacular. There is the same noise. I am sorry to say there is the same tendency towards the synthetic and unreal. Yet I believe that democratic education and democratic propaganda are an easy matter and indeed far easier than the authoritarian type, if these principles I have laid down are grasped.

It will be done not by searchlight but in the quiet light of ordinary humanism. Speaking intimately and quietly about real things and real people will be more spectacular in the end than spectacle itself. And, in the process of creating our democratic system of communications, in bridging the gaps between citizen and community, citizen and specialist, specialist and specialist, we shall find that we have in the ordinary course of honest endeavour made the picture of democracy we are seeking. And we shall have made it not only national, but international too.

3 The Nature of Propaganda

Long before the war started, those who had studied the development of propaganda were constantly warning the British Government that a highly organized Information Service, national and international, equipped with all modern instruments, was as necessary as any other line of defence. I am thinking back to 1930 and even before Hitler came to power. Over the dog days of the thirties they preached and they pleaded, with only the most partial success; and in the meantime the greatest master of scientific propaganda in our time came up. I don't mean Goebbels: I mean Hitler himself. In this particular line of defence called propaganda, we were caught bending as in so many other spheres, because peace was so much in peoples' hearts that they would not prepare the desperate weapons of war.

The Germans attached first importance to propaganda. They didn't think of it as just an auxiliary in political management, and military strategy. They regarded it as the very first and most vital weapon in political management and military achievement—the very first. All of us now appreciate how the strategy of position—the war of trenches— was blown to smithereens by the development of the internal combustion engine. Fast-moving tanks and fast troop carriers could get behind the lines. Aeroplanes and flying artillery could get behind the lines. War, in one of its essentials, has become a matter of getting behind the lines and confusing and dividing the enemy.

But the chief way of getting behind the lines and confusing and dividing the enemy has been the psychological way. Hitler was cocksure that France would fall and forecast it in 1934, almost exactly as it happened. The forecast was based on psychological not on military reasons. 'France,' he said, 'in spite of her magnificent army could, by the provocation of unrest and disunity in public opinion, easily be brought to the point when she would only be able to use her army too late or not at all.'

The theory behind all this is very simple. Men today, by reason of the great spread of education, are, in part at least, thinking beings. They have been encouraged in individual judgment by a liberal era,

They have their own sentiments, loyalties, ideas and ideals; and these, for better or worse, determine their actions. They cannot be considered automata. If their mental and emotional loyalties are not engaged in the cause you present, if they are not lifted up and carried forward, they will fall down on you sooner or later when it comes to total war. The usual way of expressing it is to say that their morale will break.

That is why Hitler said: 'It is not arms that decide, but the men behind them—always'; or again, 'Why should I demoralize the enemy by military means, if I can do so better or more cheaply in other ways?'; or again, 'The place of artillery preparation and frontal attack by the infantry in trench warfare will in future be taken by propaganda; to break down the enemy psychologically before the armies begin to function at all . . . mental confusion, contradiction of feeling, indecisiveness, panic; these are our weapons. When the enemy is demoralized from within, when he stands on the brink of revolution, when social unrest threatens, that is the right moment. A single blow will destroy him.'

Just before they entered Norway, the Germans arranged for the State dignitaries in Oslo a special showing of their film of the Polish campaign. A portion of that film was included at the end of the American film *The Ramparts We Watch*. Even a portion of the film gave some idea of the effect such a demonstration was likely to have on the peace-loving Norwegians. It showed the mass mechanical efficiency of German warfare with brutal candour. The roaring aeroplanes, the bursting bombs, the flame-throwers, the swift unending passage of mechanized might all constituted an image of the inevitable.

That is how the strategy of terror works. It worked with us in Britain at the time of Munich. I won't say the men had the wind up— in fact I should describe the male reaction as one of vast disappointment and even shame—but the women were weeping all over the place. The picture of inevitable death and destruction Germany wished to present had been successfully presented; and it is one of the best evidences of British stamina that the new united courage of the British people was welded so soon out of these disturbed and doubtful beginnings.

Terror is only one aspect of propaganda on the offensive. The thing works much more subtly than that. Here is a quotation from someone in Hitler's entourage to show how deadly the approach can be: 'Every state can, by suitable methods, be so split from within that little strength is required to break it down. Everywhere there are groups that desire independence, whether national or economic or merely political. The scramble for personal advantage and distorted ambition : these are the unfailing means to a revolutionary weapon by which the enemy is struck from the rear. Finally, there are the business men, whose profits are their all in all. There is no patriotism that can hold out against all temptations. It is not difficult to find patriotic slogans that can cover all such enterprises.'

We saw in France how groups of men could, in the name of their country, give in to Hitler. Perhaps, in the name of France, they wished to crush the popular front and keep out socialism but they gave in to Hitler. Perhaps, in the name of France, they wanted to crush capitalism in the name of socialism, but they gave in to Hitler. Perhaps, in the name of France, they sighed for some neo-medieval religious authoritarianism but they gave in to Hitler.

In the United States the German inspired organizations did not trade as such. They were always to be found under the slogan 'America first' and other banners of patriotism.

The principal point to take is that, when the Germans put propaganda on the offensive in war, their psychological opportunities were rich and widespread. They appealed to men's thwarted ambitions; they offered salvation to disappointed and disheartened minorities; they preyed on the fears of capitalist groups regarding socialism ; they preached controlled capitalism and a socialist state to the socialist minded. They harped on those weaknesses of democracy of which democratic citizens are only too well aware ; the verbiage of its parliamentary debates, the everlasting delays of its committees, the petty bourgeois ineffectiveness of its bureaucracy. They probed the doubts in the mind of democracy and inflamed them to scepticism. Everything was grist to their mill, so long as they divided the enemy and weakened his belief in himself. No one will say that German propaganda did not do that job brilliantly and well, as it marched its way across Europe. It found the population divided against itself and ready for the knife, and Lavals and Quislings everywhere drilled and rehearsed perfectly in the act of capitulation.

The Germans believed that Democracy had no genuine convictions for which people would be willing to stake their lives. They proceeded cynically on that assumption, marched on that assumption and their entire military plan depended on that assumption. Hanfstaengel actually declared at one time that this lack of conviction within democracy was Hitler's fundamental discovery—'the discovery which formed the starting point for his great and daring policies'.

It is perhaps as well that we know where the heart of the matter lies, for if lack of conviction, as they say, always results in defeatism and defeat, the challenge is plain enough. It behoves us to match conviction with greater conviction and make the psychological strength of the fighting democracies shine before the world. It behoves us to match faith with greater faith and, with every scientific knowledge and device, secure our own psychological lines. If propaganda shows a way by which we can strengthen our conviction and affirm it more aggressively against the threat of an inferior concept of life, we must use it to the full, or we shall be robbing the forces of democracy of a vital weapon for its own security and survival. This is not just an idea: it is a practical issue of modern scientific warfare.

Propaganda on the offensive is, like every weapon of war, a cold-blooded one. Its only moral is that the confusion and defeat of the enemy are the supreme good. In that sense it is a black art and in the hands of the Germans was a diabolical one. But, objectively speaking, you will appreciate that it depends for its success on a deep study of the psychological and political divisions of the enemy and is therefore based on close and scientific analysis. Catch-as-catch-can methods in propaganda can no longer serve against an enemy so thorough.

The more pleasant side of international propaganda is the positive side, where you ingratiate yourself with other countries; where you state your cause, establish alliance in spirit and create world confidence that the issue and the outcome are with you. That was Britain's great task, particularly after the fall of France and particularly in regard to the Americas.

Britain's method derives from her great liberal tradition. She is not, I am afraid, very scientific; but she does believe, out of her liberal tradition, that telling the truth must command goodwill everywhere and, in the long run, defeat the distortions and boastings and blatancies of the enemy. The Germans believe that men are essentially weak; they believe that the mainsprings of action are primarily economic and selfish; they believe that men are more interested in the *élan vitale* than the *élan morale*; and they derive the principles of their propaganda accordingly. The British still believe in the *élan morale* and hope that an appeal to the Platonic principle of justice will triumph.

I won't say Britain tells the whole truth but I think that most detached observers agree that she tells as much of it as she reasonably can. The accent of honesty and forthrightness is her principal suit. You would never find the B.B.C.—you certainly would never find Winston Churchill—under-rating the dangers and difficulties which beset the country. Germany could not get out of her make-up an element of boasting; and Mussolini, for many years, was the image of braggadocio. The British quality, and it has the mark of a national talent, is under-statement; and in the long run—if there is a long run—it is strangely penetrating and effective.

If Britain has a fault, it is that she is still the proud old nation, so sure of her cause and of her good spirit that she takes it too much for granted that other nations will immediately recognize them. You remember what we used to say about English salesmanship. The English said in effect: 'Our articles are articles of quality; they have the best craftsmanship in the world behind them and, word of an Englishman, you can take our word for it.' It was all very true, but down in South America and elsewhere there were other habits of mind and other habits of buying and the Englishman never quite got round to studying the other fellow's point of view and the special requirements of the market. He certainly never quite got round to saying 'The client is always right'.

Propaganda, some of us believe, is like selling or showmanship, a study in relativity. I don't mean that it must always, like the chameleon, take its colour from the country or the community in which it is operating. It was the German style to be, cynically, all things to all men, and that was the essence of the German doctrine; but it is not the British. At the same time, a study of the other fellow's point of view is essential.

We used to argue a good deal in pre-war England about the policy of the British Council for Cultural Relations Abroad. There were two schools of thought. One school had not yet got away from the idea that the one way to present Britain abroad was to show the Horse Guards Parade and the ceremonies of old England, Oxford and the law courts, Ascot and Canterbury, the green lawns of the cathedral towns and the lovely rustic quiet of the shires. It was difficult to quarrel with things so fine; but others said plainly: 'No, there is a world without, which wants to know more than that. You have a responsibility before the world, in terms of modern leadership, modern ideas and modern achievements. The world wants to know how up-to-date and forward looking you are. It wants to see the light of the future in your eyes as well as the strength and dignity of your past. It wants to know what you are doing to deserve your privileged position in the world; and God keep you if you do not answer them.'

If you examine British propaganda today, you will find that there are still the two schools of thought, but I am glad to say that, the younger school has been winning hands down. Never, in a sense, was

Britain a more modern, revitalized, forward-looking country than she is today.

Britain is beginning to see that accents and styles count in propaganda and that every country has its own way of thinking and its own special focus of interest. 'Other nations', says Wickham Steed, 'are not interested to hear what good people we are or how excellent our intentions may be. They are interested in what is going to happen to themselves and it should be the business of our propaganda to make this clear to them.'

On this question of international differences, I received a letter from England from someone who had seen our Canadian films. He said, was it possible that Canadians thought faster than Englishmen. I replied that when it is a problem of thinking in a straight line, Canadians think much faster; but that when it comes to thinking in five concentric circles, the Englishmen are undoubtedly the better. Our policy, however, when we send Canadian films abroad is to invite the countries receiving them to remake them in their own style and use their own editorial comment. It sounds curious but there are really vast differences of mental approach as between Canada and England. There is even a vast difference of approach as between New Zealand and Australia. He is a very optimistic propagandist who thinks he can easily pen a message or strike a style which can be called international.

London Can Take It was a beautiful film but it raises a very special issue of relativity in propaganda. That is the difference between primary effects and secondary effects. You might call it the difference between conscious and subconscious effects. *London Can Take It* created enormous sympathy for England and so far so good. The question is whether creating sympathy necessarily creates confidence. I cite that psychological problem only to indicate that in the art of propaganda many deep considerations have to be taken into account. Short-range results are not necessarily long-range successes. Conscious effects may not necessarily engage the deeper loyalties of the subconscious. In propaganda you may all too easily be here today and gone tomorrow.

All in all, however, one may be proud of many things in Britain's Information Service. It has followed its own native light and no one will say it has not been a noble light. It has not been scientific, but neither has it been cynical. To its scientific critics it has said with Sir Philip Sidney 'If you will only look in thy heart and write, all will be well'. I am of the scientific school myself and would leave less to chance in a hard and highly mobilized world. But no one will deny that at least half the art of propaganda lies in the ultimate truth that truth will ultimately conquer.

For myself, I watched the German procedure and wished a little sometimes that we could, without running over into harshness and blatancy, say a little more about ourselves and put our propaganda more plainly on the offensive. They flooded the world with pictures of action, of their young troops on the march and going places, of deeds done. In their pictures to America, they laid a special emphasis on youth and efficiency and, to people starved of belief in the future, they drummed away with their idea of a new world order. They most subtly showed great respect in their presentation of their French and English prisoners of war and emphasized the model discipline of their troops in occupied territories. They most carefully presented the Führer as a gentle and simple soul, weeping over his wounded soldiers, kind to children, humble in his triumphs. It was a calculated, impressive and positive picture as they presented it.

The Germans' careful study of the requirements of particular countries must have had particular effect in South America. They appreciated the South American objection to being exploited by alien capital and posed carefully as the outside friend who wished nothing so much as to help them be themselves and develop themselves. They knew how to pump in free news services to countries which appreciated them—by radio from Berlin, translated and typed out and put pronto on the editorial desk by local German agents. On the special national days of these countries to the south they knew how to shoot flattering broadcasts from Berlin, in the language of the country and with the fullest knowledge of the local vanities to be flattered.

The Germans knew better than to say, as a certain well-known American said of cultural relations with South America, that 'the idea was to spread the American idea to the South American Republics'. I have no doubt he thought the American idea God's own blessing to mankind, but it is worth remembering that not a few South Americans, allied to a more aristocratic and courtly tradition, still regard the American idea as the ultimate in barbarism—or as a French jester has put it, an idea 'which has passed from barbarism to degeneracy without any intervening period of civilization'. The Germans certainly knew better than to define their interest in South America with the *naïveté* of an advertisement in *Time*. 'Southward,' it declared, in a phrase calculated to raise every hackle south of the Rio Grande, 'Southward, lies the course of Empire.'

Where the Germans failed was in the fact that their cold-blooded cynicism spilled over and was spotted. You can impress other countries with your might and your will. You may even impress them with your new world order. But you can't start blatantly talking of conscience as a chimera; morals as an old wives' tale; the Christian religion as a dream of weaklings; and the pursuit of truth as *bourgeois* fiddle-faddle, without raising a few doubts in the heart of mankind.

Finally, there is propaganda within our gates. I suggested earlier that faith must be met with greater faith and that our first line of defence is in the unity of our purpose in these ideological struggles which are now upon us.

A democracy by its very nature and by its very virtues lies wide open to division and uncertainty. It encourages discussion; it permits free criticism; it opens its arms wide to the preaching of any and every doctrine. It guards jealously this liberty of the individual, for it is of the essence of democracy and, in the long run, makes for justice and civilization. But in times of stress it is difficult to see the wood for the trees. Whilst we are consulting this freedom and that, we may lose that discipline, that centralized power and dynamic, by which the principle of liberty itself is safeguarded from those who are less punctilious. When we are challenged in our philosophy and our way of life, the beginning is not in the word but in the act.

The Nazi viewpoint was that we had not found within our democratic way of life a sufficient dynamic of action to meet their challenge—that it was not in our nature to find it—and that we should not find it. 'The opposition', said Hitler, 'is dismally helpless, incapable of acting, because it has lost every vestige of an inner law of action.'

In the long run they found that was not true but it would be folly to dismiss this criticism without thinking about it. The self-respect of free men provides the only *lasting* dynamic in human society; and the most powerful and vivid statement of this proposition is to be found in Walt Whitman's preface to his *Leaves of Grass*. But we also know that free men are relatively slow in the uptake in the first days of crisis. We know that much that has become precious to free men in a liberal régime must be forsworn in days of difficulty—the luxury of private possession and private security—the luxury of private deviation in thought and action—the supreme luxury of arguing the toss. Moreover, your individual trained in a liberal régime demands automatically that he be *persuaded* to his sacrifice. It may sound exasperating but he demands as of right—of human right—that he come in only of his own free will.

All this points to the fact that instead of propaganda being less necessary in a democracy, it is more necessary. In the authoritarian state you have powers of compulsion and powers of repression, physical and mental, which in part at least take the place of persuasion. Not so in a democracy. It is your democrat who most needs and demands guidance from his leaders. It is the democratic leader who most must give it. If only for the sake of quick decision and common action, it is democracy for which propaganda is the more urgent necessity.

There is another deep reason for the development of propaganda in a democracy. The educational beliefs of democracy have been criticized. 'Universal education', said the Nazis, 'is the most corroding and disintegrating poison that liberalism ever invented for its own destruction.' This, of course, is another distortion, but there is again a grain of truth. With universal education, democracy has set itself an enormous and an enormously difficult task. We have had it for two or three generations only; and it would be crazy to think that in that short experience we have worked out a perfect technique or discovered all the principles by which it should be guided. Our system of universal education has made vast mistakes and has today grotesque weaknesses. Every progressive educationist knows that. This does not mean that we must throw the essential machinery of democracy into the discard, but rather that we must correct its mistakes and strengthen it where it is now weak.

There are some of us who believe that propaganda is the part of democratic education which the educators forgot; and that is what first attracted us to study its possibilities. Education has always seemed to us to ask too much from people. It has seemed to expect every citizen to know everything about everything all the time—a patent impossibility in a world which grows wider and more complicated every day. We believe that education has concentrated so much on people knowing things that it has not sufficiently taught them to feel things. It has given them facts but has not sufficiently given them faith. It has given them the three R's but has not sufficiently given them that fourth R which is Rooted Belief. We believe that education in this essential has left men out in the bush without an emotional map to guide them; and when men are starved of belief they are only too prone to believe anything.

If you recall the origin of the word propaganda, you will remember that it was first associated with the defence of a faith and a concept of civilization. Propaganda first appeared in the description of the Catholic office—Congregatio de Propaganda Fide—which was to preach and maintain the faith. It may be just as easily today the means by which we preach and maintain our own democratic faith. Man does not live by bread alone, nor the citizen by mind alone. He is a man with vanities to be appealed to, a native pride to be encouraged. He has a gambler's heart to be allowed a flutter and a fighting instinct which can be associated with fighting for the right. One part of him at least asks to live not safely but adventurously.

So we may usefully add a new dramatic factor to public education—an uplifting factor which associates knowledge with pride and private effort with a sense of public purpose. We can, by propaganda, widen the horizons of the schoolroom and give to every individual, each in his place and work, a living conception of the community which he has the privilege to serve. We can take his imagination beyond the boundaries of his community to discover the destiny of his country. We can light up his life with a sense of active citizenship. We can give him a sense of greater reality in the present and a vision of the future. And, so doing, we can make the life of the citizen more ardent and satisfactory to himself.

We can, in short, give him a leadership of the imagination which our democratic education has so far lacked. We can do it by radio and film and a half a dozen other imaginative media; but mostly, I hope, we shall do it by encouraging men to work and fight and serve in common for the public good. To have men participate in action is the best of all propagandas; and radio and films and the rest of them are only auxiliary to that.

Canada is a young nation which has not yet found herself but is today in the exciting process of doing so. I like to think that the breathless reception given to the King and Queen was due not so much to their presence, brilliant as it was, but to the fact that Canada found for the first time a ceremonial opportunity of raising her young national face to the sunlight. I like to think that subconscious Canada is even more important than conscious Canada and that there is growing up swiftly in this country, under the surface, the sense of a great future and of a great separate destiny—as Canada.

In other words, I believe the country is ripe, if its imagination is given true leadership, for a new burst of energy and a new expression of Canada's faith in herself. In these circumstances, I don't think it would be difficult to create a powerful sense of spiritual unity, whatever the threat may be.

4 The Documentary Idea: 1942

The first part of our work in Canada was finished early in 1942. It produced a film organization which suggested it could do great things for the country if it was looked after in good faith till the young people developcd. Much of it was pulled off the sky. On the other hand, there are special reasons why the national use of films should have fitted so quickly and progressively into the Canadian scene. The need to achieve unity in a country of many geographical and psychological distances is only one of them and not the most important. More vital, I think, is the fact that Canada is waking up to her place in the world and is conscious, as few English-speaking countries seem to be, that it is a new sort of place in the world. A medium which tries to explain the shape of events and create loyalties in relation to the developing scene is welcome. I cannot otherwise explain the measure of support we have been given, nor the long-range hopes that have been placed in this school of projection we have set up.

Stuart Legg has been such a worker as you never saw: with one film a month in the theatre series for a couple of years, and stepping up later to two. It will be easier as the research staff grows, for the key to that sort of thing is in the first place academic. There is first-rate support in the fields of economics and international affairs. This is a characteristic of Canada and will have considerable influence on the development of the group.

The *World in Action* series says more of what is going on in our minds. The films in this series develop in authority and command good critical attention both in Canada and in the States. We are concerned in these films primarily with the relation of local strategies to larger world ones. This is partly in reaction to what some of us regard as a dangerous parochialism in English-speaking propaganda: but also because Canada is moving as swiftly towards a world viewpoint as England in recent years has been moving away from it. The style comes out of the job. Since it is a question of giving people a pattern of thought and feeling about highly complex and urgent events, we give it as well as we know, with a minimum of dawdling over how some poor darling happens to react to something or other. This is one time, we say, when history doesn't give a good goddam who is being the manly little fellow in adversity and is only concerned with the designs for living and dying that will actually and in fact shape the future. If our stuff pretends to be certain, it's because people need certainty. If our maps look upside down, it's because it's time people saw things in relativity. If we bang them out one a fortnight and no misses, instead of sitting six months on our fannies cuddling them to sweet smotheroo, it's because a lot of bravos in Russia and Japan and Germany are banging out things too and we'd maybe better learn how, in time. If the manner is objective and hard, it's because we believe the next phase of human development needs that kind of mental approach. After all, there is no danger of the humanitarian tradition perishing while the old are left alive to feel sorry for themselves and make 'beautiful' pictures about it. Sad to say, the beating heart of the Stuarts was all they had left and so it is with vanishing politicos.

The penalty of realism is that it is about reality and has to bother for ever not about being 'beautiful' but about being right. It means a stalwart effort these days: one has to chill the mind to so many emotional defences of the decadent and so many smooth rationalizations of the ineffective. One has even to chill the mind to what, in the vacuum of daydreams, one might normally admire. In our world it is specially necessary these days to guard against the æsthetic argument. It is plausible and apt to get under the defences of any maker in any medium. But, of course, it is the dear bright-eyed old enemy and by this time we know it very well. Documentary was from the beginning— when we first separated our public purpose theories from those of Flaherty—an 'anti-æsthetic' movement. We have all, I suppose, sacrificed some personal capacity in 'art' and the pleasant vanity that goes with it.

What confuses the history is that we had always the good sense to use the æsthetes. We did so because we liked them and because we needed them. It was, paradoxically, with the first-rate æsthetic help of people like Flaherty and Cavalcanti—our 'fellow travellers' so to speak —that we mastered the techniques necessary for our quite unæsthetic purpose. That purpose was plain and was written about often enough. Rotha spent a lot of time on it. We were concerned not with the category of 'purposiveness without purpose' but with that other category beyond which used to be called teleological. We were reformers open and avowed: concerned—to use the old jargon—with 'bringing

The Documentary Idea: 1942

alive the new materials of citizenship', 'crystallizing sentiments' and creating those 'new loyalties from which a progressive civic will might derive'. Take that away and I'd be hard put to it to say what I have been working for these past fifteen years. What, of course, made documentary successful as a movement was that in a decade of spiritual weariness it reached out, almost alone among the media, towards the future. Obviously it was the public purpose within it which commanded government and other backing, the progressive social intention within it which secured the regard of the newspapers and people of goodwill everywhere, and the sense of a public cause to be served which kept its own people together.

These facts should have made it clear that the documentary idea was not basically a film idea at all, and the film treatment it inspired only an incidental aspect of it. The medium happened to be the most convenient and most exciting available to us. The idea itself, on the other hand, was a new idea for public education: its underlying concept that the world was in a phase of drastic change affecting every manner of thought and practice, and the public comprehension of the nature of that change vital. There it is, exploratory, experimental and stumbling, in the films themselves: from the dramatization of the workman and his daily work to the dramatization of modern organization and the new corporate elements in society to the dramatization of social problems: each a step in the attempt to understand the stubborn raw material of our modern citizenship and wake the heart and the will to their mastery. Where we stopped short was that, with equal deliberation, we refused to specify what political agency should carry out that will or associate ourselves with any one of them. Our job specifically was to wake the heart and the will: it was for the political parties to make before the people their own case for leadership.

I would not restate these principles merely out of historical interest. The important point is that they have not changed at all and they are not going to change, nor be changed. The materials of citizenship today are different and the perspectives wider and more difficult; but we have, as ever, the duty of exploring them and of waking the heart and will in regard to them. That duty is what documentary is about. It is, moreover, documentary's primary service to the state: to be persisted in, whatever deviation may be urged upon it, or whatever confusion of thought, or easiness of mind, success may bring. Let no one say that a few brighteyed films or a couple of Academy awards—from Hollywood of all places!—mean anything more than that a bit of a job was done yesterday. Tomorrow it is the same grind with ever new material—some easy, some not so easy—to be brought into design; and no percentage in it for anyone except doing the rightest job of education and inspiration we know how for the people. Considering the large audiences we now reach and the historical stakes that depend on rightness of approach, it is a privilege worth a measure of personal effort and sacrifice. If there is common agreement in the 'strategy' I have indicated, differences in daily 'tactic' will not seriously affect unity.

We should see equally straight regarding the social factor in our work over the thirties. It was a powerful inspiration and very important for that period. Without *Housing Problems* and the whole movement of social understanding such films helped to articulate, I think history would have found another and bloodier solution when the bombs first rained on the cities of Britain. But that Indian summer of decent social intention was not just due to the persistence of people like ourselves and to the humanitarian interests of our governmental and industrial colleagues. It may also have marked a serious limiting of horizons. It may have been an oblique sign that England, to her peril, was becoming interested only in herself. Some of us sensed it as we reached out in every way we knew for an opportunity of wider international statement. We did not, I am afraid, sense it half enough and we share the guilt of that sultry decade with all the other inadequate guides of public opinion. The job we did was perhaps a good enough job so far as it went, but our materials were not chosen widely enough.

Nothing seems now more significant of the period than that, at a time so crucial, there was no eager sponsorship for world thinking in a country which still pretended to world leadership. Russia had its third International and Germany had that geopolitical brain trust which, centred in Hausofer, spread its influence through Hess to Hitler and to every department of the Reich. In the light of events, how much on the right lines Tallents was and how blind were the people who defeated his great concept! For documentary the effect was important. The E.M.B., which might have done so much for positive international thinking, died seven years too early; and it was hardly, as we comically discovered, the job for the G.P.O. There was the brief, bright excursion to Geneva: there was that magnificent scheme for the I.L.O. which Winant liked but which the Rockefeller Foundation turned down: there was my own continuous and fruitless pursuit of the bluebird we miscalled the 'Empire' and the momentary hopeful stirring in the Colonial Office under Malcolm MacDonald: there was the Imperial Relations Trust, five years too late, and affected from the first by the weight of impending events. The international factor, so necessary to a realist statement of even national affairs, was not in the deal.

It is, of course, more vital than ever to a documentary policy. We, the leaders of the people and of the instruments of public opinion, have been out-thought by Russia, Germany and Japan because we have been out-thought in modern international terms. Because documentary is concerned with affecting the vital terms of public thinking towards a realistic comprehension of events and their mastery, its duty is plain. To use the phrase of these present days, you can't win the war, neither 'outside' nor 'inside'—without a revision of the public mind regarding Britain's place in the world and the larger morale that goes with a sense of being on the bandwagon of history. Thumbing a ride to the future is not nearly good enough.

I look back on Munich as representing a milestone in my own outlook on documentary. From that time on the social work in which we had been engaged seemed to me relatively beside the point. Munich was the last necessary evidence of how utterly out-of-category our political thinking was and how literally our political leaders did not know what it was all about. From that point it seemed clear that we had, willy-nilly, to relate the interests of the British people to new world forces of the most dynamic sort—physical, economic and ideological. It was inevitable that our first instinct should be to put our head in the sand and in a last frantic gesture try to avoid the implications of the future; but the significance of our indecision in regard to both Germany and the Soviet Union was plain to see. World revolution had broken out on the biggest possible scale, and to the point of having people like Churchill recognize it as such. Win or lose, the economy of Britain and her place in the world were under threat of serious alteration and, however we might presently hide our eyes, people's minds had to be prepared and made fit for them if what was great and good in Britain was to survive. It was not much use concentrating on changes in a *status* whose *quo* was being challenged from every active corner of the world and apt to be blown to historical smithereens. Internal social issues were no longer enough when the deeper political issues had become the whole of realism.

This was one person's reaction. I knew it meant the exploration of a wider basis for the public instruction which documentary represented than the reactionary régime at that time allowed. But I was altogether doubtful of where the journey would lead. I hoped, vaguely I must admit, that youth and the viewpoints their world position imposed upon them would bring a measure of progressive strength from the

Dominions. I did not know how that strength could ever be articulated in time to save documentary from its greatest setback: the official sponsorship of the old, the obstinate and the inept. That period, thank heaven, is over and, in the combined force which documentary has so hardly won, it should be possible to create a new strength of thought and purpose.

In spite of many difficulties and confusions in the public scene, I see no reason why documentary should not do an increasingly useful job within the limits of official sponsorship. Some of the difficulties are constantly quoted to me and particularly from England. We are, it is emphasized, far from articulating our war aims. We still insist on tolerations and freedoms which often, some say, merely disguise the 'freedom' to go back to Britain's *status quo ante* and the 'tolerance' of past stupidities. We have not yet learned to state the new creative terms which will give reality to 'freedom' and 'tolerance' in an actual future. We denounce fanaticism in others because we have not ourselves discovered a shape of things-to-come to be fanatical about. We still stand bravely but vaguely between two worlds and talk the language of indecision: resting our case on hopes of Russia and the U.S., the bravery of our youth, and our capacity to stand up to other people's offensives. As usual, I take the position that while I believe political issues are the whole of realism, the 'agency' of correct political change is not my concern. It may come in any colour of the rainbow, and call itself the British Council or the Society of St. George for England Canterbury Inc. so long as it is the midwife of correct political change. *Die tat ist alles.* To put it in its simplest and naïvest form—which is still good to remember and maintain—correct political change will be that alignment of political principles and loyalties which, given the circumstances of the world today, will best serve the interests of peoples of all lands, and the British people in proportion, and actively mobilize the *native* heart and mind to these ends. It will be that alignment which actively eliminates the evil forces, wherever they may be, which are against such interests and all decadent forces, wherever they may be, which are not competent to control the developing scene. That is something on which all healthy elements must agree, and the unhealthy elements present events are sufficiently taking care of. War has this grim compensation that only the successful generals are considered good ones; and there is a daily measuring-stick for leaders in that most powerful quarter of public appraisal, the stomach muscles of the people.

It is also fairly plain what areas of chaos have to be reduced to order, whatever political alignment develops. The armies of the world are carving out new geographical concepts and shapes. The processes of total war are developing new economic concepts, and more modern methods of administrative control. First things are miraculously coming first, including the food and faith of the people. Though minor social changes are not major political ones and the radish may be one colour outside and another in, the present flow of social decency must lubricate the development of state planning, corporate thinking and co-operative citizenship. The most important of the British films have, of course, been those which have seized on one or other of these changes, and it is of first-rate significance that Jack Beddington should have sponsored them. Their importance is that in explaining the shape of these developments they are exploring the inevitable shapes of the future, rough and jerry-built as they may now appear. It does not matter if the films are at first not so good. The history of documentary is the history of exploring new fields of material, always with difficulty first, then easier and better. Its chief temptation has been to abandon exploration and, doing better what has been done before, pursue the comfort of technical excellence. It will be remembered that this also was one of the reasons for Russia's attack on the 'formal arts'.

The new fields of positive material are wide and we have, all of us, only scratched the surface. The field of social changes, is not, *per se*, the most important of them. Kindness in a queue at Plymouth which means so much to the B.B.C. overseas broadcasts, does nothing about India. The important shapes are obviously those more directly related to the national and international management of industrial, economic and human forces. They are important in winning the war without. They also represent, on a longer term view, a new way of thought which may be the deepest need of our generation. In so far as documentary is primarily concerned with attitudes of mind, this aspect of the matter is worth a great deal of attention. 'Total War' is said to require 'total effort' but this has not been easily come by in nations which still have a hang-over of nineteenth-century thinking and *laisser-faire*. At a hundred points today wrong attitudes are still being taught: some in innocence of the dynamic change which total effort involves: some in conscious defence of the sectional and selfish interests which total effort must necessarily eliminate. This psychological fifth column is more deeply entrenched than any other and all of us have some unconscious affiliation with it as a heritage from our out-of-date education. Rotted in the old 'untotal' ways and in the personal pleasures we enjoyed under them, we have to examine every day anew what in our words and sentiments we are really saying. A critique of sentiments is a necessary preliminary to propaganda and to documentary as its critical instrument.

It will certainly take continuous teaching of the public mind before the new relationship between the individual and the state, which total effort involves, becomes a familiar and automatic one. A beginning has been made, but only a beginning. The capacity of the individual for sacrifice has already been well described and honoured. So has team work, particularly in the fighting services. So has the mastery of some of the new technical worlds which the war has opened up. So far so good, but it is the habit of thought which drives on towards the integration of all national forces for the public good, which goes to the root of things. Here we come face to face with the possibility of integrating these forces in a thousand new ways: in particular in the release of co-operative and corporate energies on a scale never dreamt of before. To consider this simply as a temporary device of war is to mistake its significance and by so doing to dishearten the people; for it is what people in their hearts have been harking for and represents the fulfilment of an era. Total war may yet appear as the dreadful period of forced apprenticeship in which we learned what we had hitherto refused to learn, how to order the vast new forces of human and material energies to decent human ends. In any case, there it is, a growing habit of thought for documentary to watch and describe and instil at a hundred points: serving at once the present need of Britain and the shape of the future.

Total effort needs, in the last resort, a background of faith and a sense of destiny; but this concept of integrating all resources to an active end gives the principal pattern for a documentary approach. It will force documentary more intimately into a consideration of active ends and of the patterns of integration which best achieve them. It will also force it into a study of the larger phases of public management which may not have seemed necessary before. To take a simple example, we have an excellent film from Anstey on how to put out incendiary bombs and handle the local aspects of fire-watching; but we have had no film covering the basic revolution of strategy in anti-blitz activities which the experience of blitz inspired. Britain's discovery of the intimate relationship between the social structure and defence provides an excellent example of 'total pattern' and indicates the revolution in public viewpoint required by total effort. Consider, at the other end of the field of war, *Time*'s report from Burma. 'The Japanese fought total war, backed by political theory and strengthened

by powerful propaganda. They made this total war feasible by corner-
ing economic life in conquered areas, utilizing labour power and seizing
raw materials to supply continuing war from war itself. It is a type of
war thoroughly understood by the Russians and the Germans, half
adopted by the Chinese, and little understood by Britain and America.'
If it is 'little understood' it only means that in this aspect of activity,
as in so many others, effectiveness depends on a new way of thought
which we have not mastered deeply enough to practise in new circumstances. The result of peace as well as war lies in the hands of those
who understand it and can teach it.

One phrase, sticking out like a sore thumb from the reports of the
Eastern war, reveals a further perspective. Referring to the loss of
native Burmese support we were accused of 'lacking sound political
theory'. Britain's failure to understand other points of view may again
be the heritage of a period in which we were powerful enough and rich
enough not to have to bother about them; but that day has gone.
Again new attitudes have to be created in which Britain sees her
interest in relation to others. You may call it, if you like, the way of
relativity. It involves an attitude of mind which can be quickly acquired, rather than a vast knowledge of what those interests are. It
will mature more easily from a consideration of the patterns of real
and logical relations with other countries (geopolitical and ideological)
than from exchange of 'cultural' vacua. The latter have never stood
the test of events; yet Britain makes no films of the former. In this
field, documentary might do much to deparochialize some of our
common ways of thought. There are many opportunities. Let me take
an oblique example in Anstey's *Naval Operations*. Here was a neat,
tight little film with that cool technical treatment which has always
been the distinction of the Shell Film Unit. But there are other fleets
beside the British, including the Russian, Dutch, Australian and
Canadian. They also have 'relative' importance in a total view of naval
operations. So has the German. So have the American and the
Japanese, for even if the film was made before Pearl Harbour, the fleet
in being is also a factor in naval operations. In this film, good as it
was, the relative viewpoint was not taken because the total viewpoint
was not taken, and the design of it, on the theory I am urging, belonged
to the past. I am not complaining of a film I like very much. I am
merely indicating how various are the opportunities for the relativity
approach.

Once consider that Britain is only important as it is related to other
nations and its problems and developments only important as they are

recognized as part of wider problems and developments, and many subjects will reach out into healthier and more exciting perspectives of description than are presently being utilized. The past lack of a sense of relativity in Britain has been responsible for a good deal that seems trivial and even maudlin to other peoples. However stern and manly the voice that speaks it, it is still the unrelative thing it is and in my view does not give an account of the reality of the people of Britain. The falsity of the impression comes from the falsity of the approach. It will not be easily cured for it derives from historical factors of the deepest sort, and even documentary is bound to reflect them, however objective it may try to be. The fact that it is being presently cured at good speed represents indeed a triumph of clear thinking in difficult circumstances. A deliberate attempt to relate British perspectives to others would help the process. It may be the key to it. Incidentally, this relativity approach, apart from being one of the guides to a logical and sure internationalism, is a necessary guide to retaining allies. It is worth noting that there is a difference between making a film of the Polish forces to flatter Poland, or making a film of a Dominion to show what that Dominion 'is doing for England', and making a film in which Britain takes her due place in a 'total' pattern.

So much for new materials and new approaches. Styles are more difficult to talk about for they must inevitably vary with countries. I think, however, that it is possible to make certain generalizations. Since events move speedily, and opportunities pass just as speedily, the tempo of production must change accordingly. A lot has to be done and done quickly if the public mind is to be tuned in time to what, amid these swift moving changes of public organization, is required of it. It is not the technical perfection of the film that matters, nor even the vanity of its maker, but what happens to the public mind. Never before has there been such a call for the creation of new loyalties or bringing people to new kinds of sticking points. Times press and so must production; and with it must go a harder and more direct style. A dozen reasons make this inevitable. There is the need of striking while irons are hot, and this is particularly true of front-line reporting and has its excellent examples in the German films of Poland, the West Front and Crete, and in *London Can Take It*, the Commando raids and *War Clouds in the Pacific*. There is also the need to create a sense of urgency in the public mind, and gear it in its everyday processes to the hardness and directness which make for action and decision. If there is one thing that good propaganda must not do these days it is to give people catharsis. This again, not just because 'the war has to be won', but because as far as the eye can see, we are entering an era of action, in which only the givers of order and the doers generally will be permitted to survive. Someone winced when I suggested in England that in times of great change the only songs worth writing were marching songs. This makes the same point, except that the term must be read widely to include everything that makes people think and fight and organize for the creation of order. One doesn't have to associate oneself with the German definition of order to see that their insistence on activism is an all too successful recognition of the same need. So with a spectacular flourish, is Goering's 'when anyone mentions the word culture, I reach for my gun'. It is not peculiarly or specially a German sentiment. In the name of the inaction they call culture they have permitted a wilderness, and it will certainly not be in the name of culture that it will blossom again. In its basic meaning, culture is surely the giving of law to what is without it. That hard but truer way of culture will not go by default if we search out the design in the seeming chaos of present events and, out of the experiments in total effort now, create the co-operative and more profoundly 'democratic' ways of the future. To go back once again to Tallents's Mill quotation, the pattern of the artist in this relationship will indicate the living principle of action.

So the long, windy openings are out and the cathartic finishes in which a good, brave, tearful, self-congratulatory and useless time has been had by all. The box-office—pander to what is lazy, weak, reactionary, sentimental and essentially defeatist in all of us—will, of course, instinctively howl for them. It will want to make 'relaxation', if you please, even out of war. But that way leads nowhere. Deep down, the people want to be fired to tougher ways of thought and feeling. In that habit they will win more than a war.

1 Education and the New Order

I don't think we have done very well in education. The world has been changing about us—drastically changing—and we have not kept up with it. I suspect we have held on to concepts of education fit for the last century but no longer for this and have therefore failed to create the mental qualities and capacities our generation has needed. We face one of the deepest crises in the history of human organization. There is no question of that, with the whole world at war. This in itself represents the failure of the human mind to order human affairs in our time; and this in turn represents a failure in understanding and capacity for ordering human affairs.

I hardly think education can be absolved from its part in that failure. Talk as you will of pursuing the highest ends of man and the service of God, the base of the pyramid is in deeds done and in results achieved. In that sense, education is surely never anything other than the process by which men are fitted to serve their generation and bring it into the terms of order. It is the process by which the minds of men are keyed to the tasks of good citizenship, by which they are geared to the privilege of making a constructive contribution, however humble, to the highest purposes of the community.

Grant that in so doing education does, in man's high fancy, tune the human spirit to the music of the spheres, none the less its function is the immediate and practical one of being a deliberate social instrument—not dreaming in an ivory tower, but outside on the barricades of social construction, holding citizens to the common purpose their generation has set for them.

Education is activist or it is nothing.

If that is so, the utter disorder of society in this our time does not represent a very brilliant achievement for that instrument on which society depends for understanding and guidance. We have loosed the inventions and armed the human race with brilliant physical weapons for creating a rich civilization. But we have not known how to solve the simplest problems of economic integration—either nationally or internationally. Power has been a synonym for selfishness and possession has been a synonym for greed. I do not mean that education should be blamed for this and for the wars that have resulted as night from day. I merely mean that education is the key to the mobilization of men's minds to right ends or wrong ends, to order or chaos; and that is what education is. If men's minds have not been mobilized aright, the educational process has not been good enough. If, on the other hand, men's minds are in the future to be mobilized aright, it means an increase in the wisdom and power of the educational process. So, looking beyond the immediate, the greatest task of our time is not one for the soldiers but one for the educators and, because of the nature of the problem, it is certainly the hardest task they have ever been set.

These changing times of ours do not represent ordinary changes. There are periods in history when the whole basis of truth is re-examined and when the operative philosophies are revolutionized and renewed. This is one of them. We had such a period before when the Middle Ages passed into the Renaissance. The key to that change was not in the rediscovery of Greece as the text-books say, but in something much deeper. It was in the discovery and development of the laws of quantitative measurement. Out of it came the philosophy of pioneering and personal acquisition—the philosophy of individualism and individual rights—which has ruled our minds to this day.

No period of history has been more spectacular. But I wonder if we have not for a long time been seeing the last phases of it. Everyone today talks of the war not as a war but as a world revolution. And I wonder if the world revolution does not lie in this: that the great days of unmitigated individualism and governmental *laisser-faire* are over, and the day of common unified planning has arrived.

If that is so, it means an enormous change in all our thinking and all our values. It means nothing less than a drastic spring cleaning of the concepts we teach and the sentiments by which we govern our action. At the time of the Renaissance the bases of religion and philosophy and government were altered to accommodate and articulate the deep change in human affairs. You will remember, for example, how into painting came the study of perspective and the placing of the individual in space; and into literature came the study of personal character. Personal measurement became, in varying degrees, a principle of philosophy in Berkeley, Locke, Rousseau, Bentham and the rest of them. In religion, came the Reformation with a new emphasis on conscience and individual relationship with God. The arts and the philosophies changed to give men a working vision and a working faith under the new conditions of society. They followed public necessity. The same obligation may be upon us now and I think it is.

This is not a sudden development. All the years I have been watching the educational process, it has been difficult not to be conscious of it. The only difference is that the picture which was dim twenty-five years ago is today rushing into focus.

Perhaps an illustration from that earlier period may be of some interest. It goes back to the small Scots village in which I was brought up and where my father was a schoolmaster. He was a good dominie of the old school. He called himself a Conservative, but his operative philosophy in education was a good sample of what a liberal Scottish education meant. He believed in the democratic process as Burns and all Scotsmen naturally and natively do. A man was a man for a' that. We were partly agriculture, partly coal mining, and it didn't matter where the boys came from. If they were lads of parts, he felt it his God-given mission to put them on their way. At 8 o'clock in the morning before school and at 5 o'clock after school, he was at work intensifying on the bright ones, so that they could win scholarships and go to high school and on to the university. Learning was power and he was taking his job seriously. It is still pleasant to think how he would trudge off miles into the country to prevail on stubborn ploughmen, who needed the extra money coming in, to give their boys a chance and not put them to work at fourteen.

The basis of his educational philosophy was certainly according to the eternal verities. It was deeply rooted in Carlyle and Ruskin and the natural rights of man. The wind of the French revolution still blew behind it. But it was strictly individualist. Education gave men a chance in the world. It put them in good competitive standing in a grim competitive world. It fitted them to open the doors of spiritual satisfaction in literature and philosophy. But it was in the name of a highly personal satisfaction. Behind it all was the dream of the nineteenth century—the false dream—that if only everyone had the individualist ideals that education taught, free men in a free society—each in independent and educated judgment—would create a civilization such as the world had never seen before.

Even when that kind of education was conscious of social relationships, the approach was on an individualist basis. Conservative as he was, this village schoolmaster of whom I write was something of a pioneer in the teaching of the social amenities. He pioneered school gardens and domestic science for girls at the beginning of the century. With a sense of bringing a wider horizon into the classroom, he brought to that obscure village school, more than thirty years ago, the first film show ever seen in educational circles in Scotland. He helped to build a village institute, so that his fellow citizens would have more literary papers on this and that, and particularly more papers on Carlyle and Ruskin. But the prevailing idea was as always that the individual might be more enlightened. One suspected that the end of it all was to make every workman a gentleman in a library—perhaps without too much leisure to be a gentleman and not too much of a library, but still as good as any man alive in the deep pursuit of truth and beauty.

The smashing of that idyllic viewpoint has been probably the greatest educational fact of our time; and I saw it smashed right there in my village and I saw the deep doubt creep into the mind of that school-master that everything he stood for and strove for was somewhere wrong. That was many years ago, long before the events of today made the dim things so much plainer.

As I have noted, one half of that village consisted of coal miners. The every effect of the education they were given, conservative as it might be in intention, was to make men think; and, thinking, they became less and less satisfied with the miserable pays they received. The life of the village became more and more affected by strikes and lock-outs. As amalgamations were developed, the employers stood ever further and further away and the battle for wages and safeties and securities became the fiercer as the fight became more abstract—as decisions came to depend on massed unions and massed corporations.

Somehow or other the educational process got to be beside the point. What were the delights of literature when a distant judgment by a distant corporation could throw a man into six months of economic misery? What were the pleasures of Shakespeare and *A Midsummer Night's Dream* in the evening schools, when industrial conditions were tiring the boys to death? What was the use of saying that a man was a man for a' that, when you were dealing day in day out with a war of economic forces in which only armies counted and where the motivating powers were abstract and unseen? In his local way this schoolmaster did a great deal. He started soup kitchens and got the soup kitchen principle so well established that the miners actually in one great strike organized the feeding of their whole community. Perhaps the soup kitchen idea was the one great educational achievement of his life. But before he finished I think the true leadership in education had passed to other shoulders. It had in fact passed to the miners themselves and the economists among them. They read their Blatchford and Keir Hardie and Bob Smillie; they attended their trade union meetings; and the day came when they elected their first Labour member of parliament, and, with so many other villages in Scotland, joined in the great drive for a socialist Britain.

At the time, I drew two conclusions from that village story. The first is that education can only, at its peril, detach itself from the economic processes and what is happening in the world. In that sense, if official education does not give realistic leadership in terms of what is happening and what is most deeply needed in the world, be assured the people will find other more realistic leadership. The second lesson was that the individualist dream in education is over and done with in a world which operates in terms of large integrated forces. There is nothing I can think of so cynical today as to teach a boy that the world is his personal oyster for the opening or talk, as Lord Birkenhead did, of the glittering prizes that fall to a flashing sword.

There is, and of course must be, a place for individual talents, but it becomes ever clearer that the heart of the matter today lies in team-work and in unity. Individualism, that dream of so many centuries, has given us one of the golden ages. But what was so great a force in a simple world has become a nuisance in one more complicated. By its own bright energies, individualism has in fact created its Frankenstein. It has loosed energies and forces which it is, of all philosophies, least fitted to co-ordinate and control. We have arrived at an ironical situation. The spirit of competition which was so great a breeder of initiative yesterday has become only a disturber of the peace today. Rugged Individualism, so honourable yesterday, is only rugged irresponsibility today. A philosophy in which nobody is his brother's keeper has become impossible when a decision by a board of directors hundreds of miles away will wipe out a town overnight and doom the inhabitants of a rich country to desolation and despair for years. We have seen just that, no less, in Scotland, Wales and Northern England, time and again. I need not emphasize how, in international affairs, the philosophy of irresponsible competition, governmental *laisser-faire*, *laisser-aller*, and failure to plan has landed not towns but nations and continents in the deepest disaster in the history of mankind.

I want to make it eminently clear that this is not a question of blaming any particular forces. My simple point is that the values and virtues of yesterday may not be the right values or the right virtues today. My point is that in maintaining so stubbornly the old individualist, sectional, free competitive and nationalist viewpoints, we have been holding to concepts which may have, in their day, been great and

126

glorious concepts capable of motivating men to great achievements, but which are incapable of mastering the problems of today. I regard it as foolish and unnecessary to say that financial and industrial forces have been selfish or that labour has been blind. It is similarly foolish to blame the United States for not entering the League, Britain for not supporting the Weimar Republic enough, Ottawa for making the international economic struggle inevitable in the Imperial Conference of 1932. The only real conclusion worth making is that all these events followed inevitably from the fact—as always happens in history—that we were into the new world of facts before we were out of the old world of attitudes. I am concerned to suggest that the inevitable historical process has found our operative philosophy and educative attitudes inadequate to cope with events.

To make my argument still clearer, let me say that I am not talking of the passage from Capitalism to Socialism. Like Professor Burnham, I do not believe that Socialism as we have thought of it will come at all. That surely was plain when the Workers' Soviets with all their Socialist dreams of workers' control in a classless society were driven out of industrial managership in Russia and Republican Spain, and by their own leaders. They were driven out not because Socialism did not represent a high ideal, but because, given the conditions of modern technocracy, workers' self-management represents an unpractical and inefficient one. My view, if any, would be that we are entering upon a new and interim society which is neither capitalist nor socialist, but in which we can achieve central planning without loss of individual initiative, by the mere process of absorbing initiative in the function of planning. I think we are entering upon a society in which public unity and discipline can be achieved without forgetting the humanitarian virtues. As one watches the implications of the New Deal and of what is happening today in the development of centralized planning at Ottawa, one sees that hope not only on a national scale but on an international one too.

But I emphasize the first and main point which is that we grasp the historical process and not bother about recriminations or moral strictures. Men are all the fools of history, even the greatest and best of them. A man or a nation that is historically wrong may not be evil. A man or a nation that is historically right may not be good. But when we come to consider the philosophy of education we have no alternative. As educators we must go the way with history and men's needs, or others will come to take the privilege of education away from us.

Education: A New Concept

All this carries with it the suggestion of a drastic change in educational outlook. I do not expect it to be popular. It is no more popular with me than with you, for like everyone of my generation I am imbued—I should more accurately say rotted through—with the old individualist ideals and cannot for the life of me be rid of them. I am still as soft as anyone to those emotional appeals that are based on concepts of personal initiative and personal right. I still find the greatest image in rhetoric is the single man against his horizon, seeking his destiny. But simply because we are so deeply imbued with these concepts and images, our effort must be the harder to change them. If they are not the key to the social future it is our duty as educators and scientists to forget our personal predilections of the past and build the concepts and images that are the key to the future.

We have no alternative, though we shall at least have the comfort that certain familiar concepts must forever remain, because they do represent the eternal verities. We may forget nationalism but still need the cohesion and spur of national tradition. Always there will be the concept of the people and the native pride in one's own people. Humanity will remain one of the essential dramatic concepts of human thought and endeavour. So will Justice; so will Freedom; though Justice may lose its contact with the maintenance of private property rights, and Freedom may return to the Platonic notion of freedom only to serve the community.

As I see it, the really hard and disagreeable task of education to-morrow is that it will have, willy-nilly, to re-examine its attitude to such fundamental concepts as Property and Wealth, Natural Rights and Freedom of Contract. It will have to think more cautiously when it comes to the word Opportunity and the phrase Free Enterprise. The concepts themselves will not be obliterated. They are simply due for a sea change which will leave them somewhat different from what they were before.

On the positive side, we shall find new concepts coming more powerfully into our lives; and we shall find ourselves dramatizing them so that they become loyalties and take leadership of the Will. We shall talk less of the world as everyone's oyster and more about Work and Jobs. We shall talk less about free enterprise and competition and more about the State as a partner in initiative. There will be less about Liberty and more about Duties: less about the pursuit of Happiness and more about the pursuit of Sacrifice. Above all, there will be less about words and more about action and less about the past and more about the future. Already you hear the new words in the air: Disci-

Education and the New Order

pline, Unity, Co-ordination, Total Effort, Planning. They are the first swallows over the horizon; and there are going to be more of them.

In another field, education is going to see equally drastic change. The entire basis of comprehension and therefore of educational method may change: in fact it is now changing. When we talk of bridging the gap between the citizen and the community and between the classroom and the world without, we are asking for a kind of educational shorthand which will somehow give people quick and immediate comprehension of the highly complex forces which motivate our complicated society. We are seeking a method of articulating society which will communicate a sense of the corporate and a sense of growth. No one, I hope, imagines that the new society with its wide horizons and complex perspectives can be taught in the old ways, and in fact we are discovering that the only methods which will convey the nature of the new society are dramatic methods. That is why the documentary film has achieved unique importance in the new world of education. It does not teach the new world by analysing it. Uniquely and for the first time it *communicates* the new world by showing it in its corporate and living nature.

But if you add the new words together—Work, Unity, Discipline, Activism, Sacrifice, Total Effort, Central Planning and so forth—I think you will realize where the greatest change of all is likely to happen. Education will come out of the schoolroom and the library, the literary circle and the undergraduate conference, into the light of day. At least it will come out a great deal more than it has ever thought of doing in the past. It will go into the factory and the field, into the co-operatives of production and distribution. It will express itself not as thought or debate but as the positive action within the community of organized youth groups, women's groups and men's groups. One half of education, the stronger half, will lie in the organization of active citizenship; for there can be no concept of Planning without the concept of Participation.

In particular we need to guard against the danger of making public guidance a matter of one-way traffic. The government has as much information and guidance to get from the people as the people from the government. The government can gain as much from local inspiration as the people from central inspiration. We should, therefore, insist that information work both ways and we should insist that new local organizations of every kind have constant and active representation at centre. It will be our fundamental safeguard against discipline and unity turning into something else.

When you deal with alterations that challenge the accepted and honoured attitudes of society, the path is always dangerous. I am not going to pretend that I do not realize how 'totalitarian' some of my conclusions seem, without the qualification I have just noted. You can be 'totalitarian' for evil and you can also be 'totalitarian' for good. Some of us came out of a highly disciplined religion and see no reason to fear discipline and self-denial. Some of us learned in a school of philosophy which taught that all was for the common good and nothing for oneself and have never, in any case, regarded the pursuit of happiness as anything other than an aberration of the human spirit. We were taught, for example, that he who would gain his life must lose it. Even Rousseau talked of transporting *le moi dans l'unité commune*, and Calvin of establishing the holy communion of the citizens. So, the kind of 'totalitarianism' I am thinking of, while it may apply to the new conditions of society, has as deep a root as any in human tradition. I would call the philosophy of individualism Romantic and say we have been on a spectacular romantic spree for four hundred years. I would maintain that this other, 'totalitarian', viewpoint is classical.

There is a further point I want to make: a simple dynamic change which I foresee in educational approach. In times of crisis—particularly in times of crisis—men crave a moral imperative: and I greatly doubt if education will mean a thing or will be listened to, unless it acquires a moral imperative.

The reason is plain and I hope that we shall not be so short-sighted as to miss a fundamental psychological factor in the world situation today. Down under the surface, men have lost their faith. As the war raged across Europe and absorbed one country after another, no fact was more patent, and not least to the German propagandists. Much of their technique was built on it, and successfully so.

We all know why men have lost their faith. They have seen the world going into disorder; they have had a sense of things going from bad to worse; and nowhere have they found that leadership, mental and religious, which seemed to be taking hold of essentials and clearing the way—positively clearing the way—to the future.

Now faith is a simple matter: at least simple of analysis. It is the complex of loyalties and attitudes by which men's needs are first appreciated and then fulfilled. So, if we are to help in re-creating this essential path to action and true victory, it behoves us to bind ourselves to the recognition and fulfilment of men's needs, with an unswerving loyalty which may well be called religious. For, you will remember, religion itself comes from a word which means 'a bond'. Many have recently deplored the separation of education from religion. I am making the same point, but I am also saying that religious power in education will only come if its recognition of men's needs is simple, fundamental, definite, activist and unswerving. If the religious reference is merely a return to the pie-in-the-sky motif, or if it is merely a return to rhetorical play with the word of God, I believe it will avail you nothing, for you will neither be talking religion nor giving the benefit of it.

Men's needs were never in our generation hard to see. They have to do with such simple matters as food and shelter and the good life for everyone and, more particularly, as a *sine qua non*, they have to do with the mobilization of men's will to these essential ends without any deviation whatsoever. These ends may have been forgotten in sectional selfishness and private privilege; and the privileged ones may have allowed every kind of complacent, urbane, cynical and indifferent attitude to hide from them the primitive fact that their neighbours, national and international, have been starving and dying in their midst. Or it may be that the leadership has been depressed by the progressive difficulties of a complex world and has lost its will-power and has wearily given up the task of leadership without abandoning its privilege. Whatever the analysis, if education is to find its moral imperative, it must get back to the forgotten fundamentals of men's need and take upon itself the courage and the will to realize them. It will have to clear itself, in the process, of a lot of bric-à-brac so often called culture. For example, it will hardly get away with anything so easy as telling people that they are fighting for the old way of life, even if people are reminded of its unquestionable beauties and benefits. Education will not get away with it, because too many people believe in their hearts that the old way of life is the mother of chaos; and they will settle for something short of its beauties and benefits. We will have to give a plain demonstration that we have willed a new way of life and mean it. The details, even the plan, will not matter so long as the will is patent and the demonstration real; for of all men's needs the first and most principal is hope, and it is of the essence of belief that the fact must follow.

The solution is straight and simple; and in an educational world which has come perversely to worship indecision and feel honoured in unbelief, I hope I shall be forgiven my certainty. I suggest simply this, and it is the moral imperative for education as I see it.

Go out and ask men to mobilize themselves for the destruction of

greed and selfishness. And mean it. Ask them to forget their personal
dreams and pleasures and deny themselves for the obliteration of economic anarchy and disorder all over the world. And mean it. Mean it
so much that men will know that no power on earth will stop you in
your tracks. Tell them that in desperate unity and before God they
will give the world a greater leadership—a more humanitarian new
order—than the thwarted and vengeful people of Germany can be
capable of. Say with the Prime Minister of Canada that 'never again
in our own land or in any other land will the gods of material power,
of worldly possession and of special privilege be permitted to exercise
their sway'. Mean it, and mean it so much that the people will know
that, as far as human fallibility allows, the age of selfish interest is over
and done with. Say it and mean it and think it and act on it. Make
it your religion; which is to say, make it your bond with the people.
I haven't a doubt that they will accept the new loyalties and the new
attitudes of sacrifice and effort without a qualm or a question. And
I haven't a doubt whatever that they will march with you till the skies
open and the future is born.

2 Education and Total Effort

It may seem at first sight somewhat beside the point to be talking about education when there are so many more grandiose things, like Total Effort and Getting on With the Job, to talk about. But some of us think that education has a great deal to do with total effort and getting on with the job. We even think that it was just because he solved his educational problem that Hitler achieved total effort among his Teutons. In other words, I am thinking of the educational problem involved in mobilizing the will-power of the nation. I am going to suggest that we have only begun to scratch the possibilities in this direction, and that the world events we are passing through will force us to revolutionize our educational outlook and methods on a scale we have not known for a hundred and fifty years.

This is not altogether a new story. Some of us have been criticizing democratic educational theory for the past twenty years; and, in fact, I would not be doing films now if I had not taken my criticism seriously a long time ago. The basis of our criticism has been simple but fundamental. We have seen, on the one hand, the world of citizenship becoming more and more complex. We have seen communications grow swifter and economic horizons widen. We have seen the growth of corporate entities, national and international. We have seen local considerations reach out in perspective to embrace the widest geo-political considerations. We have seen the growth of complex intelligence services and centralized controls; measuring and determining almost every aspect of the ordinary citizen's life. We have seen strange new languages growing up, attempting to give verbal and conceptual form to these changes: languages financial and fiscal, and economic and administrative, and technocratic, and even propagandist. One or two perhaps we understand well because they are our native professional languages; others we may half learn as an intellectual courtesy to our friends, others the best of us do not pretend to understand at all. We have seen the growth of many specialized fields of interest which, because they are new and have to be pioneered intellectually and actively, so much command the attention of the specialist, that he has little time for any other consideration.

We have seen problems—difficult problems—arise in all these fields. There are international problems, federal problems, provincial problems, and problems more local; corporate and inter-provincial problems; agricultural and rural problems; social problems and labour problems; there are co-ordination problems and co-ordination of co-ordination problems.

We have this changing, somewhat bewildering, world on the one hand. We do not object to it. We have it, and that is the way it is, and it is probably as exciting a circus of human effort and mutability as men have ever been asked to live and perish in. What we find curious is that our outlook on education has not only not kept pace with these great changes in the social process, but has lagged seriously behind. Nor is it just a question of lag. We think the theory of education itself is wrong, and that, in fact, it proceeds on an altogether false assumption.

That false assumption is the mystical democratic assumption that the citizen can be so taught to understand what is going on about him that he and his fellows in the mass can, through the electoral and parliamentary process, give an educated and rational guidance to the conduct of the state. In its extreme form, it is the false assumption that a man can know everything about everything all the time. This assumption, we say, has led education woefully astray and is continuing to do so. We say quite precisely that education has set itself an impossible task and therefore a wrong task; and we add that, by so doing, it has blinded itself to what is possible and therefore right. We even add that, by bringing democracy to a state of disappointment, discouragement, impotence and frustration, it has put the survival of democracy itself in jeopardy.

If the so-called voice of the people—for all the efforts of education—does not know what it is talking about, what is the citizens' actual state in the welter of events that surround him? Let me quote Walter Lippmann:

'While he, the citizen, is watching one thing, a thousand others undergo great changes. Unless he has discovered some rational ground for fixing his attention where it will do the most good and in a way that suits his essentially amateurish equipment, he will be as bewildered as a puppy trying to lick three bones at once. . . . The orthodox view of education can bring only disappointment. The problems of the modern world appear and change faster than any set of teachers can grasp them, much faster than they can convey their substance to a population of children. If the schools attempt to teach children to solve the problems of the day, they are bound always to be in arrears. ... And so ... the citizen finds that public affairs are in no convincing way his affairs. They are for the most part invisible, managed, if they are managed at all, at distant centres, from behind the scenes, by unnamed powers. As a private citizen he does not know for certain what is going on or who is doing it or where he is being carried. ... Contemplating himself and his actual accomplishment in public affairs, contrasting the influence he exerts with the influence he is supposed according to democratic theory to exert, he must say of his sovereignty what Bismarck said of Napoleon. ... "At a distance it is something, but close to it is nothing at all. ..." In consequence ... there is not the least reason for thinking, as mystical democracies have thought, that the compounding of individual ignorances in masses of people can produce a continuous directing force in public affairs.'

The suggestion made by our criticism is not that education is no good at all or that the expression of public opinion is of no use at all. On the other hand, what we are saying is that the educational system is wasteful and wrong, only because it sets itself an impossible task. What we are saying is that the belief in the voice of the people is wasteful and wrong only because it expects from the citizenry an impossible, because rational, judgment. In other words, we are not throwing Democracy out, like the baby with the bath water. What we are trying to arrive at is the point where we abandon that purely mystical concept of Democracy which encourages the illusion that ten million amateur thinkers talking themselves incompetently to death sound like the music of the spheres. We want to arrive at the point where the democratic ideal can be brought down to the realm of practical consideration and achievement.

We need not necessarily arrive at a Fascist conception. You can exercise what Austin calls the power of the militia, and a gun in the ribs is a most powerful means of persuasion. You can develop a single dictatorial party, carried along by a faith and a doctrine and giving mental and active leadership to all elements of society. This is a ready solution of the problem. As a method it has behind it the historical example of the Roman Catholic Church in earlier times, and the philosophical authority of Dostoievsky's Grand Inquisitor. But some of us believe that there are advantages to be got in the encouragement of a rich measure of mental independence, on the simple ground that, in the long run, it makes for a more civilized world of discourse.

Education: A New Concept

Our problem then has been to think of educational methods which, while suited to the complexity of the modern world, still fit this democratic conception. We do not want people to know everything about everything all the time, because it is impossible. We do not want the people to make up their minds on specialized problems, because that is asking too much. We do not want to see them given, as individuals, a false notion of their freedom in society, and have them paralyse action with the infinite din of their amateur judgments. In particular, we do not want to see encouraged a din in which the people's own best interest cannot be heard. On the other hand, we do want to see them given what they are not getting now: a service of information on the immediate needs and services of the state. We do want to see them given what they are not given now: a living sense of what is going on. If we do not want to see their rational minds set impossible tasks, we do want to see their sentiments and loyalties crystallized in forms which are useful to the people and to the State alike. Above all, we want to see our society emancipated from its confusion and bewilderment, and given some imaginative leadership in the articulation of a faith.

All this, I am afraid, is very general. These conclusions, as I said, are old ones and have been the stock-in-trade of our educational criticism for a long time. The war, however, has given them very special significance. Vast changes in the structure of the State have been wrought during the war and particularly since April 1940. Before the war we lived in what was brightly called a free society. Freedom of contract, freedom of production, freedom of investment, freedom of choice, freedom of price and freedom of the devil to take the hindmost. Perhaps it was not quite as free as that. We policed the mines and the factories to prevent the exploitation of children. We policed the grocer and the milkman, to keep the sand out of the sugar and the water out of the milk. The State had stepped in on essential matters of education, housing and public health, and it was doing so on a growing, if tentative scale. But the dream still held that the two greatest statesmen a country could have were those abstract gentlemen, Supply and Demand. It is true they could not keep the people employed, and they could not save the wheat farmer; and, in fact, they looked like causing bloody revolution all over the place; but, by and large, the dream of a free society still held.

When one thinks of the speed with which we discarded this dream, and how prepared and ready our statesmen and specialists were to discard it, we are bound to conclude that the desire for discipline and total effort, and the willingness to accept price, profit, wage and other controls, were there all the time, and not only for war but also for peace. It is only my opinion, but it seems unlikely that the very dramatic and revolutionary centralization of financial, economic and even technocratic initiative in the State will be altogether undone after the war. We may, indeed, have given ourselves just that measure of social control which social justice and the complexity of the modern world demand, and on which there can be no substantial argument as between political parties.

But I notice one persistent thought in the pronouncements of these social revolutionaries of ours. When it is a question of telling the people what they shall eat and drink, what soups they shall make, what clothes they shall wear, what nail polish they shall or shall not have, they glide happily along, knowing all the answers. But I notice too a certain respect for the original sin of the people and their imaginative capacity for bootlegging and black markets. Every now and again a doubt besets them. You cannot really control without having the militia behind you; and the problem of control, viewed realistically, involves sacrificial alterations in the personal habits of a generation that was brought up in an almost anarchical conception of freedom. Our social revolutionaries very reasonably shy at the prospect of a vast police force and, most importantly for us, they fall back on the concept of persuasion. Indeed, what the statesmen have failed to discover, the economists have, of sheer necessity, discovered, and that is the need for a vast new system of education by which the people will be made aware of the living processes and needs of the State and of their duties as citizens.

With an interesting, if academic, bow to the old democratic principle, Mr. MacIntosh of Canada's Department of Finance puts this very precisely: 'The problems of co-ordination extend very far beyond the circles of the Government Services. The achievement of a successful war effort will require not merely co-ordination within Government Services but an effective co-ordination between the public at large and the Government agencies. Such a co-ordination can be realized in part through control, but in the wider sense can be attained only through a broad policy of public education.'

Mr. Taylor of the Prices Board complements this pronouncement: 'In a democracy we need something more than technical knowledge and experience at the top; we need the understanding of a whole people—East and West—city and country—producer and consumer—labour and management.'

Education: A New Concept

I don't think anyone of us believes that the present educational system is geared to this special task. There are certain things, it is true, which the orthodox pedagogical system does very well. It teaches the elements of literacy. It teaches certain fundamental aspects of co-operation and public behaviour. In its upper brackets, it sometimes quite brilliantly teaches special skills and specialized fields of intellectual interest. The breakdown or gap lies in the teaching of citizenship: that is to say, in the gap between the citizen and the community, between the individual mind and the highly complex processes and purposes in which the State is contemporaneously involved.

There have been many clumsy efforts to bridge this gap. Once upon a time they used to teach the nature of the constitution and the State on a sort of anatomical basis, as though their forms were everlasting and permanent. We have got away from this and have at least introduced the idea of the community life as evolutionary: that is to say, as a matter of change and development. But in most of the schemes for teaching citizenship, the rational fallacy which I mentioned at the outset persists. We think we can teach the public on a vast scale to give a rational judgment on what is going on; and, trying to teach them too much, we have only succeeded in teaching them too little. We keep harping away at the idea that the only kind of judgment that matters is the rational judgment and, in that respect, there is hardly a teacher who is not, by training and tradition, an intellectual snob. But in so doing we fail to crystallize the emotions and direct men's loyalties. Whence these dreadful Cook's tours of all the world's problems which pass for courses in citizenship: like Cook's tours and Baedeckers, giving surface information only and completely out of touch with the life of the thing. Whence the derelict result that most people give up the task of trying to understand what it is all about, stick to the headlines and the funnies and the pictures on the back page, and, in their dereliction, follow anyone who has the wit to fill the vacuum of their minds with hearsay and sensation.

The adult education movement, with the best intention in the world, has fallen only too often into the same error. It, too, has insisted on being very serious and very rational. How often have the causes of the last war been analysed, how often has the structure of the League of Nations been examined, how often has the concept of Democracy been praised in a nice general philosophic way—when, all the time, the very people who were analysing and debating and arguing were moving blindfold, in mass, and at speed, to war and the breakdown of the League, and to measures of authoritarianism which, the moment a

138

country is driven to a common and total effort, prove completely logical and completely necessary.

The educational effort is not, of course, confined to the orthodox pedagogues. The newspapers and radio convey an infinite amount of information, and commentary on events. Specialized clubs hear various problems discussed. Popular magazines and specialized magazines and pamphlets and books swell the tide of information and interpretation from a hundred and one angles of special pleading. There is no lack of blue books, no lack of public relations services, no lack of material for thought thrown at the head of the benighted citizen. If the mystical ideal would only work, if the citizen could only catch it all in his head, and pick and choose, and snap off his judgments as Buffalo Bill snapped off his pigeons—one-two-three-four-five-six—just like that!! —it would be wonderful.

But what, of course, we have failed to do, and it is the most important thing of all, is to give the citizen *a pattern of thought and feeling* which will enable him to approach this flood of material in some nseful fashion. For except the citizen's mind be so predisposed and shaped in its essentials, he will find himself, as he finds himself today, utterly at sea. In this I follow Lippmann and say:

This is not an educational matter at all: it is a political matter. In other words, the key to education in the modern complex world no longer lies in what we have known as education but in what we have known as propaganda. By the same token, propaganda, so far from being the denial of the democratic principle of education, becomes the necessary instrument for its practical fulfilment. Everything else is incidental.

The State is the machinery by which the best interests of the people are secured. Since the needs of the State come first, understanding of these needs comes first in education. If the operation of controls is necessary for war or peace, understanding of these controls is a necessary part of education. Since co-operative and active citizenship have become more important to the State then amateur judgments on matters beyond the general citizen's sphere of understanding, education must in part abandon the classroom and debating society and operate in terms of co-operative and active citizenship. So the argument reaches out to wider and wider, and not unexciting, prospects. The implication of it from the first is that in determining these patterns of thought and feeling which will guide the citizen in his citizenship, education has to give far more direct leadership and far less opportunity for the promiscuous exercise of mental and emotional interests.

Education: A New Concept

The needs of the State in this great period of revolutionary change are urgent; and the citizen has neither the leisure nor the equipment for the promiscuous exercise of his mental and emotional interests.

There is another point of, I think, deep and essential importance. We cannot long keep men in a sense of mental and emotional confusion. They will go in on themselves. They will feel frustrated in their work if they do not see its end and importance. Without understanding or faith in the whole, they will exaggerate the local issues they do appreciate to the damage of the whole. Lacking faith, they will look for it desperately wherever they may find it: at the expense, if need be, of every equilibrium our civilized world has learned to hold precious. It becomes, therefore, an essential function of the State in these times of revolutionary change to give men a pattern of faith. One of the lessons we have learned in these last twenty years is that the State is in a perilous position which fails to do so.

I arrive, therefore, at certain conclusions. The first is that the State is bound to take a more direct hand in the terms and shapes of education. The second is that much of what we now know as education will become what we now know as propaganda. The third is that a dramatic approach, as distinct from an intellectualist approach, to education must increasingly develop. The fourth is that the machinery of what is called public information must inevitably be extended far beyond its present scale and purpose.

3 Propaganda and Education

Catholics remember that the Church long ago started the idea of propaganda, and they know that it was associated with the defence and propagation of a faith. Those who remember the last war remember something about propaganda, too. It was in those days what we now, a trifle deviously, call 'political' or 'psychological' warfare. It stood for the attempt of the Allies to preach the doctrine of parliamentary democracy to the Germans. It also stood for those stories in which we painted the Hun as a monster and ourselves as the exclusive children of sweetness and light. It was the instrument by which we sorted out simply and roughly the moral issues of the war and built up the morale of our fighting forces. Perhaps that is why we gave propaganda a bad name after the last war. We thought it put the world's issues in too strong a contrast of black and white. Like decent people, we wanted to understand; and we knew that there are shades of right and wrong in every individual and every nation. We knew that great issues are not exclusively moral issues, but also involve economics and national pride and race instincts and class instincts too. We revolted from the bottom of our hearts against any attempt to batter our minds into an over-simplified mould. We resisted what we thought to be an assault on human freedom.

The irony is that, in spite of all our protests, we have had an even greater development of propaganda since that time. We have seen Soviet Russia rise into world power, and one of the tremendous forces of the war, not without a great and deliberate use of propaganda. We have seen Germany emerge from the sackcloth and ashes of a defeated nation and become an even more destructive force than before, again through the instruments of propaganda. We have today reached the point where there is no longer anything particularly gruesome in the thought that Britain and the United States are as deeply involved in the war for men's minds as other countries.

We have, of course, discovered some marvellous new propaganda weapons since the last war, and particularly the radio and the film. The Nazis saw their propaganda possibilities at once and began to use

141

them on a Napoleonic scale, both at home and abroad. But, obviously, the instruments were not themselves responsible for the development which urged their use. The urge to propaganda is the important thing, and we are only now beginning to realize that this urge is somehow deeply associated with the nature of the modern state. Whether we like it or not, everywhere the new dramatic methods of appeal are being used on a colossal scale to crystallize men's sentiments and so affect their will. The relatively innocent days are over when propaganda's principal concern was whether we bought this or bought that. Today propaganda's concern is that we should feel this and not that, think this and not that, do this and not that. The scale ranges from the community which is served by a local radio station or newspaper, to the national and international hook-ups of the radio, the news services and the film. Whatever we say about propaganda, to justify or disparage it, the reality of it is with us today in every proceeding of our lives.

So it is high time we were clear what is essential or unessential about it and where it relates to those other 'old-fashioned' forces of society that are supposed to look after men's minds. I mean, of course, education and art and the free expression of opinion which the newspapers dubiously stand for in the name of a 'free press'.

One guide to the place of propaganda in modern society is its association with the idea of total effort. Wherever nations have tried to plan their society to an end, the full forces of propaganda have been unleashed. In the case of Russia there was the direction of a nation to a specific social doctrine. This involved not only the liquidation of the opponents of that doctrine, but, as Lenin put it, 'a persistent struggle, sanguinary and bloodless, violent and peaceful, military and economic, educational and administrative against the forces and traditions of society. The force of habit of millions and tens of millions is a most terrible force'. By their 'ordinary, everyday, imperceptible, elusive and demoralizing activity' they can effectively destroy the most cherished plans for the socialist-democratic state.

Lenin justified his case by arguing that particular groups of individuals in a reactionary society were so bound to false ways of thinking that they were either conscious or unconscious enemies of the good life. He urged that their enlightenment should be continuous and unremitting. He held out the dream of a society of free individuals in which the process of enlightenment had, in course of a couple of generations or so, succeeded. He reserved, however, to the leadership of one particular creed, the direction of the curriculum. In the case

142

of Hitler's Germany there was the same mobilization of the nation to a particular plan of society, but there was a different and, all democrats will say, abominable tenet: that the ordinary man did not want to exercise his free judgment or, alternatively, that he was better without it. Differences apart, both make the argument that if and when total effort is vital to society the unity of men's minds is as important as the unity of their energies, and the democracies are today accepting this principle readily as a measure of war. They, too, have discovered—or rediscovered, the churches will say—that where there is a dynamic and common faith, manpower acquires the extra mystic virtue of workpower and fighting power.

On the face of it, this use of the instruments of persuasion and inspiration is of precious value to the state and society. Under stress of war we articulate the terms of our faith in progressive democracy. We learn to integrate the loyalties and forces of the community in the name of positive and highly constructive ideals. We beat out a rhythm for our time: a hard, tough and exacting rhythm which takes the head higher and the shoulders a little further back. We bring the airplane into our imagination and blow the old map to pieces with new proximities and new neighbours. We dismiss the old frontiers of achievement as sentimental and excite our imagination on the new frontiers of communal achievement represented by medicine, science and administration. We begin to think internationally, to think not of markets but of needs. To sustain this rhythm, to crystallize these images, many have a feeling that propaganda is a positive and necessary force, providing the patterns of thought and feeling which make for an active and imaginative citizenship in the particular circumstances of our time.

In spite of this argument, the case for propaganda is by no means generally allowed, even now. Who are for it and who against? The churches are for it because the enlivenment of the spirit is their business. The people who remember the unemployment and vast dislocations of the thirties are for it. Today, they say, we begin to discover the secret of full employment and the secret of adding to the common wealth on a scale never dreamt of before. The churches were always for the mobilization of men's minds to what was right and good, and the people are progressively for it as they see in it one of the keys to their economic future. Shall we not, they say, mobilize as greatly for the achievement of the Four Freedoms as for the destruction of Nazi Germany? Shall we disregard what we have learned about co-operation on a national and international scale?

But the right of the state to use propaganda as an instrument of creative change is still deeply denied, and particularly in the United States. The heart of the matter lies in the fact that we are passing from one conception of society to another. On the one hand, we have the old conception of a society of free institutions in which the executive authority of the state is, at best, a necessary evil, to be watched over and kept from separate ambition by the Supreme Court or the Parliamentary institution. It has excellent ancestry. It derives from the Puritan sects of the seventeenth century with ideals of 'freedom of prophesying'. It suited an agricultural community in which the horizons were free institutions lived consciously on a religious and moral basis. It did not envisage a day when the community would have to act as a whole in discipline and total effort to definite ends. It did not envisage a day, after the industrial revolution and the growth of corporations, when free institutions ceased to operate on a religious and moral basis. But for many Americans this freedom *from* the state is still the most deliberate and deeply instilled pattern of political thought. It is so, although a large proportion of the population came in relatively recent generations from Europe and from far different patterns of thought about the state and democracy. The French Revolution was willing to follow the founding fathers on the equality of men and the rights of property, but it had a bigger job for the state to do than the simple police work of a widespread agricultural community. The state had a decadent old régime to liquidate and a new one to defend.

For Europe, the state has from the first represented the positive and creative force of the community, operating as a whole to positive ends. This, of course, provides a very different basic pattern of political thought, whether we are dealing with Russia or Germany or the liberal movements of Italy and France. At every turn the American pattern is challenged as belonging to the special circumstances of a new nation and as now out of date. It is challenged on the grounds that the problems of a modern highly developed industrial economy involve the creative action of the community operating as a single, integrated and unified force.

This challenge comes not least in the land of 'new deals', and Wendell Willkie distinctions between 'private enterprise' for the public good and 'private property' for selfish enjoyment. It comes not least in a country whose war effort is a model to the world of the colossal results of mass planning and mass execution, under what Henry Wallace calls the co-operation of industry and business and the 'leadership of the government'. The Wallace description is the North American rendering of a change of attitude in this matter of the state. If it does not allow the European conception of the state in full, it does allow the state a new and active part in America's political pattern of thought. It does not represent a special view. In spite of the sacred doctrine of 'free institutions'—free from the state—Walter Lippmann bears witness that as between Democrats and Republicans 'there is no issue of fundamental principle as to the responsibility of the modern state for the modern economy'.

My local paper speaks similarly. 'The truth is, it is a long, long time since enterprise has been free or since business has really wanted to be free. They didn't want it to be free when they asked for tariffs, with government agents collecting duties on their goods or giving them assistance to market their goods. They didn't want it to be free when they asked for government subsidies and grants. Nor did they want it to be free when they asked the state to provide them with low freight-rates and heaven only knows what else. Free enterprise! Scores of laws and regulations on the statute books, some of which have been there for a long time, tell how through the years government has been interfering and controlling business increasingly and nearly always because business wanted it. In a modern state and with the world getting smaller and smaller it is hard to see how it could be otherwise. In the good old days—or should it be daze?—of the stagecoach, *laisser-faire* was good enough, but no one could be so simple as to imagine that it could be good enough today. When a man says that business must be "free", that "free enterprise" must go on without government interference, he is talking nonsense. Free enterprise isn't free, and the world being what it is there isn't a chance of it being free.' My local paper is the *Ottawa Journal*. It is 'conservative'.

What we are seeing in the attack on propaganda today as a power in the hands of the state is a last reminder of the old point of view. It derives from the time when men regarded the state as only a necessary evil. Like the advocacy of free enterprise in its naïve form, it is no longer realistic. Let me add that the use of propaganda by the democratic state is exactly on a parallel with the 'government leadership' of Mr. Wallace and Mr. Lippmann's 'responsibility of the modern state' and my local paper's 'necessary government interference'. It is no closer to the totalitarian use of propaganda than subsidies, grants, low freight-rates and 'heaven knows what else' are to the Nazi system. It is, in fact, the concomitant of these departures into government leadership, for it represents the information system by which the government explains its directives and gives an account of the new stewardship which has, by democratic process, been thrust upon it.

Education: A New Concept

Of course, there are dangers in the government use of propaganda or information. There is the danger of a political head creating a public myth about himself, and the danger of a department concealing its incompetence, and the danger of a political party using the power of information to perpetuate its existence and thus thwart the democratic process. But these dangers can, by ordinary democratic watchfulness in press and parliament or congress, be avoided. They should not be used to blind people to the real nature of information as a necessary concomitant of government leadership. The possibility of abuse does not mean that proper uses cannot be allowed. In fact, they have for a long time been allowed and with the agreement of democratic institutions, simply because directives have had to be explained if they were to be effective and stewardship has had to be accounted for if it was to be understood and sanctioned.

The use of propaganda in time of war is spectacular and appears to many as a new aspect of government activity, and therefore possibly a passing one. This is not true. Government propaganda has never been challenged when it has been a question of propaganda for foreign markets or propaganda in support of a country's diplomacy. Even more importantly, it has never been seriously challenged when there was a true understanding of what propaganda should be. When it has proceeded on lines of explanation and elucidation and understanding, and when it has had the good sense to strike beyond party differences to the deeper loyalties of civic understanding and civic co-operation, parliaments and congresses have not failed to vote its funds and accept it for what it is: education in a world where the state is the instrument of the public's enterprise. Realistic observers of the nature and necessity of propaganda in the democratic state will find its constitutional authority tucked away in the files of tourist and children's and health bureaus, of trade and agriculture and labour departments, and of embassies and consulates the world over.

There is nothing new about it. It has developed hand in hand with the responsibilities of the state and has grown in direct proportion to the use of the state as a creative instrument of the community, operating as a whole to definite purposes. And it has tended, as it has found its democratic bearings, to become less and less the propaganda of legend and, more and more, part of that process of persuasion or education which is the tap-root of the democratic idea.

The chief problem of propaganda in a democracy does not lie, therefore, in proving its necessity, but rather in developing its wise and democratic use along the path of education. This, obviously, is of the utmost significance for the educational system. Government information has to deal with a wide range of materials which at every turn affect the terms of active citizenship. The educational system receives materials which are necessary to it and has, as an inevitable partner in the process, a great chance to mould the character, not only of the citizenry at large, but of the government's approach to them. By representing at many points local understanding and local participation, it has the power to affect the relationship between people and government in the profoundest and most democratic way.

Educators cannot, however, fill this role without a measure of self-examination. So far they have not fully realized the significance for themselves of the development of the state as the creative instrument of the community, nor seen that the development of government information must drastically affect them. Governments have raced ahead informing and explaining, exhorting and enlightening, in a thousand-and-one fields without the direct help or guidance of those whose native function in the state is to do these very things.

If I may say so, the educators have failed to realize their duty and their opportunity. One reason for this failure is that education is too little conceived as related to an active and participant citizenship. It is, some may think, 'away in the mind' and too much out of gear with the realities of today and tomorrow. But, I believe, the principal reason for failure is that education has not known how to absorb the vast and complex materials of civic observation and action today. Its analytic technique has been inadequate. I do not think education can assume the partnership in national information which I have outlined for it until its technique is revolutionized and fitted for the task not only of demonstrating the living terms of a living community, but of *realizing* them in action and by action. The secret of the relationship between propaganda and education in the future lies ultimately in this matter of technique, and it involves, I believe, a new consideration of the dramatic or interpretative factor in education. One cannot see propaganda become education, except it translate the materials of citizenship into terms which are capable of being grasped and which are inducive of action. On the other hand, one cannot see education conveying the duties of citizenship in a wide and complex world, except in terms of living patterns and on the level of the imagination.

Education might well have learned from its own experience. By tradition it has frowned on dramatic and interpretative methods and on the brilliant new instruments of dramatization and enlightenment which the generation has produced. It has stuck to its rational guns, and in its way it has been right. No one can disagree that the pursuit of truth is a prerequisite of understanding. No one can disagree about the need to emphasize mental disciplines in which the citizen contributes his own effort and character to the pattern of thought. Where the goodness has come unstuck is that the educational system has forgotten—in the name of these good things—to equip the citizen for the social realities in which the poor devil has had to participate. And it has avoided the imaginative and inspirational methods that would give the citizen a grip on reality, only to abandon them to the hands of others. It has as a result lost control of the real educational process and it has lost this control to the men who govern the newspapers films, radio, advertising and public information, few of whom have a licence to teach.

Not all of these men have been conscious propagandists, but all have had a propagandist effect by reason of the fact that they have used dramatic or inspirational methods. They have formulated story or pictorial or dramatic shapes. They have evaluated the good and the bad, the heroic and the unheroic, the exciting and unexciting, the desirable and undesirable. They have observed the things that interested people; they have researched into the patterns of report that commanded men's understanding, attention and desire. They have done so in the name of entertainment, news reporting, salesmanship and public instruction and, except in the case of public information, they have done it for profit. They have not always gone deep or sought to choose the most imaginative and socially valuable patterns, but they have, in fact, provided a system of evaluation for men's daily experience where such a system was lacking. They have consequently created loyalties and formed the pattern of men's thought and action. The headline has been as important in this matter as the editorial; the advertisement and the comic strip as important as the Hollywood epic. They have, to a large extent, taken charge of men's minds. The 'ordinary, everyday, imperceptible, elusive habit of millions', which Lenin called such a 'terrible force', is largely in their hands. It is, by contrast, not in the hands of educators.

The more progressive forces in education have long been aware of this situation. There has been increasing use of radio and the film for both juvenile and adult education; there has been much improvement in school-book techniques and in the use of illustrative material on school walls. The growth of contacts between school and community has been sought by bringing postmen and firemen and other representatives of community action to tell their stories to the children, and

148

submit to their examination. The children themselves have been sent to explore their community and they have been encouraged in free discussion and civic debate. On the higher levels much has been done to pursue academic inquiry on location. But these developments are still piecemeal and somehow only 'progressive' and 'experimental'.

Back in the early twenties, Walter Lippmann presented a clear picture of the limitation of the educational approach which was based on 'knowing'. He pointed to the growing complexity of the modern world, its speeding communications and the national and international horizons of every economic and social problem. He drew the sad portrait of John Citizen, tired after the day's work, being asked to express his free and rational judgment on matters he could not possibly be equipped to judge. He charged that education was on the wrong lines if it thought to produce the all-knowing and rational John Citizen of the old-time liberal dream. He suggested that in barking up the tree of knowledge, education was barking up the wrong tree.

Others—A. D. Lindsay, for example—were concerned with the same criticism. But they confirmed John Citizen, however tired he might be, in his valuable role as judge of public events. They said a man might be a great expert but not have John Citizen's 'sense of smell'—meaning that John would know best where government regulations hurt him, know best how far a government could go which was to get his sanction and support. Moreover, the expert was not so good when it came to experience and common sense, and John Citizen had the role of providing that extra measure of essential wisdom to the community's judgment. There has been in consequence, in adult educational circles in the past generation, a valuable drive for public discussion involving as many John Citizens as possible. It has provided innumerable forums, locally and on the air, and they have been a useful supplement to the natural forums provided by village pubs and country stores, and to the functional forums provided by trade unions, chambers of commerce and service clubs.

Some of us thought at an early date that these forums did not themselves provide the material on which discussion could most usefully be based. We were afraid of Mr. Lindsay's discussion becoming discussion in a vacuum. We were conscious that discussion might not in itself lead to action, but might fall off into the dreary impotence of discussion for discussion's sake. In sad fact we saw discussion in the twenties—and it was to continue in the thirties—hide from men's eyes that essential picture of the time in which the great economic and political forces were climbing into place on the horizon.

Education: A New Concept

We thought that we could reveal that picture and would meet Mr. Lippmann's criticism by providing a shorthand method for world observation. There are, we said, basic dramatic patterns in the terms of civic relationship since all social problems are bound to involve a relationship between people and forces. Revelation of these dramatic patterns is a first essential in the process of modern education. For young people and adults alike require a broad and lively picture of their society to stir their imaginations and instil the loyalties necessary if they are to face up to its problems. In short, we felt that the dramatic pattern could convey a sense of growth and movement and opposition, provide a grip on reality and secure a sense of action regarding it.

I have myself been most closely associated with this theory of education. I can at least say that I have put it into successful practice; for it was out of these considerations and this theory that the documentary film movement arose. If I recall its origin and development, it is merely to illustrate with concrete example that the educational impasse can, in fact, be broken through.

The documentary film movement has been widely noted as representing a development in film technique and it has perhaps been too much thought of as a contribution to the art of the motion picture. Certainly some fine films have come from this business of observing reality and making beautiful or dramatic patterns from everyday observations, and some people are acquainted with Flaherty's *Moana*, Lorenz's *The River*, Basil Wright's *Song of Ceylon*, and with the deep drama based on actual observation in films like *Stalingrad* and *Desert Victory*. But the 'art' of documentary is, as always with art, only the by-product of an interpretation well and deeply done. Behind the documentary film from the first was a purpose, and it was the educational purpose with which we have been dealing. It was developed as a movement, and deliberately, to 'bring alive' to the citizen the world in which his citizenship lay, to 'bridge the gap' between the citizen and his community. These are, in fact, the phrases we first used about it in the late twenties. As events have turned out, the documentary film has succeeded in meeting the need of citizens in the school and elsewhere for a living description of their community; and this is the secret of its economy and of its importance.

The idea of documentary in its present form came originally not from the film people at all, but from the Political Science school in Chicago University round about the early twenties. It came because some of us noted Mr. Lippmann's argument closely and set ourselves to study what, constructively, we could do to fill the gap in educational

150

practice which he demonstrated. At first, I must confess, we did not think so much about film or about the radio. We were concerned with the influence of modern newspapers, and were highly admiring of the dramatic approach implicit in the journalism of William Randolph Hearst. Behind the sensationalizing of news we thought we recognized a deeper principle, and I think Henry Luce at very much the same time was recognizing it too. We thought, indeed, that even so complex a world as ours could be patterned for all to appreciate if we only got away from the servile accumulation of fact and struck for the story which held the facts in living organic relationship together.

It was Mr. Lippmann himself who turned this educational research in the direction of film. I talked to him one day of the labour involved in following the development of the yellow press through the evanescent drama of local politics. He mentioned that we would do better to follow the dramatic patterns of the film through the changing character of our time, and that the box-office records of success and failure were on file.

I took his advice and a young man called Walter Wanger opened the necessary files. A theory purely educational became thereby a theory involving the directive use of films. That directive use was based on two essential factors: the observation of the ordinary or the actual, and the discovery within the actual of the patterns which gave it significance for civic education.

I may say that we soon joined forces with men like Flaherty and Cavalcanti. They had been separately interested in this observation of the actual. They were concerned with the film patterns which went deeper than the newsreel and the scenic, and arrived perhaps at the idyll and the epic. The educators have never from that day altogether strait-jacketed the æsthetes in documentary, and it would be a loss if they ever succeeded; but it is the educators who have at all times held the economic secret of documentary film and have therefore been its masters as a 'movement' and as a developing force.

The battles within the documentary movement are all illustrative of this. They have lain between the politicians and the educators and between the æsthetes and the educators; but neither the politicians nor the æsthetes have succeeded or survived for long and they have tended to scatter to the wide winds of local and opportunist activity. It was the old economic story. It was in its educational interpretation and not in its political or æsthetic interpretation that the documentary film 'met a felt want' and was therefore financeable. The point is of great importance in presenting the documentary film as a fundamental contribution to government information and to educational theory alike. It was financeable because on the one hand it met the felt want of government for a colourful and dramatic medium which would interpret the information of state; and on the other hand it met the felt want among educators for a colourful and dramatic medium which would interpret the nature of the community. One provided the audience, the other the sponsorship; and the economic circle was complete from the beginning.

For fifteen years the validity of our educational analysis has had this important proof, that the documentary film, which was one of its results, has grown to the point where democratic governments are involved in the production of hundreds of documentary films a year, and the democratic educational systems are providing an audience of progressive millions for them. The scale and nature of this development are not to be estimated by the circulation of these films in theatres, though they have done very well in the theatres, and not least in the case of the *March of Time*, the *World in Action* and the films from Britain. Civic education certainly has been possible in theatres wherever the education has been made sufficiently entertaining. It has been helped by the fact that, in these troubled times, men have had problems of citizenship on their conscience even in their moments of relaxation. It has been helped by the fact that the film industry has come closer and closer to realizing its duty as not only an entertainment industry but also as a public utility. But in the theatres there are limits. The degree of civic conscience varies with classes and theatre types and with the sense of duty on the part of exhibitors. An industry based on mass entertainment has to be cautious. The most sensible have allowed twenty minutes of civic seriousness and let it go at that. They have observed that it takes a victory like North Africa, a star like Montgomery and the spectacle of immediate battle to impose further on the mood of relaxation.

This gives the theatre only a limited place in the educational picture. It is not the best proving-ground for those patterns of exposition which must of necessity be sometimes experimental. When we bring under observation new and stubborn materials—the seemingly desolate problems of housing and unemployment and health, for example—it is difficult at first to make them entertaining and to qualify them theatrically on the ground of either entertainment or inspiration. Happily there is more seating capacity outside theatres than there is inside them. Also happily, men are creatures of mood. The very people who are united in relaxation inside the theatres are otherwise united in terms of their professional and specialized interest outside the theatres. It is in this latter field that the educational picture is filled out: in schools and colleges, in civic social services, trade unions and professional groups of all kinds. The access to the public thereby obtained is today colossal and growing at great speed in every country where governmental need for exposition is matched by the citizens' demand for it. The Canadian Government, to take an example from a country of eleven and a half million people, today maintains upwards of a hundred travelling theatres, moving from village to village and from factory to factory. Voluntary projection groups, trained by the Government, maintain services in the community halls of the cities. Repositories all across the country serve the schools and groups which have provided themselves with technical equipment.

But the scale of development is only interesting as proving the double argument: that what we once feared as 'propaganda' will no longer be feared if it is necessary education in the circumstances of our time; and that the educational system itself is reaching out and must inevitably reach further in the use of the dramatic media if it is to secure for the citizenry a true sense of their living relationship to events. What is true for films can also be true for radio and travelling exhibitions and for all the bright addenda to school walls, village halls, shop windows and factory notice-boards. They, too, are important media of the new education and waiting instruments of an enlivened democracy.

As to the nature of the service progressively provided by Government information and progressively welcomed by education, let me offer this guide. I take my illustration from what I have seen done in films, but it should be understood that the same sort of thing has happened wherever the radio, the pamphlet, the poster, the newspaper, the magazine and the exhibition have gone to the heart of the matter. We have all, without knowing it, been working progressively together, and have something to show for our labours. I knew the day when it was revolutionary to think of making 'peace as exciting as war', and I think I was among the first to hear an audience applaud the film appearance of industrial workers as though they were applauding the national flag. For there was a time when the ordinary was rejected as boring and when we were told firmly that people wanted to escape from the contemplation of their own lives and their own problems.

That obstacle was overcome. We put glistening patterns of vigour and skill and mass industrial achievement against the sky and men today accept them as part and parcel of the testament of beauty. We did so because governments wished to celebrate the essential terms of modern citizenship and because industrial corporations wished to celebrate their public utility. Behind agriculture we dramatized the desolation that comes with wasteful methods and with ignorance, and projected a new agriculture based on an affection for the soil and an understanding of its conservation and care. We did so because the soil was blowing away under the eyes of men, and governments had to do something to stop it and so had to make people understand its dreadful significance. I have seen a film on weather forecasting made which demonstrated, I always think miraculously, that men spatially distant and unknown to each other combine each day in great and co-operative dramas. The immediate reason for it was that a government wanted to prove the importance of a public service and hearten the men who operated it as a daily and pedestrian task.

Such efforts represent only the bare beginning of the educational activity of government as I have seen it develop. We have delved into social problems and tried to articulate the nature and the duty of citizens in regard to them. With the help of the ancillary information services of the public utilities, we are wise today about the problems of health and housing, nutrition and child welfare. We know more about economics because we have dramatized the dangers of inflation; and more about the place of the scientist because we have dramatized his contribution to medicine and agriculture and even to household economy. We know more about our international duty because we have all, at least imaginatively, flown in airplanes, crossed frontiers and seen our neighbours as ourselves.

Not all of this, of course, has happened out of the initiative of the governments' own information services. The free operation of the press, the radio and the film has also played a tremendous part. I am content to say that governments have not been able to avoid a vast and directive contribution to the educational process. They have not been able to avoid it because an imaginative participation of the people in the designs of the state has been progressively necessary to the successful execution of these designs.

Today, in a drive for an even greater degree of national unity and co-operation, we move into interesting new fields. The approach as ever is functional. Active participation is the end purpose. But we are less and less concerned with mere departmental information and more and more concerned with national information in the truest sense. As we face, let us say, the problem of absenteeism in industry, we find ourselves in a world of information which includes the conditions of housing and health and transportation and infant welfare under which industrial workers operate. We see these things in a new light and together, not as matters to be merely sympathetic about, but as matters essential in an organized democratic economy. What was perhaps only a departmental worry becomes a matter of deeper concern, related clearly, for everyone to see, to the life of the nation.

So with any programme of information on conservation or reconstruction or, for that matter, of national unity or national morale. These easy concepts and easy words, when they are once broken down, bring us in full view of the social and political reality of our time, with all its problems and all its perspectives and all its hopes. We do not achieve an understanding of any one of them by splashing romantically, Hollywood fashion, through the braveries of battle or by dwelling in great self-righteousness on abstract issues of might and right, evil and good. One might successfully do it in a totalitarian state, though I doubt it; we certainly cannot do it in a democracy in which we still allow to a man the right to inquire where exactly his own particular local citizenship relates to the whole, the right of every man from Missouri 'to be shown'. If we are to persuade, we have to reveal; and we have to reveal in terms of reality. Recognizing this responsibility to the local and particular, recognizing the deeper levels of understanding and exposition into which information in a democracy must inevitably reach, it is possible to appreciate that even the once-haunted concept of propaganda may have a democratic interpretation, and that its democratic interpretation makes propaganda and education one.

4 The Library in an International World

The idea of every man a gentleman in a library, enjoying in a world of quiet and genteel leisure the grace notes of human thought was, of course, an attractive notion and it is easy to see why it should have caught the human imagination. With the new world of universal and equal opportunity opening before the people, why, indeed, should not everyone have the privilege of the *seigneur* and the squire, with access to the best the human mind could offer in poetry and art? So men dreamed. All that has been wrong with the dream is that so many things the idealists did not think of have come to disturb it. We have broken illiteracy over great areas of the world. We have published books without end, we have built universities by the thousands, and we have established libraries more universally than we could have hoped. But we have also somehow managed to develop bigger and more terrible wars.

Our passion for human enlightenment has been at least equalled by our passion for killing by the million the very people we enlightened.

Far be it from me to deny the old ideal which the libraries once set before us. It is proper that all men should have access to the best thought of the ages and be encouraged to know it. It is proper that men should have, if they can, the higher understanding of man and his nature, which only the great philosophers, prophets and poets can convey. 'The languages are necessary to the understanding of the writings of the ancients,' said Descartes in his *Discourse on Method*. 'The grace of fable stirs the mind and the memorable deeds of history elevate it. Eloquence has an incomparable force and beauty. Poesy has its ravishing graces and delights and Theology points the path to heaven. The perusal of all excellent books is, as it were, to interview with the noblest men of past ages who have written them and even a studied interview in which are discovered to us only their choicest thoughts.'

This is the strength of the old conception of enlightenment. The weakness of it I can best illustrate by referring to the village I come from. We were in part a mining village and in the years before World

156

War One and on until today, we were continuously involved in the economic dislocations of our time.

It seemed to some of us that even to press these larger matters of goodness, truth and beauty had an air of cynicism under the conditions which actually prevailed; and, while I would not deny the pursuit of goodness, truth and beauty, I have thought ever since that education in a vacuum and without reference to the immediate urgency of men's lives and men's problems can only be unreal and ineffective. If the people of my village can now look forward to better lives and better conditions of work, it is certainly not because of the ideals which education set before them. It is because they thought out their economic problems for themselves and because they organized and struck and fought and finally voted the conditions of their own future. If in this process, the school and the library were valuable to my fellow-citizens, and indeed they were, it was not on the high level of Platonic discussions, but on the simple, practical levels on which human hope was encouraged, human aspirations were confirmed and the nature of the modern world was taught. It was on the levels where men and women were equipped for the business of actually achieving their hopes and their aspirations.

I cannot apologize for mentioning this now far-away village of mine, because today its striving and its strife have spread to the whole wide world. The same active dissatisfaction with slums and conditions of labour and a dollar a day are the common possession of millions in the underprivileged parts of the earth. The same liability to economic dislocations and the same sense of gnawing insecurity have spread further still, for, as we have painfully discovered, the privileged, as well as the underprivileged, are liable to both.

All over the world we are faced today with the same old disturbing questions. Why is it that our educational methods seem so far away from the realities of the human struggle? Why is it that our educational ideals do not quite seem to fit in with the actual problems which engage men's minds? Whence the dreadful gap between our peaceful intentions and the warring conditions which actually prevail? Is the way of the books—or at least the way of the books alone—outdone and outdated? Is the ideal of a literary education now inadequate? And, finally, what must we do to add to our tools of education if we are to do the job which society expects of us?

The anxiety I have expressed about the educational problem is, of course, no special reaction of mine. In every responsible circle today of politics and education, the same note is being sounded. Only the

Education: A New Concept

other day, the President of the United States put the matter as concisely as anyone. Speaking at Fordham University, Mr. Truman used these words:

'The new age of atomic energy presses upon us. Mark that well,' he said. 'What might have been essential yesterday in international understanding, is not sufficient today. New and terrible urgencies, new and terrible responsibilities have been placed on education. Civilization cannot survive an atomic war, for nothing would be left but a world reduced to rubble. Gone would be man's hope for decency. Gone would be our hope for the greatest age in the history of mankind—an age which I know can harness atomic energy for the welfare of man and not for his destruction.

'And so we must look to education to wipe out that ignorance which threatens catastrophe.'

At this point the President quoted one of the last exhortations of Mr. Roosevelt, part of a speech which he did not live to make. 'We are faced with the pre-eminent fact that if civilization is to survive we must cultivate a science of human relationships—the ability of all people of all kinds to live and work together in the same world at peace.'

'There is at least one defence against the atomic bomb,' Mr. Truman added. 'It lies in our mastery of this science of human relationships all over the world. It is the defence of tolerance, of understanding, of intelligence and thoughtfulness. It is not an easy task. It is one which places burdens without precedent both upon those who teach and those who come to be taught. There must be new inspiration, new meaning, new energies. There must be a rebirth of education if this new and urgent task is to be met. All of our educational resources— all, note you—must be pledged to this end.'

Certainly nothing ever before has brought home to us in so staggering a manner as the atomic bomb this deep relationship between the urgency of events and the processes of public enlightenment. One is of the other. If only for that reason, we may yet live to forgive the dreadful revelation of Hiroshima. The atomic bomb is the writing on the wall in letters of fire, warning us at once and for all to see, of both our infinite strength and our infinite weakness as thinking beings.

By our ingenuity on the one hand we have been able to discover and unleash a power of untold potential benefit to the human race. One scientist says: 'We can now make anything out of anything or nothing anywhere in the world in any amount, almost without measurable cost.' Chancellor Hutchins calls up the bright picture of a future under atomic energy in which 'distances and scarcity of fuel will cease to influence the location of industry and communities', a picture of new industries and new smokeless communities which can be created anywhere 'because the cost of transferring the material from which atomic energy is drawn is negligible'. As for the benefits to medicine and health, the scientists say that 'this discovery is for the biologist and the doctor as important as the invention of the microscope' and that 'we need never worry about the scarcity of radium again'.

Thus our ingenuity and strength as thinking beings, but what in this case have we done with them? Let me again quote Chancellor Hutchins: 'In this case, we elected to drop on the women and children of Japan, without warning, a new explosive against which they were utterly defenceless and which was utterly indiscriminate in its destructive power. A quarter of a million people were killed or injured by one bomb in one minute. Twenty-seven out of thirty-three fire stations were destroyed. Three-quarters of the firemen were casualties. The medical chief was killed, and his assistant was killed, and the assistant's assistant was killed. The Commanding General was killed and his *aide* was killed and his *aide's aide* was killed and his entire staff. Out of 298 doctors, only 30 were able to care for the wounded. Out of 2,400 nurses, only 600 could work. Only one hospital remained.'

There, in high relief, is our paradox, our strength and our weakness as thinking beings. It is also basically the problem which besets all of us in education today.

I shall attempt to analyse the nature of that problem and try to indicate where, as writers, artists, teachers and librarians we should go from here, if we are to meet President Roosevelt's challenge and mobilize all our educational resources, so that we can live and work together in the same world at peace. Complex and difficult as the task may be, I do not think we need despair of the ultimate result. As writers, artists, teachers, librarians, lecturers and leaders of discussion, we have a great power in the land, and, in the last resort, the greatest power on earth. It is we, in the long run, who can indicate and reveal the obsolescent ways of thought and combat them. It is we, in the last resort, who can point the way to the new patterns of thought and feeling which will make it possible to shape our strange new world in the moulds of harmonious action which are required of us.

What we are really seeing behind our problem of education today is the biggest burst of technological progress in the history of the world: a burst of technological progress which inevitably brings

Education: A New Concept

greater difficulties in mental accommodation than ever before. Aristotle said the natural community was the community which could gather within the range of a man's voice. But what is that today in a world of radio and films, in which all men are brought within each other's sight and hearing? Transport and communications have, indeed, made us all members of a single body politic; world trade has made us all members of a single body economic; and not only peace, but human welfare itself, is indivisible. But not least important is the fact that, by very reason of the new immediacy of communication and contact, all men everywhere of all colours and creeds expect today to share in the great wealth which machinery and mass production have unleashed, and to share, in a measure of equality, the social benefits which science and medicine have brought. This is not the least important development, for it is the root and basis of the troubles we see. Back of them all are eager hands of all colours and creeds reaching out for the benefits of man's ingenuity and skill; and it is no wonder at all that these hands are sometimes violent hands, that the new hopes clash with the old established interests and that ancient prejudices come between all of us and the appreciation of these new and inevitable stirrings across the world.

The solution for educators like ourselves will only unfold itself in action. We have, in the first place, to realize that the world will not right itself, that we have an *active* and *positive* role to play as educators, artists, writers and librarians. We must, indeed, absent us from felicity awhile and get out from behind our desks and institutions and make our various powers of enlightenment a dynamic force in our communities everywhere.

I hardly think that any one of us would wish to escape from the educational crusade to which we are called, in which the end is the internationalization of men's minds and the raw materials of our task are the common interests of humanity. These common interests are in themselves good to the spirit and lively to the imagination. All of us remember the flashing power of President Roosevelt's oration on Freedom of Speech, Freedom of Religion, Freedom from Want and Freedom from Fear. And all of us remember with what unanimity the peoples of the world hailed it as though together they were seeing a common vision. In the inspiration of such a vision we are the more ready and willing to face the daily job and hammer away at the local tasks which in solid and determinable fact lead to the achievement of Freedom of Speech and Religion and lead to an economic and spiritual security for all.

The Library in an International World

A further blessing is that we shall find good will everywhere. Whatever the pessimist may say, there are people everywhere eagerly reaching out for the books and the films and the radio programmes and the discussions and the mental leadership generally which will inspiringly direct their thought to the duties of citizenship in an international world at peace. As Albert Guerard reminded us the other day, the masses may be confused in their minds, but they are not confused in their feelings. They hate war and they hate oppression and they hate injustice. It is on this we can count and it is on this we can work.

We can work, too, on the fact that all men everywhere of every colour and creed are alike in the essentials of their interest. If we educators would only get off the sky and down to earth, we would realize that the people everywhere are not full of differences, but full of similarities, and, in fact, have the same basic wants and desires: to eat, to have shelter, to have homes and families and health and the friendly association of neighbours. The first charge to us all is to become more active about our educational tasks in the community; the second charge is to become more simple and more elemental about the interests which hold man together, for it is only in that way we can discover a common international language and speak across the prejudices and the distrusts which now separate peoples, nations and races.

I say this in spite of all the ideologies which now clamour for the attention and the loyalty of the millions. I am all for systems of ideals and I am all for systems of doctrine. They do help in their stolid, strait-jacketed, clumsy and slightly illiterate way to satisfy man's hunger for belief and for the spirit of confidence which attends an illusion of certainty. I like to think of Descartes's definition of philosophy, and he was no mean philosopher himself, as 'the art which affords the means of discoursing on all matters with an appearance of truth and commands the admiration of the more simple'. The admiration of the more simple is a necessary instrument of education, but when the philosophies and ideologies become actually dangerous—and they sometimes do—I withdraw my loyalty. I say a plague on ideologies, all of them, if they obscure the common nature of man's interests in food and shelter and homes and families and the good life and drive man on in hatred to mutual destruction. If they serve these common interests, they are good; and that is the measure of them and that is the only measure of them.

At all costs, let us not be bewildered by the madmen who say that this way of life or that is so exclusively noble that none other may be allowed. In an atomic war, it will be no great comfort—except in such few lunatic asylums as may remain—to say that because we wanted to save civilization we, therefore, enthusiastically destroyed it. Let us, in fact, add the conception of universal tolerance as not merely a visionary virtue, but as a necessary law and a necessary discipline for every moment of our lives.

There is, of course, one principal issue on which we shall be continuously tested in our attempt to teach and maintain tolerance; and that is the apparent clash between the ideological force of liberal democracy emanating from the United States and the ideological force of international socialism emanating now principally from the Soviet Union, but increasingly from other countries, too.

It is true that Russia has political views which many millions in the world, and particularly on this continent, do not share. Nevertheless, we must find what meeting ground we can and there is more than many people, in the first burst of prejudice, suppose. Russia is dedicated in its own way, just as the Catholic Church is, just as the liberal democracy of North America is, to the higher interests of mankind. It is as fervent as America in the exploitation of the earth's resources and of science for the betterment of the conditions of life. Its theory and its practice in the matter of inter-racial relations are of a kind which everyone amongst us who believes in the basic equality of men must warmly welcome.

It is true that in the discussion of ways and means we differ greatly. The Russians say that political freedom is an illusion if men starve. We, on the other hand, say that economic welfare is an illusion if men are not free. Ironically, both sides to the argument have a part of the truth and we are approaching the same ideal from different directions. There is no reason in philosophy why we cannot establish a common understanding in the conception that true freedom involves at once the right to seek men's highest ends and the economic capacity to do so.

What is intolerable is that each of us should deny the other's claim to truth, and, standing off from each other, create the no-man's-land of political discussion which now exists. The existence of this no-man's-land today is not only rotting our minds, but sending us off into thoughts and actions which are not only mentally stupid, but physically dangerous.

Mr. Roosevelt's words and Mr. Truman's words are spoken into the thin and futile air and there will be none of that science of human relationships which is to save mankind, if we frustrate and stifle the generous thoughts of our youth or by any action of Church or State bar them from the fullest knowledge of the ideas operating in the world today, whether they come from Russia, Rome or George Bernard Shaw.

The libraries all across the continent have an especially powerful position: they are rooted in the communities of the country. They are part and parcel of the life of the small towns and the cities and the universities. They are at the heart of the matter. In our film world we certainly command vast audiences and even the simplest film address we choose to make can look to an audience of scores of millions. But some of us have not been deceived by the illusion of power these great audiences bring. If I may cite the example of Canada in the film world, we have in these past years sought to relate our films ever more closely to the local interests of local people. We have attempted to develop the directness of approach to the educational problem which I have been urging. We have struggled, therefore, to bridge the gap between the child and the community and between the citizen and the world community, by beginning our explanations of national and world affairs on the doorstep of men's actual local interests.

Today the great drive is to make films which will help rural communities to solve their rural problems and see the actual relationship between their rural problems and the wider world without. And so similarly with the industrial communities we are trying to relate the immediate problems of labour management relationship, town planning and regional planning, nutrition, health and community living with the same issues as they present themselves in other parts of the globe.

In one matter, we are very particular: we do not believe in the general public quite so naïvely as the salesmen and the advertisers seem to do. We see the so-called general public as divided up into a thousand and one publics of specialized interests: people interested and active in rural libraries, rural community halls and rural planning; people interested in the active and actual achievement of higher standards of nutrition and child welfare and public health; people actually and actively interested in town planning and regional planning; people actually and actively interested in the elimination of prejudice and the development of inter-cultural relations. I mention these, but, of course, librarians, above all people, will best know how to fill out the list, for they are great specialists in specializations. What I stress is that we have tried to convert the problems of education into the terms of men's actual and active interests, that we have striven to take education out of the clouds and bring it to the groups from whom action and the propagation of ideas can be expected. These must inevitably be the growing points of an activist system of education.

In so doing, we have tended more and more to move out from the capital and the big cities to join hands with the community organizations. That is what the development of the non-theatrical film actually signifies. Progressively we have found that our main work of public enlightenment is in co-operation and alliance with the local schools and universities, the local women's groups, the local business groups, the local farmers' groups and the co-operatives and trade unions. Inevitably we have come face to face with the librarians across the country and have found them the natural community centres of enlightenment in a democratic society. But we have wondered sometimes why they were not with us as we decentralized our systems of information and built our local circulations and developed our forums of public discussion. I have wondered often why they are not in fact the heart and soul of the whole effort. And not just in the matter of the circulation of film, but also in the discussive development of radio, the circulation of prints and wall newspapers and all the other vital forces of enlightenment today. I cannot, in fact, think of any greater, more widespread, more penetrating or more co-ordinate and effective voice in the country today than the libraries of the country, active and mobilized, and in full possession of all the modern powers of illumination and enlightenment.

The old library outlook is over and done with. It served its day, and, indeed, the spread of popular education which the schools and the libraries have effected has been one of the initial forces making for the great upsurge of human effort which it has been our exciting privilege in this generation to witness. But the new problems involve new methods. I suggest that if libraries do not adopt these methods the essential job of popular education to which they once enthusiastically dedicated themselves will pass on to others; and it may well pass to people who have perhaps a less profound tradition of public service and a less unselfish conception of community interest. That today is one of the greatest dangers which confronts us. I do not say that the day of books is over, but the day of the books only is certainly over. It is not information that is needed today; in fact, it is not information that is sought. It is enlightenment, and that is a very different thing, involving, as it does, the dramatic process of sparking the mind and the heart into new hope, new vision, new realization and new efforts in citizenship.

From the beginning it was never the amount of it, but rather the manner of it that counted, and it is to the manner of it that we ought now to address ourselves. I shall put it shortly by saying that the complex of information today is so great that we have at all costs to present it in a form which can, in fact, be absorbed. Information in itself is cold stuff. Information of distant peoples and distant problems is particularly cold. It has to be brought alive and it has, in the last instance, to be brought home.

We ought today to be grateful for one especial gift which the technological revolution has brought us. It may have faced us with difficult issues in education, but it has also blessedly handed us the new tools for their solution. We have in radio, in film, in television and travelling exhibits and in the infinitely cheap reproduction of news-sheets, paintings, posters, pamphlets, books and wall newspapers, vital new media by which the world can be elucidated and brought to our understanding. Everywhere we are mastering new techniques of illustration, presentation and display. Everywhere we are discovering new ways of putting the issues of our complex world into the dramatic forms which people can quickly grasp. That is what 'bringing alive' means in the educational process. No longer think that the work is done if the information is made available or even conveyed. The work is not done until we spark the gap between the citizen and the world of his citizenship, bring into his imagination the great and beneficent struggle of men which we see today and finally secure his creative participation in that struggle.

To this end I would suggest six principles of educational policy.

The first is that we must internationalize the minds of men if we are to live in an international world and that we must dispose men to co-operation in a world where co-operation is the price of civilization and even of survival.

The second principle is that we cannot do this without an active and dynamic policy: that, indeed, we must all, writers, artists, teachers and librarians, get out into the hard but constructive business of directive leadership in the community.

The third principle is that we must strive for simplicity and an understanding of the elemental interests which unify all men and represent the only international language which is possible.

The fourth is that we must create a spirit of tolerance at all costs, even if we have to sacrifice the luxury of old loyalties and old beliefs.

The fifth principle is that we must bring education home and convert the complex issues of the world into the terms of local interest on the farm, in the factory, in the family, in the schools, in the universities, in the co-operatives, the trade unions, the women's groups, the service clubs and the churches.

And lastly, we must make of information and education a dramatic process of enlightenment and bring to the stubborn fact a measure of imagination and inspiration. We must, indeed, bring into our use all the bright new media and techniques which lie now in our hand in an ingenious and amazing world of new illuminations and new skills.

PART V

Future for Documentary

1 The Challenge of Peace

I do not think there is much use discussing what to do with a medium unless we are talking about it in terms of access to the means of production. I think it vain to write unless there is power of publication. I think it vain to talk about films unless there is power of production and distribution. I think it vain to paint unless the presentation of painting is at the same time organized and secured. I dismiss as out-of-date and ridiculous a position in which the creative worker lives in the hope that the blue eyes of his personal talent will serve him; and I think it possible to suggest that there is hardly a body of workers today so poorly organized for the modern world or so impotent in securing the right to work, and particularly the right to give of their best to society, as the creative workers of the western democracies.

The key to the creative worker's position and strength is of course that he should first and foremost understand the nature of the problem which society at this specific moment imposes upon him and that he should not only align himself with the forces that are shaping tomorrow but himself add his measure of creative leadership to them.

Certainly your creative worker has an astounding world to look out upon. We have just finished a brutal war and are entering upon a phase of rehabilitation and reconstruction involving not only our own country but every country in the world. This new phase calls for the very highest order of heart and mind and the workers in every medium have at this moment a crucial contribution to make to the progress of mankind. In my own lifetime and experience I have seen little else but war, and I think that by this time we know the basic nature of its perverse continuity. The wars of 1914 and of 1939 are only vicious episodes in a much longer struggle in which under-privileged nations and under-privileged races and classes have fought desperately for a share of the world's goods and the decencies of life. They have fought wisely and fought disastrously, followed good leaders and bad, but we do not see the reality of our time unless we see the class wars and the race wars and the national wars—China, India, Spain, Germany, Russia, Italy and Greece, all those dramatic images of our own experience—as manifestations, varying and various, of the single basic struggle for a more equitable distribution of the good life.

The irony of it is that the struggle has intensified and become more horrifying in direct proportion to the advance of technical knowledge and our capacity to provide a good life for all mankind. Today the situation is temporarily lightened by the defeat of Germany and Japan. We have eliminated a powerful but false leadership of the world's revolutionary forces: false, because it sought to make the world's goods exclusive. But we have still to prove that we can substitute a true leadership for that false one, and until we do so peace will have no reality. This is of all moments in our generation the most testing one. The issue was not so sharply drawn after the last war, for the peoples then had not so widely revolted and the challenge to new ways of thinking was not so desperate. But then, too, we had an opportunity to give a new deal to common people the world over. We of the rich and powerful and so-called enlightened western democracies did not do it, and the chaos of today is the measure of our failure.

It is against that picture and that problem, I believe, that all creative workers must operate and I should add that the occasion is too urgent and too concrete for the sweet abstractions on which man has founded his faith in the years gone by. Freedom is only a word till you make men free, democracy only a word till men have actual enjoyment of rights. Goodness, truth and beauty are no longer just abstractions but actualities which today men demand with guns in their hands, and actualities they properly translate into the terms of food and houses and a right to live.

I am afraid that my interest in films is limited to what they can do in and for this particular situation. If I have any complaint against the film industry, it is that it has done less than it might. It did much at a crucial juncture to mobilize the anti-fascist forces in America but, on the whole, it has not devoted the time and energy to international observation or even to national observation, which its vast international market and its great power in its own nation would seem to warrant. For a medium not given to diffidence it has been unusually diffident in assuming the great public responsibility which is its to command. Its newsreels could have been more influential and so too could have been all those short films which in one way or another observe and comment on the passing scene. As for the big films, the last thing in the world I would ask of them is that they should all be socially significant. They would be a colossal bore if they were. One can, however, reasonably ask that they should, in the patterns of their

168

drama, reflect something of the reality of our time. I leave it to the psychological experts to say if they do. I shall only say, for my part, that I doubt if the individual destiny is quite so important and the public destiny quite so unimportant as Hollywood would make them appear. I would say, just to be simple about it, that a technological society is necessarily an inter-dependent and co-operative society, and that the patterns of its drama must inevitably become patterns of inter-dependence and co-operation.

I am not going to pretend that I know better than anyone else what the documentary future is going to be and I am certainly not going to announce the horoscope of the various producers and distributors who are today concerned with this branch of film work. On the other hand it may be valuable to indicate the principles which are bound to govern the development of documentary in the future.

The documentary film has made great strides during the past fifteen years as an art form and as a public service. In Britain today upwards of thirty production units are concerned with this kind of production. Their films are in great and growing demand by the government and also by provincial and civic authorities as well as by the more important public utilities and corporations.

I emphasize the sponsors of documentary films first, because it is of first importance to see where the economy of documentary lies. In the case of governments, there has been a growing realization that the complexities of modern administration involve necessarily a new understanding by the people. Any medium which can help government to give an account of its stewardship, elucidate its legislation or otherwise help to provide a background of civic understanding is very precious to governments today. It will be more and more precious as governments are called upon for more initiative. This is not a matter in which the political viewpoint makes any difference. By the very nature of the growth of our technological society, all governments alike are involved in problems of co-ordination and management involving not only national but also international relationships.

It is in the logic of the situation that you cannot ask governments to co-ordinate or manage without giving them the right to explain or otherwise seek and secure the co-operation of the citizen whence, as we have seen, in every country, the growth of government information services of one kind or another. It is true that these services of information are frequently challenged and particularly in the United States. But they appear to be challenged only when there is suspicion of the administration seeking partisan advantage. These information services

Future for Documentary

are not challenged when they are associated with, say, progressive agriculture or when they are associated with the promotion of international trade and the support of international diplomacy. So far from being challenged, the government information services are warmly applauded when and where they relate to the reporting and better understanding of civic duties associated with recognized public need.

It is not too early to conclude that government information services are natural and necessary to modern government, that they are bound to increase as governments learn to dissociate them from political partisanship and that they are bound to provide one of the most important sponsorships for all those arts which are interested in public observation and the education of the public.

It is worth noting that the documentary film has acquired in some countries a very special relationship to this development of government information. In both Britain and Canada more money possibly is devoted to this branch of information than to any other. It may be that the documentary people in both cases have been especially persuasive but there are good reasons for the relationship. From the very first the documentary people in these countries have taken the view that the first duty of their art was to the public service. They have constantly asserted that they were public workers first and creative workers not the less for that. They accordingly fitted into the public service to the point of becoming professionals, experts many of them in the forms and problems associated with government administration.

The nature of their medium has, of course, helped them greatly. It enjoys the possibility of mass circulation but also enjoys in 16-mm. size the possibility of highly specialized and highly scientific circulation. It has the special capacity of dramatizing the fact of the matter and having an air of authority. In particular, it has the power of putting in comprehensible pattern the complex inter-relationships of the public service.

Whether the governments produce their films directly or indirectly—and there is no reason whatsoever for direct production if suitable outside production units are available and a creative relationship can be struck up between government experts and production experts—I think it inevitable that governments will provide a large mass of documentary films in the future, covering every aspect of the government's interests and therefore very many aspects of the citizens' interest. We now see only the bare beginning of the government's approach to participation in the directive education of the citizenry in all matters of social and economic concern.

170

The Challenge of Peace

I said it was best to begin with the sponsors because it is as well to know where the economy of documentary lies. Partly because of the early British example, we have got accustomed to think of governments as the most important sponsors but, although I am a government official and have spent most of my life developing government sponsorship of the documentary film, I doubt if public governments will be more important in the immediate future than those private governments which Beardsley Ruml talks about in *Tomorrow's Business*. I am thinking particularly of the documentary potential of the next ten years or so. I would guess that some of the best and most valuable sponsorship will come from city councils and state governments, from national and trade associations, from the trade unions, as well as from the big corporations and public utilities. It is the custom, particularly in the United States, to consider dangerous the educational materials emanating from corporate groups. Danger of course there is, but none that cannot be guarded against, at least in the field of technological description. Good film producers who have the concept of public service in their imaginations should always be able to direct the path of these films along constructive lines. The work of the British group with the Post Office, Gas, Shell, Anglo-Iranian, Imperial Airways and I.C.I. proves that it can be done by resolute men who serve ideals and know how to discover the creative relationship between business and the public welfare.

Doubts I know must arise in many minds and I am as conscious of them as anyone. It has been my business for many years to be conscious of these doubts. However, I suggest this for consideration. The first problem of education today is essentially one of understanding the technological world in which we live and every force which directs its development has something of importance to say. People will realize their worth all the better for knowing what railroads do for farmers, what telephones do for trade, what radio does for airlines and what automobiles do for both private amenity and public knowledge. The patterns of inter-relationship which lie at the root of modern citizenship and therefore challenge us to new ways of management have all a technological basis and I cannot think of a gas pipe or electric wire or road or ship or plane or factory that has not something to say.

The great problem of corporate sponsorship in this vital reference is, of course, that business groups are more imaginative in the matter of technological progress than they are on the human relationships which results from technical progress. In this connection much may be expected from government and much indeed has been done by governments. It is important to note, however, that nothing can be expected from governments beyond what I shall call the degree of general sanction. The degree of general sanction is not the degree of sanction by the party in power: it is the degree of sanction allowed by all the parties of Parliament or Congress. For example, in England, the degree of sanction was left of the Conservative Party in power and in Canada it is slightly right of the Radical Liberal Party which is now in power. I say, as an old public servant, that if the degree of general sanction is accurately gauged, maximum support is forthcoming for creative work. Where, however, advantage is taken and the degree of sanction is estimated on partisan lines, ineffectiveness and frustration result.

This, of course, imposes a clear limit on the creative artist working within the public service, for, obviously, the degree of general sanction does not easily allow of forthright discussions on such highly controversial problems as, say, America's record with the Negroes in the South, or Britain's record with the Indians in the East. The creative worker must not, however, simply denounce this limitation and dissociate himself from government service. If he is a practical operator and a practical reformer he will take the situation for what it is and do his utmost within the limitations set, and this is one of the disciplines which the creative artist must learn in this particular period of society.

If he wants to pursue the more difficult and controversial themes, I am afraid he must look elsewhere than to governments, and here I think it will be well to examine in future years the sponsorship potential of authorities and associations who are less ham-strung than governments necessarily are. In particular, one expects much from the trade unions and co-operative movements. One also expects much from the associations devoted to such matters as nutrition and town planning and public health. To take one example, why should Mayor LaGuardia, of the city of New York, have a radio station and not a film unit? I can imagine no more effective centre for films dealing with town planning, child welfare, public health, educational progress and inter-racial understanding than a film centre based on the social interests of the city of New York. I make this suggestion not only for New York but for every Mayor everywhere. City Councils, professional associations, trade unions, alike, are all directly concerned with the media of public observation and analysis and for the simple reason that they are all equally concerned with the growth of professional and civic understanding.

Here I am not altogether guessing. Even now there are many signs of a growing use of documentary films by these bodies. In my own experience hardly a week goes by that I am not asked for advice on how to make or circulate films by groups whose varying interest ranges all the way from physical research to stamp collecting. It is one of the phenomena of the time that there is hardly an organization that is not in, or about to be in, the documentary film business, and simply because it is an instrument by which knowledge of a functional nature can be exchanged and extended. There is one field of development which is of very special concern to all of us today. We hear a goo deal about international competition in film production and struggle for markets. We still seem to be talking the languag competition when we should be talking the language of conciliatio. and co-operation. So far as our documentary films are concerned, I, for one, do not care who makes them so long as they are a contribution to the understanding of today and the making of tomorrow. All creative work which promotes peace and goodwill is, like peace itself, indivisible. I look, therefore, for much greater concern than ever before with the international exchange of documentary films.

I hold that the I.L.O., which in the twenties and thirties did much good work at Geneva, could have done more if it had created a more living exchange between countries, of documentary material describing their common interests. I do not say that this or any other exchange would have prevented the war. What I do say is that now and in the future all international understanding must inevitably be based on a realization of the common interest of working people; their common interest in food and housing and children, and in the ordinary enjoyments that make for the good life. That realization can only be effected if the creative workers in all media see to it that it is effected. It was in our thought in the thirties that wherever a country showed a high example in, let us say, safety in mines or workers' health, the I.L.O. should have circulated that example to the whole world. In the social, economic, and educational instruments of the new international body we have, today, the same opportunity for exchange, and there will be no excuse whatever if this time we fluff it.

One thing that would result from the development of these agencies is that we would come closer to an international viewpoint in both the production and distribution of documentary films. One serious limitation in government support in the past has been the tendency to serve national interest to the exclusion of all others, and this is particularly so in the case of the United Kingdom and the United States. Whatever they may say in their diplomacy, they have not learned to come off their blaring national band waggons when it comes to information. I suggest mildly, if I may, examination of the somewhat different policy of Canada. It has been one of the interesting things about Canadian policy in information that it has really, and from the first, conceived of itself as a United Nation, and has spoken most boldly when it has talked about its international relationships and its common interests with other peoples.

I have suggested that we can look for a great development of the documentary film because it is necessary to so many people. The nature of the development of government, the nature of the development of business, of trade unions and civic associations, alike suggest a greater use of visual aids to understanding. I add that the nature of the development of education itself gives a new authority to any medium which, like the documentary film, strikes out the living patterns of modern citizenship. This association with advances in educational theory is so important that I hope I shall be borne with, if I labour over a necessary distinction between the documentary film and the simple pedagogical film.

We ought to be clear from the first that in education we are not just concerned with mobilizing new techniques for the teaching of the same old thing. We have had exciting new media made available in our day to the process of instruction—the radio, the film, the exhibition, the dramatized newspaper story, and so on. If it were just a matter of teaching more quickly the known laws of medicine and science, I suppose we could sit around and plan the effective use of these new media right away. It would be no trouble at all. The armed services and the war industries have done exactly that for the past five years. They have made efficient sailors and soldiers and airmen and mechanics in half the time that it took by older methods of teaching. But let us not be led astray by these developments, however interesting they are. The problem of education today is not one of new techniques or of visual aids or aural aids or of any other aids. These represent specific improvements in the teaching of known areas of knowledge and very important they are, but they do not go to the heart of the matter. As a matter of fact, education has done not a bad job at all in the known areas of knowledge, with or without these new devices of instruction. The technological revolution which lies at the root of all our problems is itself the miraculous result of a superb education in scientific knowledge and technical skills. Nor is the matter of literacy in question. Again education has done a very presentable job. We can, most of us today, read a little, even if we only read the headlines, the sports columns, the comic strips and True Confessions. I will go further still and say that education's problem today is not even the conveying of knowledge. The spate of knowledge conveyed daily by the various forces of education, inside and outside the schools and universities—and, of course, I include the newspapers, the radio and the film—is nothing short of colossal, and, considering the mass of it and the complexity of it, it is astonishingly well conveyed by an army of observers, analysts and mechanics who have developed very difficult skills in the matter of world observation.

In my view, the basic problem of education lies not so much in the acquisition of literacy or of knowledge or of skills, as in the patterns of civic appreciation, civic faith and civic duty which go with them. They mean nothing—literacy, knowledge or skill, the whole lot of them—if they do not make for order in the world, and today they quite obviously do not. Where I think we have failed is that we have not sufficiently realized the implications of the change which the tech-nological revolution has brought upon us. The objective nature of that new society we understand well enough but not its subjective implica-tions. We know that the old self-contained, self-subsistent and rela-tively static community is dead and done with, and no more real in our conceptual life than the tattered friezes of the Parthenon. We have obliterated the obstacles of time and space and have made the world's riches of matter and of mind potentially available to everyone. We have become specialists, in the safe knowledge that we have the benefit of the specialization of others in a new and more complex system of creation and enjoyment. They used to ask in the school books if seven men took twenty-one days to build a house, how long does it take twenty-one men. We have discovered that the answer is not seven, but probably one. We have learned the two and two makes five of the corporate and the co-operative.

But, on the other hand, we have become more and more citizens of a community which we do not adequately see. The knob of a radio set switches in the voices and opinions and aspirations of men all over the globe, but not without the thought and work of thousands of people like ourselves, which we have not yet the habit of realizing. Under our feet go wires and pipes leading to complicated supply systems we blindly take for granted. Behind each counter of our modern buying lies a world system of manufacture, choice and con-veyance. A simple weather forecast is a daily drama of complicated observation over a large part of the earth's surface, without which men could not safely fly or put to sea. We do not see it. Messages that roll easily from the local press may have come at six hundred words a minute from Moscow or may have been relayed south from London to Africa and by complicated steps north through the Americas again to overcome an atmospheric problem we know nothing about. It is a nickel buy, like an ice-cream cone or a packet of chewing-gum. Sleeping or walking, we are concerned each day in an inter-dependency, one with another, which in fact makes us each our brother's servant and our brother's keeper. This is the fact of modern society, whatever medieval theories of self-subsistence operating in the name of art or operating in the name of religion may try to tell us. This is the fact of modern society, yet we are slow to adopt the habits of thought which must necessarily go with interdependency if we are to control the forces which we ourselves have released. We operate in a new world, but are not yet possessed of it. We have given ourselves a new kind of society, but have not yet given ourselves the new kind of imagination or the new conception of citizenship which makes it tolerable. Like Tomlinson who gave up the ghost in his house in Gloucester Square, we stand betwixt and between, with the winds of the universe blowing through our empty spirits. We operate in a system of complex interdependency, but still like to think that we are simple souls face to face, and on the most personal basis, with our Maker. We have given away our capacity for self-sufficiency, but still want to be free individuals so-called—free to go our own gait and let the devil take the hindmost. Now, when we ought more than at any time in history to be talking most about responsibility and disciplines and duties, we are talking most about freedom from controls and freedom from restraints, even when they are only our own necessary self-controls and self-restraints. This is the most paradoxical fact of our time. I think it is no wonder that we are full of frustrations and neuroses of one kind or another, for we are, in fact, in the process of trying to eat our cake and have it too: enjoying the interdependence but still demand the privilege of independence.

This, of course, places a great burden and a great creative responsibility on education and on art, if we are dealing, as I think we are, with the intangibles that affect the imaginations of men and determine their will. It is no longer a problem of known areas of knowledge simply and directly communicated. It is a question of the images that direct men's vision and determine their loyalties, and we are concerned not only with the conscious processes of the mind but with the subconscious ones which insensibly govern the pattern of men's attention and the manner of their action.

The Challenge of Peace

I suggest, in fact, that the problems of education and art, and their inevitable interest today, lie in the realm of the imaginative training for modern citizenship and not anywhere else. We owe ourselves, as H. G. Wells once before observed, a thorough overhaul, not of the facts we teach, nor of the techniques with which we teach them, but of the images and patterns on belief in which these facts are framed. I am not going to suggest which images and patterns should be retained and which discarded and what new images and patterns are vital to our future. But let me say this about images and patterns. What are the images which we associate with our country? Are they the static images of forests, or the dynamic images of afforestation? Are they the static images of flat or rolling landscape, or the dynamic images of soil conservation and co-operative marketing? Do we really see beyond our personal circle to the circle of the community in such a manner that the community is the deeper reality? Must our stories and dramas inevitably follow the shape of personal fortunes, or are we learning to find new dramatic patterns in a life rooted in scientific discoveries and mass production and based on interdependence? Are we still concerned with the romantic horizons of the old-time pioneer, or are we beginning to find imaginative sustenance in the new horizons of the researcher and the organizer? Do we still see the world in a rectangle, up and down left and right, or do we really in our heart and mind see over the world and think over the world and feel over the world in the circles of common interest and actual interdependence? That, I think, is the style of question which education and art will presently be asking themselves. It involves inevitably a re-answering of Tolstoy's question as to what men live by and a re-answering which will not inevitably leave the classic conceptions in their old and honourable places. I hesitate to suggest it, but we may even have to revise our views on Plato, Milton, John Stuart Mill, and the hundred best books. It is possible that we need not take them quite so seriously as guides to the special and urgent problems of what may be, in the light of time and philosophy, a new dispensation of thought and habit —as new a dispensation as that which followed the development of measurement and perspective at the end of the Middle Ages. The key to this new dispensation may well be our use of the two words corporate and co-operative. They represent, it is possible, a new species of measurement and perspective and therefore a new species of power and thought and habit.

It is significant that the record of the educators in the imaginative training of citizenship over the past generation has been a very poor and tawdry one. They have tended to stick to the safer patterns of the known way, and the direction of the civil imagination has fallen in large part to the daring innovators of the other media—to the newspapers, the radio, the film, and the advertisements. It is significant that the leadership has fallen, in fact, to those who know how to use the new dramatic media and have had the sense to use them dramatically. Inevitably they have been driven by the very nature of their media into something approaching a living description of the new world that has grown up about us. I myself regard the dramatic pattern of the modern newspaper story as the greatest single contribution to civic education in our time, not because of the substance of it, but because of the form of it, which, it seems to me, is basically necessary to the comprehension of our time. Something does something to something. Something affects something. Someone is relative to someone. It has, more than any other single factor, turned men's thinking to the active or dynamic form without which it is difficult to conceive of any understanding of the nature of the modern world. Only less important is the influence of the radio, with the immediacy and personal nature of its contact with places and problems and people in far places.

I shall not say nearly so much for the film. The most powerful of all mass media, the mass medium most capable of bringing the disparate elements of the wide world into obvious juxtaposition and association, the medium of all media born to express the living nature of interdependency, it has stuck all too stubbornly to the drama of personal habits and personal achievements. It has, I am afraid, done all too little to impose the co-operative habit of thought. In a world holding almost with a sense of spiritual dereliction and agony to the lost cause of isolationism, it has been the naïve proponent of personal isolationism. On the other hand, it has done something to open a window on the wider world, and so widen the stretch of men's eyes, and, in the documentary film, it has, I believe, outlined the patterns of interdependency more distinctively and more deliberately than any other medium whatsoever.

2   Report from America

The other day at Princeton University Harold Laski, in one of his more downcast moments, informed us that 'The world faces a crisis of vaster proportion than any since the Reformation and despite the longing of the ordinary people everywhere for security from war it is not excessive to say that the major governments of the world stand in the position of gladiators one to another.' If I am not misreading *The New York Times* account, he went on to conclude, more or less, that there is no hope of peace in our time: that 'despite the insistence of statesmen on their passion for peace' he can see 'no prospect of its achievement in any future with which this generation is concerned'. If true, this is a somewhat melodramatic utterance when it comes from a professor of political science. It is a wholly unnatural one when it comes from an educator whose job it presumably is to accentuate the positive and lead the younger generation into the future. And I would not have brought the matter up at all except that it does present an opportunity to restate the directive duty of the educators, enlighteners and creative artists of all the media in this particular phase of Gulliver and his Travels.

We are all conscious of the crisis which Laski very properly emphasizes, though it represents no sudden melodramatic cloud upon the horizon, but rather a growing crisis that has been building up ever since the industrial revolution and in full critical view as long as one remembers. We are all conscious that the national and imperialist patterns of human development are under great strain as the necessity of a new and mutually co-operative international pattern is imposed upon them: that the paradox of our time derives from the fact that we are caught between the two: drawn to the international, yet unable for basic reasons, psychological, political and economic, to let go of the national patterns to which we are so deeply attuned. It would, moreover, be a wonder if the national concepts which have shaped our thoughts, our loyalties and actions, were to hand over suddenly and without a struggle and our minds, loyalties and actions were all in a bright miracle turned into the moulds of international co-operation.

Future for Documentary

Like all the revolutionary generations, we live in two worlds and, like all such generations, can only look forward to a considerable period of directive effort before the old is put off and the new assumed. It may therefore not be a very happy time for the traditionalists and formalists in any sphere of human action but it ought, by all order, to be a whale of a time for those who pretend to creative work. With the problem goes the privilege, as Mrs. Roosevelt more or less remarked when she saw Pare Lorentz's *Fight for Life*. Lorentz, if you remember, made a great to-do about his maternity ward and the pain and the travail were given the best dramatic outing since the 51st Psalm; but Mrs. Roosevelt thought, in her gentle way, that having babies had also 'something to do with happiness'. There, I imagine, even so high a matter as a crisis 'greater than any since the Reformation' can rest too. So far as the creative arts are concerned—and I mean all of them from teaching up, or down, which have the power to mould men's thought, feeling and action—the historical task of establishing a spirit of co-operation one to another which will fulfil our actual economic dependence one on another brings incentive and opportunity which should normally light up all our horizons.

In any case the various forces afoot will not leave us be, even if we so wanted. The technological revolution goes on apace, arming the peoples of the world with new powers but also, and in its farthest corners, with new expectations. The peoples, who, because of inadequate ways of thought and deficiencies of will, have been subject to the disasters of war and the injustices of peace are everywhere patently on the march and in increasingly good order, disturbing the equilibrium of every doctrine, faith and political formula which does not take them into most practical account. The reshuffling of the doctrines, faiths and political formulæ becomes, therefore, not altogether a matter of choice and certainly none of the world-leading doctrines—of liberal democracy, of the churches, of socialist democracy—can on this occasion hide itself away. Even for æsthetics, as we have recently noted in Brooks Atkinson's debate with the Russians, there is no coral strand these days in which to conceal its fair-haired, blue-eyed little noggin. This is perhaps what makes so much of the high intention of the gentlemen in the libraries only grimly deceptive and, for no reason at all, I think of Chancellor Hutchins of the University of Chicago and his *Hundred Best Books*. The essays that once broke men's minds out into the future from just such crises as ours appear now only in support of the formulæ and definitions that will not budge, piling up behind them all the influence and power which a natural affection for the past or a frightened affection for it can all too easily create. Touchingly, we are invited to the lumber room of the human spirit, to go over the old snapshots and the old occasions when the world was young, with Plato to Milton to John Stuart Mill, matching the nostalgic baseball memory of Tinker to Evers to Chance. Against the express warnings of the Ancients themselves, the net effect is to confine the living terms of thought in the strait-jacket of other times and other conditions which were specialized, local and static in a way that has little bearing on the mastery of international forms in a swift-moving time.

An important example of this is the reiteration of the older definitions of democracy and freedom which do more at the moment to confuse the public mind and paralyse the public will and make international understanding impossible than any other educational influence whatsoever. Faith is found, says Michelangelo in one of his sonnets, only in the creative processes of time: which I take to mean where the actual forces of the future are shaping. It would seem on the face of it that this other world of technical and economic relationships, which is patently upon us, imposes, as it requires, other and relevant patterns of thought and sentiment if we are to bring it to order, and that is to say, if we are to live spiritually in it.

This suggests to me a certain drastic re-examination of all the media in the light of the very great new responsibilities placed upon them; and I mean a re-examination different in character and kind from the normal re-examinations which artists and critics at all times affect. For example, much of our æsthetic approach, and here was the indissoluble difference in the Atkinson debate, is still reflective rather than directive. If this analysis of the crisis is correct—and in spite of all the regard we owe to the courtly cultures and all the secret wishes we may stifle that they will in grace return again—there is no alternative at this time to throwing dear old Wordsworth and his 'recollections in tranquillity' out of the nearest metropolitan window.

In the field of enlightenment all the barriers break down between the media and all become one *in education* as the creative process becomes a directive one.

In actual fact we are nearer to this position, and in all the media, than many people realize. Not only are the policies and viewpoints in the theatre, in films, in the press and in education itself coming closer to an urgent sense of the public service and of their directive function within it, but larger, more co-ordinated, more activist forms of organization, reflect an appreciation of the magnitude of the task. There is a powerful image of this in the council room of the United Nations at Lake Success. The crescent-moon table faces the general public and the world's press with a new sort of directness and there is an altogether new scale and character in the facilities demanded by the various instruments of world communication and permitted to them: in the floodlights for the cameras and in the glass-fronted silence loges for the operation of both the radio people and the film people. One has only to pull a switch and here under the searchlight we have this new international democratic process under highly organized world review. The machinery of world observation has actually begun to exist. Perhaps it is not yet adequate enough. Melodramatic and immature forms of reporting distort some of the important issues and suppress all too many of the pedestrian but constructive achievements. The direct participation of the scholastic system as one of the mass media of equivalent power and influence is not yet sufficiently organized. Nor is the participation sufficiently organized of that even more powerful mass medium of enlightenment which is represented on the community level by the churches, youth organizations, women's groups, business and service clubs, trades unions and all those other organizations which provide direct and immediate leadership of functional civic interests. The participation of the arts is, as usual, not organized at all. None the less, the picture is already impressive and the more so as critical forces in all the media reach out for qualitative, as well as quantitative, improvement in the handling of public affairs.

In the field of books there are a hundred and one new experiments in cheap publication and quite remarkable developments in the attendant fields of visual illustration and presentation. Even the school books are becoming exciting and the range of their inquiry extending enormously. In the press services a new generation of international observers is coming along, matured in the complex deliberations which inevitably attend the complex relationships between peoples. The mass magazines are reaching out from the trivial into considered commentary on matters of public importance. As significant as anything of the general stir is the debate of great moment which is now ranging across the nations on the principles determining the freedom and the responsibility of the press. In radio the F.C.C. insists on higher standards of public service and one is not unaware of the general influence in the educational departments of the networks. N.B.C.'s strong support for the establishment of a U.N. world network in which an objective news coverage of international discussion will be made available everywhere, represents a maturer sense of responsibility and statesmanship.

The film, of all the media, has in the past concentrated most on entertainment and least on these deliberate processes of enlightenment with which we are now so progressively concerned. It had, it thought, no pressing reason to do so. It was from the first a simple and easy way to spread the popular drama and the romantic story to the small towns of the nations and this it has done with such enormous success that there has never been any pressing commercial incentive to reach out to larger considerations. Yet in spite of this, and for twenty years, there has been an increasing drive, both inside and outside Hollywood and the other studio centres of the world, to make the film a vehicle for ideas and a more deliberate instrument of the public service. Achievements have been scrappy to say the least, but they do include a considerable measure of experiment on the popular level by men like Warner, Wanger and Zanuck.

There is at this time an interesting debate going on, led by Louis de Rochemont of the *March of Time*, in which the influence of American films abroad has been brought seriously under review; and it is significant of a perturbation, if not of a new critical spirit, which is affecting in varying degree every level of film production and film organization, national and international. 'I wish to report', Mr. de Rochemont says, 'that the French, for instance, think that we Americans are somewhat off our rocker. Their impressions of the American Army remain those of force, effectiveness and swift purpose. They cannot understand how such military power grew out of the civilization which Hollywood depicts for them, a civilization in which the chief values are luxury, ostentation, opulence and frivolity, and in which constructive action and concern for the rest of the world and its problems have no place. To them it all adds up to complete irresponsibility. We are giving Europe an eyeful, to be sure, but an eyeful of what?

'In Europe the American way of life is under attack, and the attack goes to the very roots of our American existence. The extreme Left calls us imperialist and without conscience. Moderates fear we are unstable, easily swayed and planless. The renascent Fascists are convinced we will eventually be a soft touch. American films, our last best point of contact, lend themselves handily to the confirmation of these suggestions. . . . The European public is hungry for American films, and any reasonably good film can add millions of francs to its distributor's blocked balances. But beyond the European's willingness to convert his vanishing currency into an hour or two in the house of illusion there is something more profound. Europe is asking us for spiritual and emotional bread, and we are giving it a glittering cascade of rhinestones.'

This criticism, severe as it may sound, is matched by much that is being said in the Screen Writers' Guild, by the film critics both here and abroad, and by those who in the highest quarters are striving to develop those non-theatrical uses of the film which have been so largely ignored till now. It is true that Hollywood insists on staying close to the mass public in its fancies and its foibles, and I am one who agrees with this insistence, and for the good reason that the *realpolitik* of the human spirit demands it. Now, as at all times, one must go where the people are, and whatever creative work we seek to do must be done, not in superiority over them, but in co-operation with this our larger self. It would be not only a poor future but a fascist one, which did not take the people along with it. Apart from that, the film industry is becoming conscious, as never before, of the experimental films which are breaking through the meretricious formula of the studios. The greatest success of *Open City*, a film on the Italian resistance, has been in the professional circles of the industry, and nowhere are the realistic qualities of the British film style so much noted. I do not consider *Henry V* greatly contributive to the problem with which we are concerned, but it is at least remarkable that its special standards of quality have drawn from the salesmen an effort of distribution which has never been known before for a film of this kind.

Best signs of all are the plans of the major companies to develop the use of the film in education and create side systems of distribution outside the theatres. They have been a long time in coming to their decision, but I think it certain that they will progressively conceive of the medium as a medium capable of many other uses than the simple uses of amusement: as a medium, in fact, which will join with the schools and universities, the youth organizations and the churches, the women's organizations, the business clubs and workers' groups in a considered effort to support community leadership.

Some sign of the new attitude comes from the Eric Johnston office, which is already pledged to an experimental programme of films for schools and promises that this is only a beginning. The Independent Producers' Association under Donald Nelson has moved similarly to ally the facilities of the industry with the requirements of the teacher. All the films of general interest in education previously gathered in the Bell and Howell library were significantly bought up recently by one of the Hollywood majors as a basis for the thoroughgoing nationwide service of films of specialized interest. In fact, in spite of the industry's everlasting and weary defence of its old traditional position, there are happenings within it which contradict its complacent assertions. The cynics may hold that it realizes that a new market is opening up and that it is merely reacting to a new opportunity for profit. A simpler explanation is that the people of the motion picture industry, like every other section of the population, are becoming progressively concerned with the march of events and that the younger generation which came through the war is reaching out beyond the elders to wider worlds of public responsibility.

There is another factor of even greater importance. In film as in all the other media—of press, of radio, of education itself—it is not just the medium which decides what it will do. Governments everywhere are too deeply concerned in the state of opinion within their borders to avoid active consideration of the instruments which affect the minds of their people. Even if Hollywood would like to, it cannot avoid close examination as it crosses the borders of every state outside America. And even inside America, the forces of public opinion and of public demand are everywhere learning to require new services and new standards of performance. While Hollywood has been sticking to its formula of entertainment, a host of others have been exploring the documentary uses of the film to further the interests of agriculture and industry, to promote public health and child welfare, and perform a hundred and one educational duties which cannot be gainsaid by any force whatsoever in progressive communities.

This development which has been most scientifically matured in Britain has been responsible for the creation of very large audiences outside the theatres: in schools and universities and in the clubrooms of the various specialized interest groups. In Britain it is a common observation that there is more seating capacity outside the theatres than there is inside the theatres, and when people think of non-theatrical distribution they think of the specialized interests and activities of people in their local communities. As a result, the Film Service of the British Government plays to an audience of some 27,000,000 people composed of thousands of little groups, gathered together in the ordinary service of their communities and their professions. In Canada, the Government Film Service, operating on a similar approach, plays to an audience of over 12,000,000. This is the measure of the new development which is now emerging in the film industry of America. The potential here is an audience of something like 250,000,000 people a year. It will not be an audience mobilized by the film industry as such, but an audience mobilized by the educational community organizations themselves : and if these organizations show even a modicum of intelligence in regard to this development, they will be in a position to direct the whole force and character of the film services which are developed.

What now appears likely is the creation in every community of community visual councils, centred possibly in the public libraries. As I see it, the universities, schools, churches, youth organizations, business and service clubs, trade unions, women's groups and professional associations would be represented on these councils, and each council would maintain an information service by which all documentary and educational films, and from all over the world, which are of pertinent interest to any one of the contributing groups, would be described and routed to it. I imagine these visual councils of the communities as having, in turn, a National Council, through which producers would be told what films were most required. This pattern of development is already apparent in Britain and Canada, is under examination in other countries, and becomes more likely everywhere, as the United Nations reaches out for national and community instruments through which its overall international service can effectively operate.

I would be the last to say peace it's wonderful, but every medium, I suggest, is going through, as the film medium is going through, an important phase of self-examination and reconstruction. The fierce words of negative criticism are valuable but they are also deceptive. Whatever the noise of protest on the inadequacies of the past, all media are showing signs of extending their services on a dramatic scale : improving the spread of their communications, widening their coverage to the ends of the earth, and invading new fields of responsible public service. No one can say that the advances are adequate enough for the task in hand, and the best service that any critic can do is to hold all the media of understanding to still higher standards of achievement, but no one who has the duty of illumination upon him need lack in prospect.

1 Documentary: The Bright Example

A good deal of gloom surrounds the British documentary operation in this summer of 1947. I think the situation is urgent and warrants an immediate official inquiry if a great national asset is to be saved from damage, and most important needs of the state in the field of information are to be imaginatively fulfilled. But first let us see the problem in proportion.

The documentary film development in Britain is still the one bright example to a great many countries of how the film can be mobilized in the public service to give image and perspective to the national and international scene. Canada demonstrates possibly a more orderly use of the film but not yet a more extensive or more penetrating one. In the *A.C.T. Journal*, there is a register of thirty to forty companies which, in one way or another, are concerned with films of reportage, or instructional, or documentary qualities. This scale of the British operation is important because it means that the demand for production, of whatever sort, has been established.

Looking from the outside, I think also that we miss the point if we do not realize how deeply and uniquely bedded in the public service the British documentary film has become. I hear grumbles about the cold hand of bureaucracy, but show me please anything elsewhere like the acceptance of the documentary film's uses by all the branches of government. This represents a great step ahead, whatever the problems of growth, or of order in growth, or of quality in growth may appear to be.

The complaint takes various forms. Something—the best ones say—is going out of documentary, and in fact why are they so dull and why did we not make such a show at Brussels as we once did with *Song of Ceylon* and sundry other minor masterworks of the moment? Far too many units, it appears, are going into instructional work in plain avoidance of the difficulty of revealing in dramatic or poetic or other creative form the stubborn social material of the day.

The films are slack for lack of fire, and so are the boys who make them, runs the criticism. There are shocking stories of people of talent

187

doing nothing for a year and losing their competence. Production procedure lacks the tempo which is essential for creative work and there are endless dying delays as between the film-makers, the sponsors and the people of the Treasury. Committee production, I am told, has raised its ugly head to the point where films are killed in the script by bureaucratic indecision.

It is said that the economies and administrations of the units are not always as orderly as they might be, and that many of their efforts could be better co-ordinated. It is doubted in some quarters whether production by thirty to forty units with separate overheads and sometimes insufficient resources can represent an efficient system. One comment is made that pettifogging independences are turning the documentary business into a small shopkeeper's business and that failure to concentrate ideas and energies and plan their more intensive development is not in keeping with the times.

There is criticism on both sides. The units charge the sponsors, and particularly the Government sponsors, with a lack of decisiveness and a lack of imagination. They say they have lost the conception of a total driving plan for the use of the documentary film in the urgent service of the nation. The sponsors, on the other hand, say that the film-makers are too independent by half and cannot be relied on to deliver efficiently or even to deliver what they have undertaken to deliver, and finally that the boys are so full of small politics these days that nary a one of them has time to throw his cap over a steeple.

It is all a little like quarrelling with your wife, except that there are some sponsors and producers I know who should make honest women of each other, and vice versa.

That is the sort of criticism I hear. If I am to believe it, the great art of sponsorship which Tallents and Leslie and Jack Beddington and Wolcough have represented in the past is now progressively usurped by the little people playing for departmental exactitudes and personal safeties; and that we, on the other hand, have only created a regiment of directors capable of making competent pictures which, for all their technical adequacy, are dead in the eyes. I doubt if the problem is quite so simple. My notion is that it is a deeper one than people, be they sponsors or film-makers, and goes to the heart of the historical moment. If so, it is not to be solved by disappointment, or complaint, and certainly not by flurried excursions into denunciations one of another.

The documentary film was conceived and developed as an instrument of public use. It was conceived, moreover, as an instrument to be used systematically in all the fields of public instruction and enlightenment. It is true that we hoped that individual artists would have every opportunity within the framework of the public service; but the other half of our socialized or public conception of art was that we could only secure this larger hope by tying our effort to the organized forces of social growth under whatever form they came. No one ever said that the said forces would automatically love us for our blue eyes. Some of us have even insisted that the developing process was bound in its nature to be positively difficult, and this has always been the catch in our continuing argument.

The organized forces of social growth, be they the Departments of State, or the great corporations, or the trade unions, or Rank, or even the Boy Scouts and the Y.M.C.A., are not necessarily tutored in the arts nor even sensitive to what the arts might do to increase the national life. I myself have served many Ministers, yet some of the best of them were æsthetic yokels. I have lived most of my life among bureaucrats only to wonder why, in the name of planned economies and the increase of human welfare, so many of the unelect should come to inherit the earth. But this itself is the very condition of the planned economies which are of necessity being imposed upon us.

Inevitably, there has been a great and swift expansion of the public services, and with every expansion goes the need for systems of budget control, personnel control and all the other paraphernalia of large-scale administration. Inevitably, too, new bands of specialists arise, not all of whom have a classical education, nor even any width of education. It is to these new hosts, and they come often in uncomfortable form, that the artist working in the public service must expose himself today, and it is with these hosts that he must enter into understanding and collaboration.

The new patronage of the arts has to be worked for. Because, like all other socialized forms, it has to be built out of the new and rising social forces of our time, it cannot come either by miracle or in the simple innocence of expectation. There are still, it seems, remainders in the artist's mind of the days when he was the king's or the queen's player and a stroller generally, and waited for his betters to take notice of him. This has obviously no part in the democratic or socialized times in which the artist now operates.

We in the film world are in a specially difficult position, for we work in an expensive medium and make a larger claim than most on the public economy when we seek the freedom of art. It is, therefore, more important to us than to others that the socialized patronage of the arts should be successful. We cannot, even if we would, turn away from it for, by the nature of our work, if it is conceived on any large and commanding scale, there is nowhere else to turn.

I agree when people say that, without imaginative support from the sponsors, imaginative films are impossible. I even sympathize a little when people talk of throwing up the government relationship altogether and re-discovering their freedom. But I still conclude that it is a suicidal attitude and not realistic, either socially or æsthetically. Our stuff is where the public process is and nowhere else. What we could spin out of our own little tails in a time like this would be little and not for long.

I therefore suggest that the solution does not lie outside the terms of public sponsorship but, on the other hand, lies in deliberately and patiently working to make that sponsorship an imaginative sponsorship. This is where the emphasis should now lie. Criticisms which do not recognize this task, and defections which are merely impatient, do not greatly help.

The situation calls for a new measure of mutual confidence and a new measure of leadership on both sides. As for the documentary people, I would have them count their blessings, even if they find their rations short. Where elsewhere has the documentary idea been so richly maintained even when a good deal of formless stuff which neither taught nor revealed was passed off in its good name? Where elsewhere have so many companies been maintained in such continuity of public work that they have come to expect it, no matter what administrative shapes they gave themselves?

As for the sponsors, they are fortunate at this time to have a school of film-makers at their disposition who, whatever their foibles, have made a profession of this realistic field of cinema and have remained faithful to it. With better organization, they represent an essential asset to Britain at this juncture, because there is much in these days of change on which the British public needs to clear its vision and strengthen its will for the job ahead.

Perhaps the documentary people are not at the moment so vigorous in new ideas as they might be, but who, pray, is? The new forms and the new fates were not educated for by the schools, the churches or the arts—not even by the schools, churches and arts of Whitehall—and the gap created is a spiritual one which is evident everywhere. The documentary people are part of a larger picture, and there is no great difference between the frustrations of the C.O.I. and the frustrations of the units who think they are afflicted by it. Neither are yet at the stage of seeing where the positive way of the public will lies, and who can blame them when the leaders themselves flounder in equal uncertainty?

There was recently at Cannes and Brussels a cynical and widespread comment as the films of the Western nations passed under review. The upshot of it was that if the great economic slump had not yet come, the great spiritual slump certainly had. The American vitality was considered as ever an empty vitality, but I caught the feeling that even the Henry V's and Hamlets and Nicholas Nicklebys were regarded in some critical quarters as representing no more than the genteel recollection, in anything but tranquillity, of another generation's creative strength. I would say that the so-called 'dullness of documentary' is not yet a disaster. Only its defection from the service of reality could be.

This contact with reality lies, as we know, in using the medium, with every disciplined effort possible, as intensively and imaginatively as possible, and on as wide a scale as possible, in both aiding the public enlightenment and, through the great images of creative action of which our medium is capable, firing the public will.

In this matter, the documentary people have, of necessity, to look to the brightness of their creative weapons and the methods by which they work. The situation calls for an examination of what they are doing on every level of talent to take the documentary film beyond the level of mere technical proficiency and into the world of imaginative interpretation. They cannot continue to live on the word 'documentary' itself, nor on its successful contribution to educational theory, nor on its reputation of practical achievement in the hard days of the war.

The whole idea was that we should make of this medium an instrument so sensitive to the needs of the public service that we would always be level with the problems of the time as they came along and, if possible, just a little ahead of the time. The idea was that we should so understand the problems of these sponsors of ours that we would be ahead of them in realizing their creative implications so far as the documentary film was concerned. Our freedom was to come, surely, from our demonstration that we were, in the practical issue, a necessary force for public understanding and public order, and not from any simpleton thought that, because of this and that in the way of acquired prestige, we were doing someone a favour. The condition of our freedom lay in fact in the capacity to be so expert in public issues that our need of Whitehall was matched, in normal human terms, by Whitehall's need of us.

We knew very well from the first that the day we did not command that expert sense of what was deeply required, the men of the camera were bound to return from whence they came, and that was from behind the camera, shooting to another's ideas and another's direction. I begin to suspect that this is what has begun to happen, and for the reason I state.

I do not want to push the point too far in a difficult situation, but I do not like the loss of direct and confident relationship between the artist and the government official; and I am bound to think that if something is going out of documentary, it is because something has gone from its essential underpinnings. Ground has to be made up. A notable understanding of the needs of the nation is the first condition of a positive, fresh and imaginative contribution towards their fulfilment.

The second condition may lie in recognizing the need to reorganize the documentary business, and radically, from an administrative point of view. The documentary people have lived a charmed life in some ways, though on the other hand it was also worked for. They came up before the full shock of Britain's new economic position in the world was felt, and they have disposed altogether of the largest sum given, in our time, to any band of creative workers.

They prospered because of the new Great Britain-Dominion relationship created by the Statute of Westminster. They prospered again as they, rightly enough, discovered images in the general will towards social reconstruction. Above all, they were equipped to serve most usefully, during the war, in the mobilization of the fighting front of democracy. They were politically correct; and they were politically correct because they were liberally correct. There was never a time when anyone could say of the documentary people that they took personal advantage from the work they did, or served their own comfort. I have been told a hundred times over that this was silly and that we could never hold a group together on such a basis. But the documentary people did so, and, even when my friend C. A. Lejeune speaks dividing words now, this she must allow.

Where Miss Lejeune has something, and where I must at this moment speak out, is in saying that now is not the time for complacency. I do not think the documentary people can afford the independent luxury of so many units. I do not think they can afford the present high cost of films. I do not think they can afford the present laboriousness in which a film is conceived, or the present tempo in which it is made. We cannot afford it for the simple reason that we are shooing our sponsors away.

Documentary: The Bright Example

It is not in films only that realism is wanted, but also in the manner of their making. The realism of that manner—and no matter what arguments are advanced for spiritual or æsthetic holidays with pay—is strictly related to the enormous amount of work to be done on the one hand, and, on the other, to the present situation in Britain and what the actual economic traffic will stand.

Here I had intended to bring forward the idea of the commission of inquiry, but I see with pleasure that others have already been talking along the same lines. Miss Lejeune's recent piece in which she says it would be a good idea to 'pause for a moment in the study of the "finest documentaries in the world", and consider what people are effectually doing to them', represents a sensible and helpful warning.

Short of a proper inquiry, I have myself no conclusions to offer. I simply want the documentary film in Britain to be even better in the public service than it has been before. I want the documentary group to be in the vanguard of the national effort and an example of good sense and discipline in the creation of the future. Above all, I do not want the documentary group to wait around for things to happen to it from the outside, when now, as it has always done, it can write its own brave ticket. It requires, however, a special effort; and I think now, and not later, is the time for it.

2 Progress and Prospect

It is difficult to review the progress and prospect of documentary at this time (August 1949). Yet I do not feel to blame if I have not been able to see easily where the light now leads for the situation economic, affects us all and the inspirational side, for reasons economic and other, is dust in the throat.

Good things there are and we had better begin with them. The new establishments of documentary are holding and developing well. The last batch from Canada—collections they call them among the *couturières*—was very good; nothing stupendous but a standard of free-line drawing, so to speak, which meant good heart; and that is very much something these days. One weakness which I shall return to: a certain reaching for the metropolitan which may yet unstick the National Film Board from its roots in the great spaces and take the country shine from its notable complexion.

Similarly in New Zealand, with its one-a-week essentially local reel, representing an outstanding national service for a small unit. Australia keeps steadily on, and considering all the political difficulties of that toe-tramping continent, the Stanley Hawes epic in personal persistence is one for the book.

South Africa, moreover, has asked for a design for government film work and this will go ahead in the fall. The Government interest there and the willingness of the present established government film interests to stand down for a wider plan of development give promise of putting South Africa in line with Canada and Australia.

India it is too early to reckon on. There is much discussion of the use of films and many people have passed through over the year to look at the shape of our work in Britain: some to stay and learn, in spite of the incompetence of our present arrangements for overseas students. But it is too early in India. All the problems are huge and not least the problems of education and national planning which affect the film medium most. It would take a brave man to write a plan for India at the present time, and Nehru, who keeps returning to the film problem when he can, is right to hold his hand until the native genius

194

in the matter has sorted itself out. I add that a government film unit is grinding itself in in Rhodesia and that first flickers of interest begin to appear in Pakistan. Indeed, so far as the Dominions are concerned, all are more or less conscious of the value of the film and all, at different speeds, are seeing to the establishment of the film as an instrument of national policy.

Most encouraging too are the signs of life in the countries overrun by the war. One gets the warmest of impressions in Germany, although there is, and properly, a good deal of reserve. Most striking is the sense of latent power there. It was evident in the unit of young men working to the British Information Office in Hamburg. They were certainly feeling their way but they were at least feeling, which is more than even the fortunate people are doing today. The camera work was outstanding in sensibility, although perhaps there was a note of Wertherism too. I remembered Dostoviesky's, 'when you are sorry for all the world, you are only sorry for yourself'. I still regret that we cut the Airlift film to a reel and did nothing much with the Refugee film. We murdered the Airlift film to get it a fast place among our one-reel theatre reports; and the Refugee film similarly did not connect with usability.

They set, as so many films do, the problem of either designing for established uses or so developing distribution that it provides organized presentation for all kinds and species. With the flow from different countries becoming ever greater and ever more various, our catch-as-catch-can system of distribution—founded some of it on amateurism and some of it in narrow purposes—appears ever more inadequate. It poses the major question perhaps in film organization today.

The other day in Paris I sat in at a show of films by the Brussels Pact Powers; and this Pact, incidentally, looks like having a film result in the next two or three years. The U.K. was represented by *Daybreak in Udi*. It went well enough. It is a good film but for sheer movie there was stuff from both France and Holland that returned the eye to the old excitement. Most interesting of all, if you please, was a Dutch picture of a Gas Works. I haven't seen better shooting for years, and that is the measure of what appears to be happening in the Western Union countries. While we are retiring from behind the camera and shooting from the deck chair or something, the directors there have got themselves excited, as in the first chapter, by the old bag of tricks itself. It is important, and not only as indicating technical fervour, but as representing too an energy of approach which undoubtedly is reflected in the freshness of the films themselves.

As for France, you never know: for, in spite of the failure of the

Government to plan and finance, and in spite of the notable chaos of its film operation as a whole, there always seems to be an individual or an individual group round the corner to take something exquisite from a pigmy or a peasant. Art spills out of the French like blood, although in what illicit adventure so unlikely a people got that kind of blood I have never been able to figure.

But, by and large, France, of all the great powers, is furthest behind in the ordered use of the film in its national process; and its exceptions, pleasant as they are for the film societies, are a false guide to the film's contribution to national momentum.

Holland is in better heart, much better, with Dr. Vroom of the Department of Education a powerful imaginative and far-seeing driving force. So too is Denmark. In both cases the idea of government planning, borrowed it may be from Britain and Canada, has taken firm hold. The Dutch governmental relation with the film industry has something to teach us all.

The British set-up in some ways is far and away the most developed, yet its present qualities in production are noticeably less spectacular than in Russia and Italy. Our films are for the most part technically adequate but not more technically adequate than the Canadians. We reach particular high points in, say, the *Cornish Engine* from Shell, *Daybreak in Udi* from Crown and *Atomic Energy* from G.B., but not more particular high points, for all our extra strength, than France and Holland. The reasons for this we had better analyse at this time, lest among the swings and roundabouts of the Edinburgh Festival the root of the matter is lost sight of.

Compared with the other countries—outside the Soviet group—Britain is certainly more strongly planned and more widely organized for documentary. In sponsored production it has approximately half a million from the C.O.I. alone, more from the Colonial Office and the Boards of Coal and Transport. Television disposes of an increasing amount of film money. So do Shell, I.C.I., B.O.A.C., the Travel Association and the odd sponsors. Adding the monies of the commercial operators, the total available for actuality and documentary must reach to a million a year.

When it comes to distribution we appear on the surface to be in a state of considerable disorder but I doubt if that is the correct analysis. It does not appear so much a state of disorder from countries overseas but rather a profusion of non-theatrical interests which require to be integrated, representing the rich initiative of a hundred and one interests. What has happened is that we have developed our non-theatrical distribution out of all sorts of motivations and purposes and have not yet taken time to work out the total strategy for the development as a whole. Thus we have the film society movement developed from local groups interested in the art of the film, and the scientific film society movement deriving from academic and professional interests as well as the general interest in scientific progress. We have the education people, the agricultural people, the health people, the local government people, the Co-ops and the political parties, etc., similarly establishing, even if sketchily, film operations to enliven their services and their causes.

The Government, because of its various interest—save the political party side—and because of its own specific interests, has developed a central library and created a regional system of travelling units. In complement, G.B. and Pathé have established production and distribution services for a large variety of films from both national and international sources. The Government, moreover, has set up not only an organization (C.O.I.) to look after the film in national information, but also two organizations (British Film Institute and Educational Foundation for Visual Aids) to look after the film in its relationship with culture and education.

No country, in other words, is better served in local and professional zeal or in government support of the pretensions of the film as an instrument of specialized purpose.

The theatre may be another matter. Certainly we do not enjoy the dictates which, with Hitler and Mussolini, made the film a national must in the Fascist theatres; but there is a quota law which, by and large, gives theatre circulation for 200 films a year. I do not think it is more despite the wishful thinking of the producers and, even then, some of the 200 do not circulate widely, in a field which has double-feature programmes and does not want much in the way of information anyway. Yet 200 represents a helpful outlet for those who can gear documentary to the necessary fast-moving shapes of the theatre programme or, otherwise, in novelty and spectacle, command its curious attention.

What then is wrong that, with so much opportunity, we do hardly as well in film itself as we expected when the field was developing? Let me take distribution first, and for the reason that distribution makes not only the life of a film but the spirit of the film-maker. It requires sorting out from the film-makers' point of view and it calls, as I say, for integration. Sorting out it needs in the sense that we must make up our minds what precise relation we have to our audience, and especially which audience we serve. At the beginning I deplored the Canadian Film Board's ever reaching for the theatre audience. It derives, I am sure, from a local need to show cause to the Treasury and bring in an extra couple of dollars. I am sure too, that the illusion rears again its ugly head that the odd spot among the theatre millions is worth more in public information than the persistent influence of the community groups that in every known way lead the opinion of the community. What disturbs me, however, is the limiting and rotting effect of a theatre distribution policy for documentary as a whole; and it was ever so from the beginning.

It is true that theatre distribution can be improved for documentary. The Government, by diktat, might, e.g. force a one-feature programme, although I think there is not much chance of this as yet. Or it might insist on one reel in every programme being devoted to national information or encouraging the national effort, although the time is hardly ripe for it. Or the mobilization of the independent theatres in a third circuit might nurture the supply of a third series of films outside Pathé-A.B.C. and the G.B.-Rank group, although this will take the time of local Wardour Street politics and it may be government diktat again. Or the theatres might be 'educated' to documentary, although this, after twenty years of it, gives no hope of sudden revelation. Or a super theatre distribution effort, say at the C.O.I., might carve its way publicity-wise through the catch-as-catch-can shorts booking methods of the trade: although why dog should eat dog and a highly financed operation should eliminate the independent units that are trying to get along, it would be difficult to defend. Or the Government might buy the best, from whatever source, and give them away to the theatres, though the theatres do not necessarily want give-aways of however high æsthetic an order. Many thoughts there are and many *a priori* possibilities, but the fact of life would appear to be that there is room in the theatres for 200 reels at most. Pathé is planned to supply a minimum of sixty-eight; G.B. what with one thing and another, thirty, and C.O.I. has a present guarantee of twelve and an inevitable presentation of thirty plus. Altogether they occupy enough of the available field to make you think. Against this consider the theatre hopes of so many independent units today.

It isn't simply that the space available is limited. We ought, I think, to make up our minds now that because of the special laws of the popular theatre and because the exhibitors do not largely share our special hopes of documentary, much of what we do and want to do has no relation whatever to theatre distribution.

Progress and Prospect

In fact, the biggest and silliest curse that has come over us is the thought that the success of documentary as an idea means any difference to its prospect in the theatre : save where the theatre laws—not the documentary ones—apply. These laws demand for the spot on the programme, which is not necessary anyway, a maximum in novelty, spectacle or journalistic urgency. Bugs Bunny is not accidentally the top theatre item in American shorts. *March of Time* does very well, with the Luce organization behind it, to stay where it does. But witness the struggle even in so large a market to make ends meet with the Disneys. The only certainty I know in Britain is an intimate study of Prince Charles. For the rest, given the costs involved and all the other circumstances, the opening is for fast journalistic types in the form of direct report or in the form of magazine specials.

But what all this has to do with documentary, except in its journalistic aspect, it would be difficult to say. The true secret lies, I am sure, with Shell's *Cornish Engine*. It is the film of the year, except for *Daybreak in Udi* which shows at least that the larger stuff of documentary is there for the finding. *Cornish Engine* is the film of the year for the good reason that it knew from the beginning what it wanted and has achieved it superbly. Somebody liked Cornish engines—probably Elton with Wolcough concurring—but realized from the beginning that the only people who could possibly share their regard were the engineers and engineering fans across the world. In setting themselves this audience they could accordingly lavish all their affection on the subject without twisting it here and sugaring it there to serve the Philistine. Even *Udi* has the curse of talking down upon it. It is so busy being simple for the ordinary—the last error of authenticity—that it misses time and again the poetic or other rich far-reaching note. The common sense of it is that the ordinary ordinarily expect the poet to be extraordinary and that we serve the ordinary with nothing less.

It is a simple proposition but I will let it stand : that the qualities will come again to our work if we will only define our projects in such a way that the affections are engaged and will be warmly supported. This means in the first place a *volte-face* from the theatres altogether to the non-theatrical audience of our original documentary persuasion. It means returning ourselves to the local bailiwicks of the film societies and other specialized audiences and serving them directly and fully without further wandering around in the fields which we neither command nor have interest—outside reportage—in commanding.

I do not know whether a post-mortem is worth while at this time because it seems to me so much error has to be undone that it would be better to have it undone than say why. To my mind there were two stages of illusion. The first one came with people like Harry Watt who wanted to reach out to what appeared to be the greener grass and larger life in the studios. With Watt it was all very well. He had a natural flair for theatre and a natural distaste, which his great father would have gorgeously approved, for the film society and the specialized audience. I can see him now reaching for the great liberal horizon of all mankind, as is his way. Very properly too, the war was his, for it gave him the perfect combination of dynamic event and serious intention and a public reaching for both.

But few enjoyed either the driving talents or the driving illusions of Watt. With Watt it was a question of storming the studio with documentary and nothing else and this he has done and will continue to do. Less must be said for his followers. The stormed citadel quietly and effectively absorbs them and God only knows what ignominy of melodrama and passable second feature awaits them.

The second stage of error in my view came in Britain with the wartime and somewhat wanton success of documentary. It was profusely financed and fanatically supported by Jack Beddington. Its success—again in a period of dynamic event and serious purpose—was superb. But one feels today that in the very urgency of the event there was no time to consider where the roots would very differently lie at the war's end; and the M.O.I. did not prepare for it. Nor did the film-makers. What was only a temporary command of the marquee was taken for granted as a sign of ultimate conquest. Read in these dimmer days the Hosannas surrounding the wartime achievement and take note. The trouble is that so many people believed it all; and off they were to the fun and the fair of the studios to take their shilling.

Even now the truth is only beginning to dawn on them: that in times of urgency, yes, documentary is a national asset which even the theatres will recognize, but in lesser times, no; it belongs to where the serious purpose is continuous; and that is where the community leadership of all kinds quietly and continuously lies. I wish the Canadian example was properly understood where, with urgency less pressing, the whole development was geared, as it could be geared, to a long term conception of documentary's relation to the national service. It will be a pity if, falsely interpreting its success, it too, but more gratuitously, falls into the error of following the wrong signpost.

As it is, we have three major fronts on which to work. Non-theatrical has to be built up with new thought and energy—a new overall strategy I suggest—so that it will justify both the cost and energies of serving it. The non-theatrical audience is in and around twenty millions a year at present. We should aim at fifty millions in the next three years. To that end we have to organize specialized audiences as never before: in terms of their functional needs as well as in terms of general cultural interest. Essentially a supply of cheap projectors—under £150 —has to be established. Regional Film Councils and Film Locals have to be organized to see that each specialized interest in the community is organized and served. Here the B.F.I. has a lead to take, but there must be such support of it from all quarters that it has the real financial wherewithal to do its work.

Production must now free itself from false leads and forget any notions it may have had that documentary is God's gift to the exhibitor except where film journalism is concerned, and that success in it is a short cut through the looking-glass to the studios and the Screen Writers' Bar. A stop there must be on this utter confusion.

Documentary's freedom and quality lie where they always did lie— in the simple process of serving where service is wanted, however modest the prizes may seem to be. It is not by accident that the camera work is less fresh and moving today, the cutting less dynamic, the sound less exploratory and inventive than they were ten years ago, nor is it by accident that the writing in general is terrible and the habit of work less satisfactory to all concerned. In the confusion of ends there is neither concentration of energy nor the happy exercise of special *fortes*. In the organization of non-theatrical distribution and the sorting out of all the many talents in regard to it there is much hope. I could only wish that A.C.T., that haggard echo of the great illusion, would see it that way. Television, so to speak, is here with us, and no voice in the wilderness or wild honey about it. If it inherits, as it surely will, the great B.B.C. tradition, at least half of what we have wanted is secure. We have had to take it the hard way, finding sponsorship in government and elsewhere when the ways of commerce failed; and we have had the advantage of giving our work a real and practical consideration. But the television way with film must by its very nature be freer of foot. Good people and good things will be allowed for, if the Third Programme is any guide, but even at that it will not allow for all. There are deeper and fresher interests still which even now make the Third Programme sanctimonious, old-fashioned, right, long after the right time and stupid with academic humbug. That other interest we must surely guard and keep for ourselves. Many specialized groups and interests there are which will be served as the

B.B.C. now in sound serves them; but again there are others which television on a general service cannot be expected to reach.

So the broad road forks out today. Some will be wise to take the path of television before the West End theatre boys get hold of it and frivol it for good. Others like myself must keep to sponsorship and not only out of the long habit of living with the hair shirts that go with it. Contact with government has its own special privilege, even creatively; not less in these days when governments begin to make definition of æsthetic. Where, however, the way of the artist lies it would be difficult to judge. It will be a hard way either way.

All I know is that a daffy civil servant—like Sir Stephen Tallents—is the nearest thing to the Medici the free artist is likely to find in these difficult times, and I am glad beyond words that he has been invited to open the Edinburgh Festival. It is the opportunity for the free artist that needs most to be emphasized today, when reorganization of so drastic an order has necessarily to occupy our minds so much.

3   Documentary: A World Perspective

Because of Britain's unique contribution to the development of the documentary film in the thirties, there is still a tendency in England to judge the documentary film today by the British example. That would be wrong. Documentary films of one kind or another are being produced all over the world. The total world production may be in the region of fifty thousand films a year or more. Britain produces two or three hundred only. Think of all the different categories of documentary production, e.g. public reporting, scientific films, technical films, instructional films, etc. Think of all the governments and government departments which in various countries have their own film programmes of public information and education. Remember all the hundreds of state and civic authorities, industries, laboratories, colleges, hospitals which make films for their own special purposes. The largest producers are bound to be those most concerned with intensive technical education (e.g. Russia and the U.S.A., possibly China). The most organized production countries are bound to be those with national planning systems for both education and uplift. I do not know the figures for Russia and cannot get at them. Poland, Czechoslovakia, Yugoslavia, East Germany and Hungary have each an annual production of some hundreds.

The original British documentary school made much of 'poetic' documentary and 'humanist' documentary. This type of film is very much in a minority today in contrast to the flood of documentary films in the above mentioned more practical categories. By and large the most distinguished documentary films æsthetically are to be found in Poland, Czechoslovakia, Canada, Germany, Holland, Italy, France and the United States. There are occasional good ones from odd countries like Brazil (Santos) and Bolivia (Jorge Ruiz). Australia is always on the edge of good documentary in this æsthetic category. The British contribution is not as relatively important as it once was.

There were two reasons for Britain's original importance in the documentary field.

One. It was the first country to use the documentary film in an organized way to implement governmental and public purposes (E.M.B., G.P.O., health, slum clearance, town planning, popularization of scientific discovery, Commonwealth relations, international communications, colonial education, etc.). No one should think now that because of its success this was an easy and smooth development. The Treasury was always against the idea of the government participating directly in film production. In fact it got out of it after the war but not before presenting an example to the world of government sponsorship and, by its own example and teaching, encouraging the creating of good independent production units outside the government service. British documentary's most interesting period was in its early stages when individual ministers were directly and personally interested in the documentary film (Kingsley Wood, Walter Elliot, etc.). Its most powerful period was during the war when the Treasury guards were down (Crown Film Unit).

Two. The early British approach to documentary was from the beginning both complex and ambitious. The film-makers sought finance in the name of public information, public relations, technical instruction, etc., but at the same time sought to develop the æsthetic forms of the documentary film within the framework of public information. The first film in that category was *Drifters*. Other good examples were *Song of Ceylon*, *Night Mail* and *North Sea*. Others had made documentary films before the British school developed (Flaherty, Ruttmann, etc.). The unique British message to film-makers was that good documentary in its æsthetic forms could be achieved within the limits set by public information and with some prospect of a share in the vast financial support which public information offers. It was this possibility proved practical which lit up the film-makers across the world. In an important way the British documentary idea discovered for film-makers everywhere the prospect of making a living at it.

The official acceptance of the relationship between public information and the film-makers was, of course, limited in England. It depended very largely on personal persuasion at the higher levels (ministers and senior civil servants, i.e. people like Walter Elliot and Sir Stephen Tallents). The constant critical influence of *The Times* had also great effect. The writings of the documentary people (Paul Rotha and myself mostly) piled up and so enlarged documentary's public authority. It is notable that in other countries it has been relatively easy, following the British example, to secure government support for straightforward reportorial and instructional films and for straightforward propaganda documentary. But documentary as an art form has emerged in the public information field only where the same forces as in England operated, i.e. personal persuasion at the highest levels and the support of important newspapers and good critical writing generally. The best example overseas is Canada where the Prime Minister, Mackenzie King, gave me his personal backing and almost a blank cheque in support. Other examples today of government sponsorship at a high level are to be found in Poland, Czechoslovakia, Yugoslavia and Holland. The power to deliver has, of course, also to be taken into account. In every successful case there were the artists present to deliver on the æsthetic promise and within the framework of public information purposes.

The wartime achievement of the Crown Film Unit is not a true guide to the general line of development. The conditions then were favourable to effort of any dramatic order and, as I have noted, the Treasury guard was down. In the thirties we could only with care and persistent effort get over it. Around 1934 and 1935 there was a logical attempt to expand the range of documentary from communications (G.P.O.) to health, housing and labour relations—in fact an attempt to bring in the Ministries of Health and Labour. It failed. The effect was to drive us to such other sponsorship as would allow us the same relationship between public information purposes and documentary in its various forms—with informational forms as the mainstream, æsthetic forms if possible. It was for this development that Film Centre was set up and independent production units, based on the principles of the original documentary group, established (e.g. Realist, International Realist, Strand, Basic and Data). This was spectacularly successful. The Shell organization welcomed the idea and started on a documentary film career which has been as influential as any anywhere. The Gas Light and Coke Company for years did first-rate work in health and housing. The Films of Scotland was set up to organize independent sponsorship in Scotland and operates to this day. The example of these earlier leaders in the field has been followed by other industrial sponsors—B.O.A.C., I.C.I., The British Transport Commission, etc. But only in the case of British Transport has there been the same drive towards æsthetic result.

This acceptance by industrial sponsors of the British government's example involved an important development of their normal ideas in publicity and propaganda. It meant: (*a*) The acceptance of the idea of the long-term persuasive power of æsthetic forms as distinguished from the shorter-term effect of mere publicity and propaganda; (*b*) A study by industries of the wider implications of their public responsibilities and public image. This acceptance has had in time a considerable influence on both government and industrial film-making in the United States largely through the American film-makers who learnt directly or indirectly from our teaching and example. In Canada the industrial and other non-governmental sponsors had the present example of the work of the National Film Board to follow which, of course, was of our own founding. Here again the government film-makers became the leaders of a more imaginative sponsorship in the non-government world.

I don't think there is any question that British documentary's principal claim to importance in the history of the cinema is in what it taught about the wider and more organized uses of the film in the public service, and about the more various and deeper aspects, the documentary film might take in the public service. In these matters it went far ahead of anything before it and in fact was something different in kind. There is, of course, nothing comparable to the organization of the so-called documentary 'movement' in Britain and the missionary zeal with which it set out first to expand its range in Britain and then explain its doctrine to countries outside Britain.

The once so-called British Documentary School may not be important in Britain today nor are British documentary films as distinguished or distinguishable as they once were at the international festivals. But, I repeat, the limitation today means only that the British Documentary School did not stay at home but, because of its nature, spread abroad and particularly to those countries where the need for it was most deeply rooted (in young countries like Canada and in the under-privileged countries which like Malaya, Ghana, Egypt, Iran, Iraq, Venezuela and India, had much to do in building the future—and in those countries like Poland where the central planning and direction of the educational forces were most intensive). The real continuity of the original documentary idea lies in fact elsewhere and logically so.

Here are the influences which propagated the British documentary idea overseas.

One. The overseas film distribution service of the Foreign Office, Dominions Office and, at various times, of other government agencies —largely inspired by the early documentary movement—did much to show the British documentary example across the world.

Two. The critical attention given to British documentary films in Britain influenced critical attention elsewhere. Here the attachment of *The Times* to the documentary development was important. So were the critical notices of specialized film journals, e.g. *Cinema Quarterly*, *World Film News*, *Sight and Sound* and *Documentary Newsletter*. Our own documentary writings had world-wide circulation and translation, particularly those of Rotha and myself. To this add the influence in international film meetings of the British Film Institute and the Scientific Film Association.

Three. The Imperial Relations Trust had a lot to do originally with the setting up of the National Film Board in Canada, Australia and New Zealand and in turn the example of the National Film Board of Canada had a most powerful influence in setting up similar organizations to meet national needs in many countries. This participation of the Imperial Relations Trust (Lady Reading and Sir Stephen Tallents had a lot to do with it) which is almost totally forgotten today, is quite a fascinating incidental chapter in the total story. I personally owed it much for its co-operation at an important juncture in documentary development.

Four. The establishment of film units in the colonies by the Colonial Office, particularly in Malaya and Ghana and the sending of documentary teachers to India and the creation of non-theatrical distribution systems in many of the colonies should be taken into account for the examples they provided to other under-privileged countries.

Five. The world abroad of Film Centre working with Shell has been very important. Sir Arthur Elton was chiefly responsible. It involved the setting up of units and the training of native documentary groups in Iran, Iraq, Egypt, India, Singapore, Nigeria and Venezuela. It is a fascinating story of modern missionary work undertaken in the name of industrial public relations.

Certain incidental factors contributed to this development apart from the original international potential of the documentary idea itself. The first flush of documentary in Britain was sustained by such practical realities as the drive to a new conception of Commonwealth relations after the Statute of Westminster, the swift growth of modern international communications, the growth of international interdependence on scientific levels and of course by the wave of social reconstruction in Britain which in the thirties affected government policies no matter what party was in power.

Driving forces of this kind have either diminished or have not been mobilized as they once were for documentary purposes. Perhaps there has been a diminishing of the creative will. Certainly there has not been the same sense of relationship with government and other sponsors on high levels of public policy. Certainly there has not been the same wish on the part of new documentary film men to be part and parcel of the larger public purpose.

Note that the government after the intensity of the propaganda drive during the war most deliberately demobilized its propaganda forces. Government sponsorship passed to the bureaucratic committees of the various ministries working through the bureaucratic controls of the C.O.I. So far as documentary films are concerned there has been no first-rate imaginative approach to government sponsorship since the war. Oddly enough it was the Labour Party which carried out the demobilization. I think only one Labour minister really realized what was creatively involved. That was Sir Stafford Cripps.

This has not been the total disaster it might seem. It is true that the documentary films produced on the old sponsorship basis do not make the same impact today on the international scene and are outshone by films of many other countries, except in the case of the scientific films of the Shell Film Unit. On the other hand, much of what was best in the documentary movement has been taken over by the B.B.C. To get a fair picture of British documentary on its wider fronts you must take into account not only the international development noted above but the national development in the television field.

It is clear that in the straight reporting field and in the editorial field inherited from *March of Time* and *World in Action*, work is being done in British documentary television as good as any in any other country. On the reportorial level consider the excellence of the coverage on the Coronation, the crowning of Pope John, the Rome Olympics, the wedding of Princess Margaret, the return of Gagarin and the Moscow May Day Parade. On the editorial level consider the impact of the B.B.C. reporting of the Electrical Trade Union story. Remember the first-rate stuff on the American presidential elections and Anthony Lotbinière's 'The Candidate'. In other categories of documentary take into account 'The Magistrate's Court' (Ross-Atkins); 'Unmarried Mothers' and 'Prostitution' (Morris-Calder); Dennis Mitchell's 'Morning in the Streets', 'Night in the City', 'Strangeways Gaol', 'Chicago' and the trilogy from Africa. There is John Schlesinger with his 'Innocent Eye', Benjamin Britten and 'The Class'; Kenneth Russell's 'Prokofiev' and 'House in Bayswater'; Cawston's 'On Call to a Nation' and 'The Lawyers'. There is John Ormond at the B.B.C. in Wales with 'Borrowed Pasture' and 'Once There was a Time'. You would certainly have to include Philip Donellan's work in 'Joe the Chainsmith' and Robert Barr's in 'Medico' and find a special spot for many excellent documentary vignettes in 'Monitor', 'Panorama' and 'Tonight'.

Documentary in television makes, you see, quite a story. There are some first-rate documentary people at the B.B.C. on any level of criticism and don't forget the people behind the scenes like the editor behind 'Monitor' (Allen Tyrer) and that powerful woman on many fronts of production, Grace Wyndham Goldie.

You have still more to take account of in ITV with Granada's Report on the Pill and Homosexuality and A.R.'s 'Two Faces of Japan' and 'The Quiet War' by Peter Morley and 'Main Street, America' by James Breedon.

Here a note in parenthesis about the group which called itself Free Cinema. It is easy to dismiss it but in my point of view it will turn up again and in more powerful form. It was an attempt to fill the gap left by the after-war failure of government sponsorship but in fact it found no alternative source of finance for ambitious documentary films and perished like the French *avant garde* in the late twenties and for the same reasons. Its origins were mixed. It was partly influenced by the neo-realist movement in Italy and by the *Nouvelle Vague* in France. It reflected—oddly in Britain—something of the spiritual pessimism of a defeated France. It was conscious too of the neo-anarchism of the beatnik movement in America. In so far as it was English it was close to the lower middle-class protest against upper-class privilege of the so-called Angry Young Men. In so far as it adopted a working-class motif its affection was a little like the Jewish affection for the Negro cause in the United States. What was best in it, and most native, turned up in the theatre with two or three very considerable talents—John Osborne, Arnold Wesker, etc.—to give it reality and with an economic root that proved a practical one. I haven't a doubt that you will hear of it again as the group's success in the theatre emerges as a phenomenon of the commercial cinema.

In fact the story of the British documentary film is only weak if you look at its continuity under British government sponsorship which is pretty awful these days and under industrial sponsorship which is no longer as inspired as it was. This latter may be partly the fault of the film-makers who may have gone too commercial or just plain complacent.

Look at the British documentary overseas, look at it under B.B.C. television auspices, look at it as it is coming up via neo-realism in the theatre and you may have a very different picture.

4 Learning from Television

What had I learned in five years of television? Quite a bit I thought. Now I am not so sure. Reckoning it up, much of television is derivative, not to say parasitic, which is Sinatra's word. There is nothing necessarily wrong in the derivative. It is good, for example, that more people should see plays. What's wrong in being derivative is when you debase the original tradition. The great tradition of the theatre is not greatly served. The tradition of the cinema is quite shabbily served, except in the case of the newsreels, the sports reports and the actualities generally, which are done better. Yet even news and political and public commentary are more thoroughly done elsewhere. As for television as parasite, it is a continuously uncomfortable and ugly thing: invading privacy on what the victim, poor devil, has thought a privileged occasion, exploiting personal emotions and human weaknesses as nastily as the dirtiest of sideshows; the B.B.C. with even more unforgettable and unforgivable instances than its commercial competitor.

But then again there is much to put in the balance. I think immediately of the horses and the fights and Real Madrid and Cliff Michelmore: Michelmore and his like a phenomenon one only glimpsed at the *Deux Ânes* and the *Dix Heures* and patently one of the unique gifts of the new medium itself. I think too of the unexpectedness that goes with television. You never know what is going to turn up: something you never thought to see, or even thought seeable: someone precious you never thought to meet. Nor may one deny to television that with all its faults and failures, superficialities and vulgarities, it is widening the horizons of observation and of consideration, on a vast scale, and making people just a little more fit to be citizens of a modern society.

For the present I confine myself mainly to two points that interest me personally. The first is the visual tradition deriving from the cinema and what is now happening to it in television. The second is the nature of the television relationship with people. I carefully don't say the 'public' because I have a notion that television has other and more

210

intimate relationships than the word 'public' denotes. I will take the two points separately.

A recent article in the London *Times* made the announcement that 'pure cinema is dead'. 'There it is,' the article repeated, 'pure cinema has perished,' but pure radio, i.e. sound radio, has not. It was a thoughtful article, devoted to the proposition that television, like the talkies, is a bastard form so far as visuals are concerned, but that steam radio is a purer medium altogether, with 'therapeutic and restorative' powers to which television cannot aspire.

It is this notion that the cinema has been killed off along the way by the talkies and television, which fascinates as a point for argument. I won't take advantage of the fact that there never was a purely visual or silent cinema, for there was always attendant noise of some kind or another. Indeed the more the silent cinema came to take itself seriously the more seriously its exponents took their musical scores. Round they went to the theatres and, in many cases, it was a matter of compulsion to play them. What matters, however, is that we consider a little more carefully what really happened to this visual art of ours with the coming of synchronized sound, and what is happening to it now with television. It has been enormously affected, but is there something *sui generis* and precious which has actually and inevitably perished?

There has been from the beginning something special and, if you like, *sui generis*, in what the motion picture could do. The old simple arguments are still valid, e.g. the camera can get around and so provide new vistas of things observed. Not the least of these new vistas was in the comedy that got out and about and into the streets with Mack Sennett. Add the various kinds of lenses and there are other worlds again open to the cinema. Speed the action and slow it and you not only add to your possible effects, dramatic or other, but the range of human observation is extended still further. Develop the idea of the 'Kino-eye', consider the infinite possibilities of varying the viewpoint of the camera, develop the possibilities of the 'montage' and you finish up with an array of powers, all native to the cinema, capable of bringing it to the point of æsthetic measurement. These were the elementary principles on which we all in the early days operated. They are probably so obvious to everyone today that they have been lost sight of, by being taken for granted like Chesterton's postman. It may be that what was once exciting because it was a new kind of observation is so much part and parcel of our common observation in television that many no longer recognize it as cinema, not to say pure cinema.

211

International

Certainly there have been developments in the cinema which have affected movie as movie for better or for worse. For example, one influence of television on the film business has been to drive it to very large-scale films and diminish the production of 'B' films and 'C' films. Here is an observation on that by Norman Holland in the *Hudson Review*. 'Hollywood unfortunately has come to prefer the impure or un-film: the meticulous redaction of Broadway plays and best-selling novels. To some extent, of course, Hollywood has always drawn on the novel and often with consummate success (*Sierra Madre*, *No Down Payment*, and so on). But within the last four or five years, this kind of safe-A film has almost blotted out the B's and C's and X's that worked from less successful (therefore, less fulfilled and exhausted) novels and treated them more cinematically. It used to be idle—or scholarly—to compare films to the novels from which they were taken; now, one can scarcely avoid it. The index to the change is the difference between Stanley Kubrick's *The Killing* (1956) or *Paths of Glory* (1957) and his *Lolita* (1962). The earlier films were real films; *Lolita* is in the current style of the un-film.'

This would seem to make a point in our correspondent's favour but we have *The Times* in yet another moment of judgment noting with admiration—presumably cinematic admiration—the work of Bunuel, Bresson, Antonioni, Bergman, Godard, Truffaut and Fellini, with an accolade for Hitchcock that could only possibly go to his devotion to cinematic technique. And *The Times* might well have noted at the same time the work of the Polish, Czechoslovakian and Japanese film schools. On this balance it would seem the battle for movie as movie is taking a long time to get lost.

One thing must certainly have made our correspondent gloomy. It is the ponderous record—in the dramatic story field—of television with its cameras. It is, to say the least, a simple record and even at times a simpleton record. One reason, they say, is that the cheapness of television's methods—the sometimes appalling and appallingly un-necessary cheapness of television methods—drives it inevitably to what we can only in visual terms describe as amateur theatricals. But there are other factors involved. The medium itself is in some ways pre-disposed, and properly predisposed, to the amateur. Then again there is in England a far-reaching suburban preference for the uncomplicated in art; and this æsthetic laziness reaches even to the highest quarters of criticism: as when T. S. Eliot is preferred to O'Neill on one of the greatest theatrical occasions of our time; as when the Royal Academy declares itself on Picasso. Indeed the amateur and/or suburban is so much less challenged than it is say in France or America that many might claim that the predisposition to it is, in its shabby, proud sort of way, a national or Anglican characteristic.

This, of course, affects in the first place the choice of theme and subject matter and to that extent makes many people like myself restive in the presence of television programmes and of the dramatic programmes in particular. I simply do not share their sense of importance. On the other hand the picture is not altogether dark. There is an obvious challenge coming up from below in the choice of subject matter which, even if it is not critically articulate as yet, is making a rough impact of the suburban complacencies. One notes cheerfully the presence of 'foreigners' like Sydney Newman in our midst and the growing strength of talent with a more continental sense of dramatic value.

The same relative optimism does not however apply to the visual presentation in television. If there is one generalization one may make with something like certitude it is that in certain categories of production television is just not good-looking enough and, after any considered experience of the cinema, uncomfortable to look at. In fact our wonderful peripatetic cameras are not getting around any more, at least not enough. The special powers of expression resident in the multiple possibilities of the camera and the multiple possibilities of recorded sound (just as important and just as native to the cinema) are largely ignored. You might think sometimes that we have hardly gone a step forward from the days of *The Co-optimists* and *Rookery Nook*. That was over thirty years ago.

Yet here again the picture is not all dark. Dark it is in the dramatic field and deep dark it is in the matter of visual poetry, but there have been other visual developments in television which positively delight. For one thing Newman, who is after our old persuasion, is not likely to forget the number he first thought of and there has been sign of this; and I seem to remember in the comedies things from Charlie Drake and Arthur Haynes and Benny Hill and, on occasion, from Hancock, harking back to the more joyous technical days of cinema comedy. Michael Bentine is as movie as they come and so, they tell me, was Spike Milligan in his Australian programmes.

As for the visual record of television in the matter of actualities, it is positively first rate. Television's newsreels are better than we ever had from the cinema. Its sports reporting is in a different and higher class and not just because of television's immediacy: it is better and far more knowingly shot. Its 'editorial' reportage, deriving from the

International

March of Time and *World in Action*, covers a far wider and more penetrating front than we could pretend to, though the present proponents are not, I think, as visually conscious as we were. I am sure that must come.

In general, we can say that in England today the documentary film has in television its most powerful sponsor. I think British television *as producer* has largely failed documentary in its wider and more æsthetically important aspects; on the other hand, it has to be said that television is its most appreciative and powerful presenter and exhibitor. It may be that in television today there is a relative ignorance of what these other more æsthetically important aspects are. Some of the boys down below know very well and, given a chance, show it; but how little, relatively, are they given that chance. The very success of television with its reportage and actualities today—derived, note you, from a movie tradition—has it would seem blinded television somewhat to the larger reaches. When it comes to the poetics these bright young fellows in their new high places just don't want to know and say so openly. Much as one must admire their achievements, it represents a sort of blind ignoring of other possibilities which makes one shudder. Will it last? Of course it won't, and let this be a first cheerful shot across their bows to remind them that they are under observation. The issue is for me deeply important. I just hate to think that all the good things in the poetic line of documentary are coming from foreigners: the more so in that it was from England they first learned to follow it.

Summing up so far, I get a picture of television as a very mixed bag of tricks in a pioneer situation with a strong and positive challenge to mediocrity in all aspects of reportage and a fair prospect of better things even in drama; with visual developments in television far behind reasonable expectation in every field except actualities. I discount to some extent the excuse of budgetary limitations on the ground that others, before television, have done well with their visuals and on similar short rations; and here I cite early Chicago and early Hollywood, the French *avant garde*, early British documentary, early Russian cinema and the best of the American 'B' and 'C' pictures. As they say on the motto of that Girls' School in the Parliament Hill Fields 'It's the low aim that does it', not the nature of television as such. That anyway is my view and I propose therefore in a separate note to have a look at the television medium to see where possibly it may of its nature be limiting or enlarging to the larger creative ambitions.

Television involves a vast and various service and with much of that

Learning from Television

I need not be concerned. It is altogether proper that it should provide a hundred and one diversities which may be thought to be superficial by some but are welcomed by many. As I have noted, television has a predisposition to the amateur in the sense that it provides a platform for people and for problems which we could never conceive of the theatre or the cinema accommodating. This I find excellent, for it means that we, devoted no doubt to the tittle-tattle of our own community, share the equally vital tittle-tattle of others. Without disrespect, let me cite the gardening programmes as representing that splendid category of television interest, at its best.

But even if we allow that television is correct in giving all these ordinary services to ordinary people and utterly right to see that nobody monkeys around with their blessed ordinariness, there are other fields in which television operates and must operate which of their own nature carry the implications of creative effort and public responsibility. It is at that point and only at that point that the low aim becomes important and the excuses, pointing to the 'inevitable' limitations of the medium and the 'inevitable' limitations represented by the TV audience, obnoxious. To begin with, I doubt if we know much about what the medium is greatly capable of, dramatically or in general æsthetically, for the simple reason that we have only superficially tried it out; and with first-rate creative visual artists only oddly, and in only one or two categories of effort.

Then, too, I doubt if we know very much about that so-called audience, for the equally simple reason that the television conception of audience is the most blindly derivative of all television derivatives. It comes directly from the mass approaches of the film business, not in its best aspect but in its worst. As I watch them count their heads, whether on ITV calculations or the B.B.C.'s, I find myself having the same doubts we once had in our early movie days, when we initiated the Film Societies, the specialized cinemas and the non-theatrical distribution of films. And now are added new and even more powerful doubts. I ponder the thought that heads in a movie emporium are not heads in a home, and far from it. I look at my own ratings and I am supposed to jump with joy if, as indeed has happened, the rating beats the Sunday Palladium in my own bailiwick. I don't, and for the simple reason that a programme like mine would be dead by the dyke-side if I worked on that sort of measurement. Whatever league it is in, it is just not in that one.

As for the greater visual development of the medium I am in some critical difficulty. Confining myself to the categories of drama, comedy, dramatic documentary and poetic documentary, and allowing even for the possibility of spectacle, I am bound to think the medium cannot be developed properly as a visual medium unless it uses the complete apparatus of film techniques in both image and sound : in other works, unless we put television into the business of film-making, either on celluloid or tape, when tape can be as subtly managed as celluloid. This is of course an expensive and frightening prospect if we are to take our measure from the present relatively parsimonious budgets of television. I can say—a little lamely—that the production values of the cinema were never altogether measured by expenditure. I can say with Leonardo, more or less, that you don't buy your golf or your cookery in the shop. But, however ingenious or brilliant the use of film techniques to give size and depth, expenditure is involved and on a scale not now thought practicable. This drives me however not to the thought that television cannot be less developed in practice but that television must inevitably become part and parcel of the film business and in its larger creative efforts in certain categories merely a means for the distribution of the art of the cinema. I have thought from the first that pay-as-you-go television is inevitable in our economic society ; and I am more confirmed now as I note the complacency in creative mediocrity which prevails in the categories I have cited.

Whatever laws of popular appeal television may have derived from the cinema, there is one which it may not finally avoid. It is the law of 'importance also', the law which discovered that the Western was the more powerful for being an epic, the law that even Elizabeth Taylor is the better for being also Cleopatra. If, in its present organization, television cannot provide this 'importance also', the whole history of the cinema is there to say that the vacuum will be filled.

Now to the subject which fascinates me most in television—the nature of the television audience. As I have indicated, I believe that the same visual laws must affect the creative future of television—in certain categories—as have controlled the creative cinema and force television to make the appeals represented by the Film Societies, and the specialized cinemas as well as the popular emporia. But the exciting thing about the television audience is that it is a far more various phenomenon than we ever dreamt of in the cinema world, even in our most ambitious and various approaches to non-theatrical distribution. In some ways it is as various in its interests, curiosities and tastes as the readership of the newspapers and the magazines. Television inevitably follows their obvious lead and not least because it has been able to call richly on newspaper and radio skills and, above all, has been able to meet many of these audience requirements cheaply. What has been less obvious is the thought that in certain aspects the television audience is not really an audience at all, much less a public audience.

This possibility has not been greatly grasped. You have that over-emphasis on T.A.M. ratings and the reduction of all programmes more or less to a simple quantitive measurement; and even the B.B.C., for all its great traditions, is guilty of this error, and in fact more guilty today than it was. I can realize why professional people who come in from show business are not likely to think otherwise, but I find it odd that people who come in from other quarters altogether and with other and different interests should fall so quickly for the thought that they are in the self-same way public figures with a similar public relationship. What if we are not public figures at all but strictly private ones in the television relationship? It could be an important distinction, not least because it would alter not only our expectations but also our attitudes, both in our television appearance and in our public one. I whisper the possibility that there is a point where publicity—which of course has some impact on our sponsors—may not be as useful as it would seem, and a point too where the old 'production value' is the one commodity which we least require. I add that in this other private realm of the television relationship even the letters we get may not give us a valid account of ourselves, and that the relationship with the people in the street which is inevitable may be in character far removed from the relationship very properly established by the public stars and the truly professional public performers.

I am, of course, following up on the notion that one essential, and it may be unique, aspect of the television relationship is that we are dealing with two or three people gathered together, and in the very special circumstance and atmosphere of their home. These two or three people gathered together may be thought of not only in their domestic unity but as separate individuals: their ages different, their experience different, their range of interests different, their sensibilities sure to be different; the will to see and appreciate varying accordingly. They may be one as a family or as neighbours, but it is possible to think that each is seeing and listening quite privately, as when they read a book.

New modes of address and behaviour immediately suggest themselves, quite different from the ones we ordinarily adopt in show business or face to face with a large public. You will avoid a live audience in the studio like the plague, lest you, consciously or unconsciously, catch the mood and manner of addressing a public audience. You will behave, in short, like anyone entering someone else's home and measure your address to the normal courtesies. You will not take undue liberties and you will know that a show of cocksureness or arrogance or even of superiority can be deadly. You will in fact appreciate that it is not a situation in which you ordinarily preen yourself. Some do and the very nature of the embarrassment they induce is highly significant.

When you think further of this particular television relationship, you are bound to draw a sharp distinction between the practices of education on the one hand and, on the other, the arts of persuasion and finally of inspiration. Your educator, even your so-called popularizer, will not necessarily command these arts, but of course is wonderful when he does. As often as not, for all its earnest intention, the educational approach may actually appear in this connection patronizing and intrusive: the religious one apt to be the most painful of all.

If, as I think, the approach in this unique television relationship is by persuasion and inspiration, it is worth noting that the powers involved are not as unique as many—on both sides—suppose. The world of suggestion is one in which everyone operates to some extent. We can drop a hint or take it and a nod is as good as a wink. We know how to catch on and are fast or slow on the uptake as the case may be. We not only arrive at conclusions but jump to them. We can get wise to a situation, get the message or get with it; and of course a line is not the less effective for being thrown away. Indeed we have a hundred and one expressions by which we indicate our common power to appreciate from the merest nuance or innuendo—with, I notice, soupçon coming up fast on the horizon.

It is of course the profession of the publicists and propagandists to know their way around in this magic wood, but television is revealing another kind of operator—and from the most unexpected sources—who is even more subtly at home in it; and 'home' is the *mot juste*. Where more notably than in the home does the power of suggestion operate? It is the very citadel of suggestion, the one place where you don't have to spell things out and in fact would go up the wall if people did.

A fuller realization of the possibilities of this relationship must I imagine greatly enrich the whole operation of television. In the meantime there is much to admire and many exponents of them who positively delight. If I mention Michelmore specifically, it is only to indicate the sort of personal or relatively personal relationship involved. There are others who according to one's sensibility or fancy are equally our familiars, and so much so that an actual form of affection goes with them. I do a bit of a pitch myself in the territory and therefore know with a measure of specialized understanding how good they are; and this also means that I can talk more objectively than most about the affection they command. In the nature of things people talk to me just about everywhere as I get around, not only about my own programme but even more about others. It would be impossible not to catch a sense of the relationship they enjoy and the power they either command or potentially command as the result of it.

Mind you, there are differences of degree. If I myself make my pitch quite deliberately and almost exclusively to the two or three gathered together, this derives in part from personal predilection but also, in part, from the fact that it allows me one of the most economical gambits on television and therefore one of the freest. With another economic pattern I could interpret the relationship somewhat differently as indeed others do. The argument from the two or three gathered together applies similarly, if not equally, when you think of the neighbours of a local community, the familiars in a local pub or the private interchanges in a factory. I will swear that it is on this measurement and not the more grandiose measurement which applies to really public figures that we have the secret of our most warmly regarded television personalities.

The larger implication? That here, in the relatively intimate and devoted neighbourhood audience, much multiplied, is a fundamentally new factor in mass communication, to be prized, to be understood for what it is, for what it means and might mean. We may not be in the big big world of art, but we are certainly in the big big world of persuasion.

What have I myself learned from television? I have learned that in this league the law of Tao operates with deadly accuracy. 'He who stands on tiptoe does not stand firm; he who strains his stride does not walk well; and he who reveals himself is not luminous.' I have learned, and to my constant surprise, that we don't know very much about the powers of appreciation we confront; and that much more is possible than we ever dreamt of, in a medium which is God's gift to the operator who commands its relatively private relationships. I shall say also that it is a realm in which, as in sport, you recognize immediately and as of Providence the 'naturals'; and a realm in which you don't know much if you don't know how to admire and respect your betters. In this we are, blessedly, a world away from the catch as catch can of the show business we came from.

Postscript

I know that the dead bodies of coral insects make a South Sea island but I doubt if the dead bodies of old pieces make a book. The Scots doctrine has it that we are saved not by works 'but by grace' and, personally, I prefer books in the usual way, like locomotives with big journeys ahead of them. This is more like a night's shunting in the yards at Crewe.

I had some misgivings when my friend, Forsyth Hardy, wanted to make this selection. I never kept my stuff nor thought it important beyond the critical battles of the moment which, I am happy to say, were always plenty. It may be that I have hewn out some theory in my time, affecting the principles of education and affecting the use of the film as a vital instrument in public information. But writing, for all of us in the documentary movement, has been incidental to the business of making the word flesh. I must now, myself, have been associated in the making of maybe a thousand films or more. I have also had something to do with the machinery of their financing and distribution in different parts of the world, which is a greater labour still, considering the cross-purposes that attend the present phase of our somewhat romantic democracy.

Writing has no doubt helped us clear our heads and renew our spirits as we went along, but the most important point about the ideas on which we have speculated is that we have worked them out in practice. In fact, one must see the writing of the documentary group as somewhat strictly related to action. I have grown so weary of the distant nonsense of Laputa that I have almost come to believe it is the only kind of writing worth doing in our time.

In any case, I agreed to Forsyth Hardy's venture. I was moved that somebody should have gone to the labour of digging out my pieces from the old journals and the old files. But more conclusive was Hardy's insistence that a few people might get a better sense of what others, besides myself, have been driving at over the years. I hope they do and that Hardy's faith is in some measure justified.

It is clear that Hardy wanted this to be a serious book and myself

Postscript

a pretty serious character, and there is a way the Scots use the word 'purposive' with the accent on the second syllable, which rushes out of my diabolic infancy to frighten me everywhere I go. Among the best things for me in film have been the clowns and the comedians, the dancers, the horses, the poets and the dolls. By the witness of these pages I might never have delighted in W. C. Fields and Fred Astaire nor fallen in love for ever and a day with the great Miss West. The documentary group would not have gone very far if it had been all for public observation and reform and not started with an affection for the living quicksilver of the medium itself.

One special word should be said about the documentary movement. It has been greatly fortunate in its men and in its friends. We have held together as no independent movement in art has done in our generation: across the years and across the distances, physical and psychological, which separate nations. I could say it was the idea which held us, for it has at its core the secret of the co-operative spirit and no consciousness of boundaries to the common interest of mankind; but I have also the best reason to know how unselfish men can be.

Hardy emphasizes the long struggle to build a documentary movement and the intensity of effort it sometimes demanded. Certainly not all our decisions to open new horizons have been correctly understood or correctly supported. Certainly there were always people around, and in sometimes exaggerated estate, who, as they might say in Brooklyn, knew strictly and consistently from nothing. On the other hand, difficulties have been incidental to the fact that the British Government supported us throughout and over that long and necessary period which permitted us to mature our ideas as well as our techniques and our teams. In the light of events, that was crucial.

Some strength we may have got the hard way, by out-writing and out-speaking our opposition and, on occasion elbowing a piece of it into bankruptcy, after the gentle manner of Hammering Henry Armstrong, who was a principal inspiration of our day. But no one should forget the support we always enjoyed, and from the most unlikely sources, in both Whitehall and Parliament. Nor could we pay the debt we owe to the understanding of *The Times*, the *Manchester Guardian*, the *News Chronicle*, the *Express*, dear Lejeune's *Observer*, the *Sunday Times*, the *Yorkshire Post*, the *Spectator*, the *Glasgow Herald*, and Forsyth Hardy's own *Scotsman*; nor to the B.B.C.; nor to the trade papers, the *Cinema* and the *Kinematograph Weekly*, which, from 1929 on, were away ahead of the field in our support.

And what are you going to say when you have people about you

Postscript

like Stephen Tallents, Robert Nichols, Walter Elliot, Stafford Cripps, H. G. Wells, Charles and Lawrence Wright, Colonel Medlicott, Jack Beddington, S. C. Leslie, John Marshall, Niven McNicoll, Norman Wilson and, among the Canadians, Mackenzie King, Charles Cowan, J. W. Dafoe and George Ferguson? Each one of them has, at one point or another, made a fundamental contribution to the continuity of what, because of its continuity, is now called the documentary movement. I say: how could we have missed? I am glad indeed to have this chance to salute the people who trusted our purpose and pay them my affectionate due.

JOHN GRIERSON

1946

POSTSCRIPT TO THE NEW EDITION

In developing the documentary approach to film-making it is now obvious that we served a useful purpose and, it may be, more purposes in more places than we foresaw. A sense of purpose was certainly at the heart of the matter and, I think, still must be if the documentary film is to command wide and various public support and do justice to its æsthetic potential. While documentary's uses are today widely appreciated all over the world and even to the point of being taken for granted, the original driving force which pushed it over the years into some notable æsthetic achievements has weakened in some quarters. Indeed, any afterthought I have at this time is concerned not so much with the celebration of the world-wide success of the old campaigns, but with the failure on that one front, the æsthetic front, which has given some of us in the past our greatest satisfactions.

From the beginning it was clear, at least to me, that there was a limit to what could be expected from the commercial film industry. This, of course, was before the socialist countries had come to plan their film production in the constructive interest of their cause and community. In the West, the industry was concerned primarily, then as now, with mass entertainment, and the private profit motive, then as now, largely dictated its character and quality. A place was found, logically enough, for the 'actuality' film in newsreel and travelogue and in the format of lightweight film magazines. But there the road to realist observation stopped. There could be exceptional cases when exceptional films by exceptional men broke through to the public screens, but one was always conscious of the discomfort that went with

222

it. The observation in depth which we hopefully thought possible was not welcome because the commercial industry, then as now, had no place for it. Even my own relatively pleasant experiences with distributors could not conceal the fact that there was no true economic root for the documentary idea in that quarter.

For me the greatest single discovery in the development of documentary came with the realization that its logical sponsorship lay with governments and with other bodies conscious of their public responsibilities. The second was with the realization that there was more seating capacity outside the commercial cinemas than inside them. In the event, television demonstrated that in this matter we were all too modest. It has provided an access to the means of production and distribution which has revolutionized the prospect for the documentary film and happily so, but only in direct proportion to the sense of public responsibility which has been forced upon it.

That first economic rule still sternly applies. Nowadays, backing for the documentary film in its journalistic, informational, educational and propagandist forms has become relatively easy to arrange; but it has still for its larger result to look for sponsorship where that larger result is actually wanted. This in turn involves it, now as then, in a constant effort to ensure that it is wanted. If these early writings have any significance it is in the measure that they reflect that effort. If we got anywhere—and we did—it was because, on every level of public persuasion including the ministerial, we saw to it that the documentary idea was taken seriously.

Looking about me, I merely note that the documentary men are not now organized as they once were for the purpose of ensuring their larger creative future, and themselves ensuring it. Their patient dependence on the fortuitous goodwill of the back-room species in government departments and television authorities, I sometimes find a trifle surprising. I could never get myself to believe in fortuitous goodwill from any source whatsoever. You get what you command.

Past experience would seem to suggest that one way out of that impasse is to make a cause of it, or better still many causes: the kind of hooks you can hang big hats on. The better economic circumstances which permit so many good things on the lighter levels should fool no one. The fact is that in some countries which should know better the great things we once expected are not being made; or, when they are, they are as rare and accidental as in the primitive days.

None the less while the difference between sponsorship in the socialist countries and the private enterprise countries is profound, it can be misleading. By and large, the best documentary production on the æsthetic level is today in Poland, Czechoslovakia, Yugoslavia and Hungary which is to say that more good things get done there and as a general rule than anywhere else. On the other hand the record of the British Government was at one time excellent as the record of the Canadian Government is excellent and to this day. The industrial sponsorship of great international companies such as Shell has been, and as a general rule, inspired. However they manage it in the by guess and by God conditions which govern their sponsorship of the arts, these odd ones round the corner in France and Italy, and Holland and America continuously demonstrate the power of the individual effort. It is a power that applies in socialist countries as in others, just as complacency there can be as enervating as anywhere else.

My own prejudice is for régimes which have abandoned the by guess and by God approaches. I am for what they call in the best quarters 'the regular development of society', including the sort of contribution to it the documentary film can make, though I hold an absolute reservation in favour of the especial freedoms due to seers and artists. Obviously in one régime or another much will always depend on the powers of persuasion of individuals on the film side and on the creative goodwill of individuals among the sponsors. In the documentary development I know best good work has always derived from these special personal relationships. But in the last resort I would insist that they are better based on genuine national aspirations and such. If there is a truly creative understanding the art will look after itself. In short, we either belong to the creative mainstream of our society or we do not. If we do, it is for us to assert where and how we do belong and speak and act with a due sense of our role in the social leadership.

JOHN GRIERSON

Kinsale
12th September 1965

Appendix

The dates and original sources of the articles, reviews, and other writings and addresses of John Grierson included in this volume are listed below.

PART I: A MOVEMENT IS FOUNDED

Drifters by John Grierson: *The Clarion*, October 1929.
The Russian Example: *One Family*: *The Clarion*, August 1930; *Earth* by Dovzhenko: *The Clarion*, November 1930.
Flaherty: *Artwork*, Autumn 1931; *Cinema Quarterly*, Autumn 1932.
First Principles of Documentary: *Cinema Quarterly*, Winter 1932; *Cinema Quarterly*, Spring 1933; *Cinema Quarterly*, Spring 1934.
The E.M.B. Film Unit: *Cinema Quarterly*, Summer 1933.
Summary and Survey: 1935: *The Arts Today*, London, 1935.

PART II: DOCUMENTARY ACHIEVEMENT

The Course of Realism: *Footnotes to the Film*, Peter Davies, London, 1937.
Battle for Authenticity: *World Film News*, November 1938.

PART III: DEVELOPMENT IN CANADA

The Film at War: Broadcast from Ottawa, 30 November 1940.
Searchlight on Democracy: *Documentary News Letter*, 1939.
The Nature of Propaganda: *Documentary News Letter*, 1942.
The Documentary Idea: 1942: *Documentary News Letter*, 1942.

PART IV: EDUCATION: A NEW CONCEPT

Education and the New Order: The 'Democracy and Citizenship' series, pamphlet No. 7, 1941, published by the Canadian Association for Adult Education.
Education and Total Effort: An address at Winnipeg, Canada, 1941.

Appendix

Propaganda and Education: An address before the Winnipeg Canadian Club, 19 October 1943.

The Library in an International World: An address before the American Library Association, Buffalo, New York, June 1946.

Part V: Future for Documentary

The Challenge of Peace: An address to the Conference of the Arts, Sciences, and Professions in the Post-War World, New York, June 1945.

Report from America: *Theatre Arts Monthly*, December 1946.

Part VI: International

Documentary, the Bright Example: *Documentary 47*: The Edinburgh International Festival of Documentary Films, 1947.

Progress and Prospect: *Documentary 49*: The Edinburgh International Festival of Documentary Films, 1949.

Documentary: A World Perspective.

Learning from Television: *Contrast*, Summer 1963.

Index

227

Index

228

Index

229

Index

230

Index

231

Index

232